LAUNCHING COMMUNITY PRAYER MOVEMENTS

The Case for Community Prayer Leadership Teams

P. Douglas Small

PUBLICATIONS

Scripture quotations, unless otherwise indicated are taken from the Holy Bible, New King James Version, Copyright – 1979, 1980, 1982, 1990, 1995, Thomas Nelson, Inc., Publishers.

ISBN: 978-0-9896525-4-4
Copyright © 2014 by Alive Publications
Kannapolis, NC 28082
All Rights Reserved
Printed in the USA

CONTENTS

FOREWARD

SECTION ONE

The Stories

SECTION TWO

Wading through the Statistical and Philosophical Bog

SECTION THREE

Research Suggestions

SECTION FOUR

SECTION FIVE

FOREWARD

This is a *preview edition of Launching Community Prayer Movements – the Case for Community Prayer Leadership Teams.*

In these pages, you will read the stories of people who, often as the result of some jarring event that served as call to reality, concluded that their community would not change unless someone stepped forward to lead such change, and they often felt themselves the most unlikely person to lead such change.

In fact, their humility and need to depend on God became their greatest asset along with a teachable attitude. The characters here are fictitious, but represent a composite of real people across the nation who are wrestling with community issues, which can only be solved by a spiritual solution. Components of these stories arise from real-life incidents. Across the nation, an invisible army of prayerful, heart-driven change agents is rising.

The purpose of this book is to fan the flames of the movement, to offer ideas for those just beginning, and propose, a means to connect these grassroots prayer and impact movements.

Various terms are being used – 'Prayer Councils,' 'Servant Leadership Teams,' 'Community Prayer Movement,' and the term recommended for the movement as a whole, the 'Prayer-Connect Community Leadership Network' – PC²LN. The name 'Prayer Connect' brands the movement, tying it to the official vetted international and national prayer movements. Frankly, the name chosen by the local leadership team is not important. This is a bottom-up movement.

From a national perspective, members of the National Prayer Committee, created in 1989, have been watching the growing number of flash points of unity and prayer across the nation. It became apparent, more than a decade ago, that it was important to find some means of connecting, without controlling, this current groundswell of prayer, which is growing evidence of a move of God. The National Prayer Committee is a collage of national prayer leaders and organizations whose representatives work in local communities across the nation. Moreover, while the national leaders of these various prayer efforts meet at least annually, there is no parallel fraternity to connect these diverse prayer movements locally.

Here is the simple goal. To encourage each community to identify national prayer ministry representatives along with para-church and congregational prayer leaders; and gather them at the same table to work toward

> **The Mission**
>
> To facilitate a network of diverse and widespread community-based prayer teams that aim at global renewal and revival, with a local, measurable flashpoint in view; through unified, consistent, unrelenting prayer that strengthens individuals and families along with Christian ministries; the focus on the prayer community emphasizes transformation by incarnational and proclamation of the community.

creating a seamless community prayer effort and transform prayer events into collaborative process. Nationally, the goal is to connect these local efforts, one to another, in a voluntary national relational construct, under the umbrella of the two organizations above. To point out resources. To provide templates as models for their efforts. To champion their story. To facilitate communication. To fan the flames of prayer-based community transformation.

There are other critical considerations.

- Few disagree that *we need a Great Awakening* – a national spiritual revival that breathes new holy vitality into the church; and impacts the culture though significant numbers of converts and re-centering social values. While the need is national, the flashpoint of such renewal is local. It is measured by community change. Cities lead nations.

- Currently, *we have no neutral national construct that connects and empowers such grassroots movements.* Consequently, they tend to be silos, struggling alone. At times, a local effort rises to prominence and becomes a national top-down movement. However, that's not the goal here. The paradigm shift is to local initiative, the 'one church' in the city, orthodox in theology, missional in nature, generous in spirit, gracious to opposition, and that is a game changing transition.

- *Our goal then is not to seed a 'bit more prayer' into the current failing model, but to intensify the rhythm of prayer and godly collaboration in a new Ezra-Nehemiah paradigm* that empowers pastors through prayer and unity; and elevates laity as leaders and missionary peers in the marketplace. Prayer is foundational, but our goal is beyond mere prayer – it is establishing a rhythm of relentless prayer out of one's daily personal discipline of prayer: Weekly Prayer Connections; Church Prayer Gatherings Monthly; Quarterly Community Prayer Gatherings; Annual Days of Prayer. This relentless drumbeat is a national call to prayer – daily, weekly, monthly, quarterly, annually.

- *Beyond prayer, the call is to move to coalitions of care. And collaborative evangelism. Prayer-Care-Share.* The Great Commitment of prayer,

  > *I exhort first of all that supplications, prayers, intercessions, and giving of thanks be made for all men, for kings and all who are in authority, that we may lead a quiet and peaceable life in all godliness and rever-*

7

ence. For this is good and acceptable in the sight of God our Savior who desires all men to be saved and to come to the knowledge of the truth (1 Tim. 2:1-4).

Such prayer empowers the Great Commandment, *"And thou shalt love the Lord thy God with all thy heart, and with all thy soul, and with all thy mind, and with all thy strength: this is the first commandment. And the second is ... love thy neighbor as thyself"* (Mark 12:30-31). That opens the door of hearts and changes the very character of the Great Commission, *"Go ye therefore and teach all nations, baptizing them in the name of the Father, and*

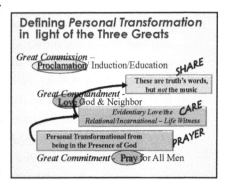

of the Son, and of the Holy Ghost: Teaching them to observe all things whatsoever I have commanded you: and, lo, I am with you always, even unto the end of the world" (Matthew 28:19-20).

- *Prayer is forever the foundation of all we do,* the first act of obedience and alignment; the power behind effective ministry; and the last act of worshipful gratitude. Unity and humility are at the heart of the relational construct created. Love is the driving force expressed through a caring people and caring congregations in collaboration. Mission completion - the gospel lived and shared, resulting in conversions, baptisms, on-going discipleship and cultural impact - is the non-negotiable command that Jesus gave.

SECTION ONE
The Stories
Ordinary People:
Extraordinary Possibilities

CHAPTER 1
Prayerville, USA

Meet the Threads and Strands of our Story:

Edgar and Edith Davis - *Living quietly and minding their own business, Edgar is rattled by fresh and uncommon violence in the city. As he begins to explore the spiritual and moral condition of the city, he uncovers issues that deeply trouble him, and folks who share his concern that inspire him. His wife Edith, a retired school teacher, joins him in his journey.*

Dr. Rogers and his wife, Elaine – *a dedicated Christian couple, Dr. Rogers is a physician. His wife Elaine has been involved in a number of Bible Studies across the city. They share Edgar's concern for the spiritual vitality of the city.*

Pastor Reggie – *Edgar's pastor, who is moved by the heartthrob of his friend and member, and comes alongside to advise, cover and rally pastors to the cause.*

Benny and Betty Jarman – *Benny is a successful businessperson who is respected across the city and beyond. He, from time to time, has sponsored breakfast events for businessper-*

sons, and hundreds have been part of these faith-laced, positive experiences. His wife Betty is deeply involved in an interdenominational Bible Study network.

Darren – *An on-fire young collegiate that is passionate to reach high schoolers and college-age peers. He is not a youth pastor, but has found favor with them. He is connecting with kids and mobilizing them for prayer and to be a witness for Christ.*

Isabel Ford – *Isabel is the veteran intercessor of the city, known and respected widely. She is a walking repository of failures and successes of revival activities, the ebb and flow of the spiritual-moral life of the city. She has around her a small effective group of intercessors who have persisted in prayer over the years. They have watched efforts mobilize and dissolve, offer promise and pay-off, and others with much thunder and little rain. Still, she is one of the most positive and faith-filled people on the team.*

Prayer in Prayerville

Edgar Davis has lived in mythical Prayerville all his life. He attends First Church. Recently, three nearly back-to-back homicides happened in the quiet community, not far from his boyhood home. The city on average, like other cities and towns, has five such incidents yearly, still far too many. Edgar for the first time, at least to such an acute degree, became concerned about his city. With three homicides in the neighborhood in which he grew up, he was more than shaken; he was stirred. When the police were not immediately able to find the shooter, for weeks the neighborhood lived in panic – one senseless killing after another over a thirteen-day period. Edgar joined his pastor, Reggie, and hundreds of others in a candlelight vigil. His mother still lived alone in the

12

neighborhood, but she refused to leave.

So shaken was Edgar, that his blood pressure escalated, he had dizzy spells and vision issues. His doctor noted the potential problem as stress, and Edgar, knowing that Dr. Rogers was a believer, opened his soul. To his amazement, the doctor sat down and listened. Edgar recalled, "I was crying! At one point, I thought he might cry, as well. We prayed together. And he told me, one way to reduce stress is 'act on it,' of course in a positive way." 'Act on it,' the words echoed for days.

Edgar told his wife, Edith, "Maybe I am supposed to do something". The next Sunday, he found himself at the kneeling rail following communion at church and he could not leave. "I was bro-

> **I was broken. Not for me, but suddenly for my city. ━ ━ ━ ━ ➤**

ken. Not for me, but suddenly for my city. With the wafer and cup in my hand, I said to myself, 'Jesus died for me, yes – but he also died so the senseless violence would stop. He died for the city, indeed, the world.'" He had always privatized his faith, now he was beginning to see a corporate dimension he had not seen before, at least, so clearly, and in such a compelling manner. Then he asked himself a question, "What am I doing?" He made an appointment to consult with his pastor, Reggie. "It keeps coming to me that I ought to pray more. We all ought to prayer more. At least, that is where it begins." Indeed. Within seventy-two hours after the prayer vigil, the shooter had been arrested. However, Edgar knew there was still more that needed to be done. With some leads from his pastor, Edgar began an intense investigation about the status of prayer in and for the community.

After reflection, he felt that the recent tragic events were indicators of a loss of the spiritual-moral compass of the community. The murders intersected with the neighborhood crime watch needs, fatherless homes, poverty, racism, drugs, gun access by teens and gangs, and a lack of maturity in relating skills in families and the community. But those were not the things that moved Edgar. He felt that something else was at the bottom of the problem – a lack of community spiritual health. The one place he felt leverage could be applied was by a citywide prayer movement. He began to survey every prayer effort in the city, and then the county. His wife, Edith, a teacher for a years and now retired, also started making some contacts about the community crisis and levels of prayer beyond those in congregations.

Edgar began to notice that the prayers on Sunday were very self-interested. He realized that even his church rarely prayed for the city or the neighborhood around them. He called Dr. Rogers again, and then met with him and his wife Elaine who headed a prayer and Bible study network. In the meeting, Elaine Rogers gave Edgar the name of Benny Jarman. Benny had led a series of 'Success in Life' breakfast gatherings for businessmen in the city for nearly a decade. Soon Edgar was seated across from Benny and his wife, Betty. And they were dreaming about how to call the city to prayer. Betty was part of a network of women's prayer and Bible studies in her denomination that stretched across the county.

In that meeting, Edgar learned about Darren, a young prayer mobilizer that would jolt his frame of reference. Darren had emerged on the local campus of the Community College as a Christian leader. Darren was young enough to be the grandson of Edgar, what a pairing, and his enthusiasm, as well as his knowledge about the spiritual status of students, seemed endless.[1] Not only did he have his fingers on the pulse of 'See You at the Pole,' but also on the growth of Bible Clubs, and before and after school informal connections along with a unique outreach to the small private college that Edgar had almost forgotten about. Darren's eyes lit up, as he noted that over 200 students at the local college were foreign, and most had never heard the gospel. Darren along with about two dozen others was already prayer walking the campuses of the county. Edgar and Edith invited Darren and a small group to their house for dinner – and they listened in amazement as the prayer efforts on middle and high school campuses not only in their county, but also beyond the county were described by Darren. Edith, as a former teacher noticed an immediate role for herself. Darren, who was not from Prayerville, saw a connection with the broader Christian community he had not realized as possible before this moment.

Edgar continued to reach out, making calls and having coffee. He turned over every lead he was given. He refused to be independent. The phone was ringing constantly and their house had become a busy place for connections. One morning, Edith, jarred him, "you are in over your head!" Edgar went back to Pastor Reggie! "I need a covering; accountability!"

Finding Motivators

Edith connected again with Elaine Rogers and Betty, who introduced her to Isabel Ford. Isabel was regarded as the premier intercessor in the city. In the civil rights era, she had organized black-white prayer teams, and for fifty years, she seemed to be at the heart of every prayer effort in the city. Edgar and Edith felt like they were making progress.

It was clear; it was time to bring all the folks they had met and dialogued with to the same room for a face-to-face meeting! Each would bring others from their stream. There were Bible-study prayer groups in the room, several pastors, intercessors from Isabel's network, youth pastors who were involved with Darren and others. The National Day of Prayer coordinator was present as was the Global Day of Prayer representative. There were numerous para-church prayer representatives. Edgar and Edith made sure that blacks, whites, and Hispanics were invited. Their invitation list included young and old, evangelicals and Pentecostals, and a handful of Christians whose reputation and influence, as Christians, was known in the city, beyond their congregation.

Simple Questions

While the evening was casual, there were a list of key questions. "What is happening now?" And they went around the room looking for answers from key leaders who had a bird's eye view of the city and county. "Does the present level of prayer and unity represent progress or are we regressing in view of the past?" That was an Isabel question! Next, they asked, "What should be happening?" The responses ranged from mild complaints to moderate expressions of hope, and not a few stories about failed attempts at unity and collaboration.

"What is possible?" Edgar asked. Darren shared about the global prayer effort and city transformation. Others shared regarding large prayer gatherings that were happening in other cities, pastoral prayer groups, concentrated intercessory efforts, and its positive effects.

"Could that happen here?" Edgar asked. "If so, how? If so, who? If so, when? If so, what are our next steps?"

Next Steps

They outlined their next steps:

1. Continue to learn and to explore their own city, levels of prayer and the spiritual health of the city.
2. Find more information from the outside – from other cities who might be exploring a similar process.
3. Keep telling their story, doing informal vision casting. Do

this in different streams – among pastors, youth, people of prayer (particularly intercessors), and marketplace influencers in each of the 'Seven Mountains.'

4. *They developed a 'must see; must tell' list! In addition, key leaders in the group took responsibility for getting to these individuals and sharing what was developing in their city.*

Next Meeting

At their next meeting, the number had doubled, but their circle of influence had quadrupled. They saw three areas where they needed to focus:

1. What was the level of countywide, unified prayer, and how could they grow that?
2. Where was the community experiencing pain not felt by Christians and not responded to by the church?
3. Where were the unreached people and the unengaged congregations? In what sections of the city/county were they found? What demographic sectors? What were their ages and economic profiles?

It was now time for serious homework.

- First, a group of three key leaders was charged with forging a vision and mission statement. A pastor, and a great wordsmith; a key layman; and an intercessor. Edgar was a consultant to the group.
- Another group of three was urged to develop a prayer plan – their first steps toward a serious community-wide prayer blanket.
- A third group was commissioned to continue research and exploration.
- Finally, a 'special forces' unit was commissioned to find missing members, crucial to the success of the team. Who, they asked, is not at the table, who should be at the table?

This team of about a dozen would now shoulder the greater responsibility of moving the process forward.

Together Again

When they came together, the prayer team had forged a basic and simple prayer calendar.

1. First, they noted national prayer efforts that occurred in their community throughout the year, some of which were sponsored, and some that were not. (See Appendix for a sample of Annual Prayer Days.)

2. They noted 'the seasons of prayer lapses,' the months in which little unified prayer was happening, and they had a plan, first, to call for quarterly prayer gatherings, 5th Sunday night prayer events, that would move around the city, possibly hosted by different congregations. They also heard about the idea of establishing a rhythm of prayer - daily personal prayer, weekly prayer connections, not less than monthly church-wide congregational prayer meetings, a quarterly community-wide prayer gathering, and an annual day of prayer.

STORY

Will is the pastor of an independent church in Freedom. When he heard about the pastors in a nearby city that were going away for an extended time of prayer, he asked if he could join them. And he came back to the little town of Freedom of about a thousand population, fired up. He made the rounds, contacted all of the seven churches in the little town. And he managed to get six of the seven pastors in the same room. Will determined to find a way for them to connect, at least to pray together. Over the months, relationships devel-

*oped. They began to have a community unity ser-
vice every fifth Sunday. They identified the theological hot potatoes. For them, number one on
the list was the doctrine of the security of the believer; another was their different views of Spirit
baptism and its evidence, and finally, church government. They agreed, in that fifth Sunday event,
none would use the opportunity to promote the
doctrines distinct to their own congregation.*

*Half of them had food ministries, and they
discovered that, at times, the same families
abused all the pantries, so they combined their
efforts to create one church-sponsored, community, food bank. They also found that a handful
of families had been members of at least three of
the churches in the community and were often at
the heart of church splits. They joked about starting a church just for those maverick sheep. What
they did do, was enter an agreement to minimize
destabilizing church splits. When visitors came,
they would obviously welcome them, but if they
discovered that they were members of another church in town, they would openly say, "Yes,
your pastor is a dear friend of mine." And if the
newcomer wanted to join, they would ask for a
letter of commendation from the previous church.
In no case, would they welcome a splinter group
without working on reconciliation issues. It was
a bold idea. They forged a covenant of trust, and
committed to serve one another, and not only
their congregations, but also the community.
At one point, the mayor asked, "Are you taking
over the city?" They smiled. Church attendance
increased across the board. Members of several
churches enjoyed fellowship and service opportunities not possible before. The pastors met each*

Monday, and often shared ministry duties– visiting the hospital one for another, caring for emergency needs. Even members, not being able to reach their own pastor, would call another, and he would respond to the need – all with honor, none trying to steal sheep.

3. They had found two pastoral prayer groups and had connected to the hosts of those gatherings. One was primarily white and evangelical; the other was a group of black pastors. They encouraged these pastors to inform and engage other pastors, but they also realized the need for a back-up plan. Both these groups were settled in terms of attendees and their routine and focus. If new pastors were to be engaged in the process they envisioned, it most likely would not come from these groups, at least primarily. They needed additional avenues for connecting with pastors and discovering their interest. The local ministerial fellowship was quite diverse and included non-evangelicals. It was emerging as an all-faith council.

4. They launched the process of discovering 'local church prayer representatives' and the congregations that had a Prayer Team, and quickly learned that those churches were no more than five-percent of all the churches. Sadly, prayer leadership was languishing in the very place where it should have flourished, inside the churches.

5. Youth pastors were exploring the possibility of the creation of a 'prayer house' for teens. This could alleviate some of the Friday-Saturday night youth mischief. And redirect youthful energy, and create a setting for prayer that would allow for uniquely youthful expression.

6. They realized that they had not even touched the need for a citywide network of intercessors, intentional prayer walking and missions, adopting causes and people for prayer. There was so much to do.

Cautious Humble Feet

Suddenly, all the information and ideas became overwhelming, and as often happens, as excitement about particular pieces of the vision emerged, so did competition and questions about sequence. What had been a joyful journey suddenly became like the Israelites complaining in the wilderness. "Who is in charge?" the question was boldly asked. Edgar confessed, "I think I have taken this as far as I can; I am in over my head!"

The group was now at one of the most important junctions they had faced. "Who is going to lead this? Should this be formally organized? Is this a pastor-led or a lay-led initiative?" In the end, a multi-person panel along with pastoral advisors and other 'consultants' emerged. Each member of the leadership team would serve a segment of the Christian community that needed to be mobilized.

- There would be a 'Congregational Component' with an emphasis on congregational and pastoral prayer, youth prayer efforts rising out of local churches, including campus prayer initiatives, intercessory teams in local congregations (prayer groups).

- There would be a 'Marketplace Component' that investigated how believers might interact in the city/county, as believers – not as Baptists or Methodists, Pentecostals or Calvinists – but as Christians who saw the need to be more effective as salt and light. The question was, apart from the congregations and denominational la-

> The culture is shaped by seven mind-molders or mountains in society.
> - Media
> - Government
> - Education
> - Business
> - Church
> - Arts and Entertainment
> - Family
>
> ▬ ▬ ▬ ➤ Bill Bright

21

bels, how would these Christians connect? They would begin with the so-called seven mountains, expand the categories and redefine, if necessary, to fit their local situation. Their goal would be sector vision leaders and the establishment first, of a prayer component in each sector and then throughout that sector, followed by a care and evangelism component.

- They would build a 'Care Coalition' – a consortium of churches and para-church organizations that had aggressive care-based outreach programs. Their goal was to educate one another, both to community needs and existing resources, and to forge new ways to collaborate. One of the things they planned in the first year-to-eighteen months was the sponsorship of a 'Care Fair'. To coordinate that event, they created an 'ER4C Squad' (Emergency Responders for Christ Squad); that soon became the Emergency Responder 'Force' – and then, 'the Force.' Before the Care Coalition meeting, three churches that each had an emergency responder team caucused to determine how they could be proactive in the county and do more collaborating.

The group rallied health care specialists in the county for a forum and a hundred responded by coming to the half-day conference. They assessed their collective strengths, surveyed the group to discover unmet needs in the community with a focus on senior care, divorce after-care, hunger, fatherlessness, poverty, the high school drop-out problem, drug related health and relating problems. They quickly found an action team of mission-minded men and women.

In addition, they cultivated a small but significant police-pastor connection through their chaplaincy effort. Their youth pastors launched a 'gangs' initiative' in connection with the local schools. In addition, youth pastors took hall monitor training and agreed to become school volunteers.

Church members became 'readers' for elementary schools. In the area of the city in which drop-out and achievement rates showed the greatest need, a group of churches, and teachers opened a 'once monthly' Saturday clinic. Christian schools participated, as well.

A number of churches combined their food and community service ministries.

As they gained momentum, the task again suddenly seemed overwhelming. There was only one thing to do, take one-step at a time.

1. They divided the city into zip-zones.
2. They pegged every church in the county in terms of their location. They coded the churches – RED: involved, on go. ORANGE: on the edge, and considered essential. BLUE: not involved, the least hopeful. Moreover, they prayed for the code-blue churches and guarded against being judgmental. They knew some would come later, rather than sooner; some were not ready for such bold unity, and that made their own example and demeanor even more important.

They looked for 'PACE' churches in each zone. A handful of churches, they felt, transcended the zones. Gradually, around the 'pace' churches, dream teams developed that were to focus on issues inside each zip zone. Their first goal was self-education – inside their zone. This was a challenge, since not all members lived inside the particular zone; and yet, the church was to be a good neighbor itself. Church members began to realize how oblivious the church was to their neighbors – and that often the church neighborhood was the one to which they paid the least attention. Was the church a good neighbor?

They developed the concept – one county: many towns and cities; one city: many neighborhoods. In addition, they began to ask, "How many neighborhoods are you part of?" There was the *residential* neighborhood of homes and apartments, the *congregational* neighborhood with homes around the church (attendees and non-attendees) where they worshipped, the *vocational* neighborhood where they worked, the *marketplace* neighborhood where they shopped, their *children's* neighborhood (school and park areas), the *recreational* neighborhood where they played or relaxed. And of course, there were the *neighborhoods of family and close friends*. Seven neighborhoods! They knew, to be concerned about one and not all was naïve.

3. A proclamation team considered how they might engage the county with the gospel over the next decade.

4. Prayer teams explored how they could cover the city in prayer, 168 hours a week. (Four Prayer Rallies a year were projected as a part of the process). They embraced the concept of the rhythm of prayer – daily personal prayer, weekly prayer group connections, not less than monthly congregational prayer meetings, quarterly community prayer gatherings, and annually, the National Day of Prayer. Daily. Weekly. Monthly. Quarterly. Annually. A persistent cadence of prayer.

5. Each zip-zone team identified its schools, and began to pair intercessors and churches. They looked at the crime statistics where the gangs operated and they began to determine how they might impact these territories. They researched the state of the family, poverty and crime, the presence of drugs. They charted bars and nightclubs, liquor outlets, exotic clubs. They noted cults and occult outlets and activities. They were deeply into the research of their city, learning things they had hitherto ignored, never seen as significant.

6. Intercessors started cursory spiritual mapping – a conscious exercise in awareness that they had previously ignored. They explored the sources of light and hope, as well as the dark spots. They asked, "Where is God in our

area? Where is his light? His love? What is the degree, the depth of longing for him? They came to believe that a 'light' problem was a 'love' problem, and a 'love' problem was a 'longing' problem – and that was a 'prayer' problem.

STORY

Diane had just finished a mammoth spiritual mapping project on the city. And her research was stunning. Pastors gathered for the briefing. Maps highlighted the data. It was too much to take in at once. Could there really be that much prostitution? That much illicit sexual activity? That much witchcraft? That many occult churches and bookstores? Was it really true that the largest churches were marginal, and there were few of them? Did that many abortions take place in the city annually?

The pastors of the city launched a monthly 'Discover the City!' tour with Diane. They crowded into a van or more than one if necessary, and traveled to this site and to that. Diane pointed out the spiritual features and activities of the city most of them would have missed, even if they had been looking directly at it – this was a tour with a veteran intercessor, trained in 'reading a city.' At times, they pressed into occult bookstores and walked the aisles, looking at the books, often coming out stunned. They visited sites where animal sacrifices had occurred. They looked at seedy areas with hotel rooms rented by the hour. As they exposed their hearts to the moral disorder of the city, they found their passion increased. Their resolve deepened. Their rose-colored view of the

25

city faded. The reality of sin, the commitment of those who sought a profit at the expense of others, was a stinging experience in contrast to the casual commitment of the typical Christian.

'Discover the City!' – Quite an idea for a prayer tour.

These intercessors began to pray about misplaced and misdirected 'longings.' They recognized that only God could satisfy these longings with his love. And what was needed was for the light of God to manifest, for God's revelation to become clear – and that came by prayer. O, what is wrought by God through a humble group of pray-ers!

7. Marketplace leadership teams (Nehemiah) began to emerge out of several of the professional-vocational tribes. In the medical community two doctors, a radiologists, two nurse practitioners and hospital administrator began to meet to consider how to connect believers in their vocational tribe. A number of Christians in retail connected as well. A principal who had been quietly praying with a handful of teachers decided to expand her effort to reach out to believers in the educational sector. Strange-

---

━ ━ ━ ➤ Ancient societies were most often organized by kinship tribes. To evangelize them, meant necessary access to the inside of the tribes. Missionaries developed relationships and lived among the tribes. Our society is organized by professional tribes. We need a missionary force that lives on the inside of each professional-vocational tribe, knows its customs, speaks the language, wears the label - and loves it.

ly, a group of Christians who worked at a local brewery emerged, calling themselves, "Christians – Working in the World."

Their movement connected with another small group in media, and a couple Christians in other vocations who admitted that their work environment was not always kind to their faith. At least four vocational teams emerged to consider how they could make the place they worked a 'prayed-for' place, a place where God's love and care were manifest at least quietly in their lives, and a place of witness to the end that others might know Christ.

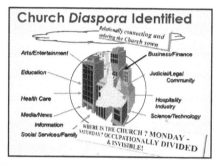

8. It became apparent that they needed a central place to connect, to store the data. A vacant office was donated for their use in the downtown area of the city. There, they began to chart their data with wall maps. Another wall became a collage of news-clippings from the present and the past. Almost weekly, a church van loaded with intercessors drove to various places in the city to see things first hand, to get a better understanding of what was emerging in terms of data. They recorded their insights, their prayer experiences, and began a shared journal.

The Search for a Core Theology

One of the first significant challenges to unity that surfaced was over theology – a sincere layman approached his pastor after being in a room with a diverse group from across the city, and exclaimed, "Pastor, they don't believe like us!" At times, Edgar and the pastors had noted minor detours in which the people did comparative theology work, and graciously teased one another about differences, but the spirit of unity had remained intact. Some of the pastors in the circle were fiercely committed to their denominational positions on theology, and indeed, a few had served their organizations in significant and trusted levels before returning to pastoral ministry. These were not men who were soft on theology or ready to abandon the traditions in which they had been raised and educated.

The leadership team decided that the pastors, who had demonstrated unity across denominational lines, should at some point address the concerns over differences which had never been a serious threat to the group, but none-the-less were significant for other reasons.

'Core' theology is a term that refers to the central beliefs at the heart of the Christian faith.

Pastor Reggie took a moment in one of the leadership meetings to distinguish between the different levels of theology. He spoke about 'core' theology, the central beliefs at the heart of the Christians faith. These were non-negotiable – "So is all the rest", someone in the back of the room shouted. Everyone laughed. Without attempting to set-forth a declaration of faith, Pastor Reggie talked about the core of theology as being so integrated, that when one piece was removed, it threatened the integrity of the whole.

Then he spoke about the theology that made each denomination special and suggested that each group's tendency was to 'center on their exceptional slice' of theology, rather than the core. After all, it is the particular slice of theology that makes each denomination distinctive. In previous years, Christians attending conservative churches embraced the core, there was little argument. It was just assumed, but that is not true today. Now ortho-doxy itself is threatened. Moreover, he remarked, the center is not mere orthodoxy, it is a living center, Christ Himself, exalted, su-preme, and incomparable. "If we will exalt Christ," he proposed, "agree to disagree on the slices of theology that make us unique, it is the centrality and supremacy of our focus on Jesus that will keep us united. Our goal," he said "is not to evangelize one anoth-er, not to persuade each other to our positions, but to glorify Christ in the city, and reach those who are unreached. We have reached a point at which the goal must now be to fill the city and county with Christians – regardless of the brand, if indeed, the brand is orthodox."

Pastor Reggie ex-plained yet one more slice of theology - the differ-ences that mark us due to culture, conscience, style, gifts and callings. "There are in these areas of theol-ogy noticeable differences.

There are questions that Scripture does not answer – mysteries to us with regard to cultural lines, issues of personal conscience. Those must be left as open questions. As Paul points out, eating meat may be wrong to one, not to another. The right-wrong issue is not rooted in a clear Biblical declaration but is a matter of the heart. Our problem comes," Pastor Reggie explained, "When we attempt to take a position on these discretionary issues and force all others to conform. Or when we press into the 'core' of theology our own denominational beliefs, ideas and practices unique to our movement, and force on others conformity. What we desire is for our differences to enrich us, not divide us; for the value we place on Jesus to be so compelling, that we are drawn to him across our

29

differences – and the world sees in that, our love for Him and one another."

The Mission

To *facilitate a network of diverse and widespread community-based prayer teams that aim at global renewal and revival, with a local, measurable flashpoint in view;* through unified, consistent, unrelenting prayer that strengthens individuals and families along with Christian ministries; the *focus on the prayer community emphasizes transformation by incarnational and proclamation of the community.*

Critical Assumptions

1. Nothing less than *a culturally transforming revival* - a great awakening - is acceptable as a goal. We must see some 10-15 percent, thirty-to-forty-five million of the gospel resistant or the functionally unchurched, swept into the church in revival. That number might would certainly include a number of the casually committed, but without a significant number of the genuinely unengaged, the revival would not see its needed impact. 'Sinners' have to be saved!

2. They also acknowledged that they had to reach the ethnic pockets in the county.

3. They made a commitment to reach the local college, and high school and middle schools, with the knowledge that if they failed, the next generation would be lost to the church and the gospel.

4. Conversions were not enough; they had to disciple the harvest or only pollute the church with a deadly pluralism.

5. Unity and collaboration were critical. They knew the mantra: Noble efforts + disunity – a Common Vision = a competitive model that produced ineffective results.

6. This unity had to become citywide, not only between pastors, but between Christians.

7. The church *gathered* had to be more effective; but the church *scattered*, the church *diaspora,* also had to be effective – salt and light, scattered throughout the community. First, that church had to be identified and recognized. It became apparent; to influence the health care community or the educational community, one congregation could not accomplish the task. However, when Christians from a given professional sector are gathered, despite their denominational or congregational affiliation, they are typically a formidable group. Sadly, they have never been convened, never been charged – as a group – in forging a prayer-based, care-laced, great commission concern for their professional peers. Only as individuals have they considered, if even then, the responsibility of praying at and for their place of business as an intercessor, the task of being salty salt and light, incarnationally; and then the discernment and discovery of opportunities to share their story. All over the city, such gatherings need to be sponsored, until there are groups of Christians, who now identify one another as Christians, and gently hold one another accountable.

As the leadership team continued to dialogue, they began to imagine:

- Prayer events that involved more than a narrow segment of the community.
- A process of prayer – 24-7-365 – a prayed-for community.
- Prayer Leaders, from diverse organizations and denominations at the same table, consistently, relentlessly.
- Pastors – praying together; Lay-leaders praying together.
- A seamless network of intercessors across the entire city.
- Networks of prayer connecting one city to another.
- Embedded intercessors in every segment of society;

31

prayer missionaries to every professional and vocational tribe.

- The Church of the City – actively engaged in prayer and witness, every day of the week.
- Prayer teams that adopted the Mayor, community leaders, schools, police, fire and safety personnel for prayer.
- A prayer-crisis line for your city.
- A youth and children's prayer movement for your city.
- Intercessors who are informed with accurate research on the city, its pain and promise, praying for the destiny of your town.

Imagine ... A Great Awakening!

STORY

The mayor of the small town learned that a group of citizens was planning to drive the streets and pray. Passerville is hardly noticeable. There is the big church on the hill, a few shops here and there, no real downtown. Their post office is less than 500 square feet. Most people, who speed down the four-lane road between Memphis and Birmingham pass through Passerville, and never notice it. "To do real shopping," the mayor noted", we have to drive at least forty miles. When you pray, pray that we'll get a WalMart." Some cities fight against the location of a Walmart in their community. Not this mayor. A group of intercessors drove up and down the four-lane praying that Walmart would be attracted open a store in the little town. Walla! Walmart came within a year.

1   There are 4,140 2-year, 4-year, public and private colleges and universities, some with graduate programs. Some specializing in professional training. Attending them are 17,487,475 students; 724,000 from other nations.

CHAPTER 2
How It Begins:
A Catalyst

Meet the Threads and Strands of our Story

Cole and Karen – *Now living in their hometown after getting married and moving away for a time. They have been recently stirred to do more than attend church, be quiet 'good Christian' folks. They are concerned about the moral and spiritual condition of the nation. As a result, they determined to launch a movement to unite believers in prayer.*

Pastor Monson – *Now retired and in his '80s. He was Cole's pastor in previous years and is still respected across the city. He has been a steady and consistent advocate for revival and renewal. After leaving the active pastorate, he chose to settle in this community.*

Ellen Goodwin – *Ellen, like Pastor Monson, is quite senior, also in her '80s. She is the 'Anna' of the city who has prayed long and hard for spiritual renewal to come. She is still fiery, and as solid as a rock. Not only do local folks seek her out for prayer, she is known across the country as 'the intercessor' in Hometown. Around her, a small group of intercessors has emerged who persist in prayer for the city.*

<u>Frank Graham</u> – *Coordinator of the Annual Day of Prayer that hundreds attend. In the months prior to the event, he cranks up his organization, replaces vacant or tired players, and plans for the annual event which is always an inspiration to the hundred or so that attend.*

<u>Megan</u> – *15-year-old daughter of Cole and Karen. She is involved in a teen prayer movement in the city called 'Friday Night Fire.'*

<u>Eric Swanson</u> – *Eric is a pastor to other pastors, though he would not call himself that. He is unassuming. He does not pastor the largest church in town, but it may be one with the biggest heart, especially for its size. Eric was a key leader for a pastoral prayer movement that showed great promise for the city. It is still an oasis for the three-dozen or so pastors that regularly or infrequently attend the pastoral prayer gatherings.*

<u>Lee Casey</u> – *A community businessman. He is a well-known Christian and positive influence in the community. He is one that realizes that the city needs prayer, but not one that has acted on that understanding.*

Cole and his wife, Karen, moved back to the town both of them grew up in about five years ago. Standing in a crowd of some two-to-three hundred people at a community prayer event, he scanned the crowd. There was a former pastor, retired, and still living in the area. Pastor Monson had been such a comfort when Cole's father died. There was Ellen Goodwin, now in her late '80s, a veteran intercessor. She was on a walker, did not get out much, but she was present for the prayer gathering – unbelievable.

There were many familiar faces, most of them with gray hair. In a community brimming with churches, why were there only a few hundred at this event? Still, he never remembered attending this event when he lived in the area before, and he had only been in attendance once in the five years since he moved back. 'We're all far too busy!' he reflected, 'so busy we are missing the critical and about to lose the nation!'

A Student of the City

It was that afternoon that Cole decided to be more than a passive participant; more than just another Christian who lived between his home and the church where he worshipped ignoring the spiritual life of the city. He looked in the crowd for significant community leaders, and there were far too few, just a relative handful of concerned believers. In the next few days, Cole called Frank Graham and invited him to coffee. Frank was the organizer of the annual event. He explained that, in the early years, the event had drawn almost a thousand for a few years, then numbers had declined, but he assured Cole that a crowd approaching three-hundred was a good turnout. Cole affirmed the effort, but shared his concern that even if a few thousand attended the once-a-year event, he feared it was not enough.

Karen was involved in a network of women's prayer and Bible studies. Just a few of those individuals had attended the prayer event, and some, sadly, were not even aware of it. Cole and Karen began an informal investigation. They asked dozens of their friends if the church they attended had even mentioned the prayer rally. While their results were less than scientific, they found the number was far less than half.[2] Cole and Karen had attended the church of Cole's youth for a year or so after they had moved back to the community, but it was not a good fit for their teen-age kids, so they began to attend a very large church on the edge of the city with a sprawling campus and Christian School where their kids attended. Cole had lunch with one of the pastors. Yes, they knew about the day of prayer, but the pastor noted that they had not found cooperative community ventures the most productive use of their time. They typically conducted their own similar prayer efforts. Had it not been for a friend, Cole would not have known about the prayer event.

He called Frank Graham again, and this time he was armed with new information and a ton of questions. "How is the prayer event publicized," he asked? Frank apologetically noted, "We have limited funds – so the Christian radio station helps us as much as possible."[3] Cole knew a bit about publicity. A dozen or so public service announcements the week prior to the event would not reach many people. Only about 15% of the Christian population listens to Christian radio daily – and they certainly do not hear it all day long. "And we have a website that gives the event time, place and date." The area did not have a Christian TV station.[5] "We also send a flyer out to all the churches, and we send notices to those for which we have email contacts. Our organizing team is only a handful. Our best response is among prayer leaders and small group of pastors who pray together regularly." Cole made copious notes.

The comment about pastors praying together encouraged Cole, and he assured Frank he was not being critical, but was sensing a deep stirring that he could not dismiss. They prayed together. Cole was grateful that Frank was not threatened by his persistent concern. "I have been praying for someone else to catch the vision and share it with me." They agreed to meet again and stay in touch. And Frank promised to get Cole a few names of the pastors in the prayer group.

Karen was also feeling a sense of intensity, as was their fifteen year-old daughter Megan, who is part of a prayer group at her school, and one that is not content to pray for their own needs alone. The young prayer group has done extensive prayer walks, prayer outreach events, and all-night prayer called 'Friday Night Fire' with dozens of young people from different churches in the area. Megan began her own research, inquiring about the passion for prayer among youth groups in various churches.

Meanwhile, Karen found that there were more than a dozen women's prayer and Bible study groups in the network with which she was associated. She asked if she could call the leaders. One by one, she contacted them. As she did, she discovered that each had a great appreciation for prayer, and each leader emphasized the critical importance of prayer in their group meetings. But Karen also noted that the focus of prayer in these groups was mainly personal, prayer requests for one another's needs, for crisis situations, and of course, at times, for personal growth as related to their studies. Who was praying for the city? For a Great Awakening? She knew the focus of the group, its primary purpose needed to retain its integrity, but she had the sense that even the leaders did not have a passion for a community-wide movement of prayer focused on spiritual awakening. Prayer was embraced in a personal but far too narrow way. "I am not suggesting that you change the purpose of your gathering", she assured one leader who was a bit defensive. "I am only exploring the extent to which the prayer movements and groups in our city are not only aware of the importance of prayer in its role of changing the city and its potential power for a great awakening." Most leaders acknowledged that prayer could bring change, but they did not see it as primary to them. It was as if there were across the city all these 'prayer parts,' all legitimate, all serving an important role, all personally fulfilling to those who attended, but all disconnected from one another and content to remain independent, and more tragically, content not to challenge the cultural status quo. Karen grew insightful, "If our prayers only help us personally adjust to the growing darkness around us, that is both wonderful and terrible – wonderful that prayer changes us, but terrible that it does not give us the courage to challenge the darkness. Prayer must be more than a tool for reactive adjustments; it should empower us!" For a moment, she was amazed at her own boldness. But she wasn't finished, "Do you think the Holy Spirit only wants to help us cope with a cultural condition that is worsening? To accept the darkness, passively? I think he may be calling us to stand against the tide, and that begins with bold faith-filled praying." To her surprise, her friend winked, "I am with you!"

Cole took the list of pastors that Frank had given him and made the first call. "Pastor Swanson, Eric Swanson? My name is Cole. Frank Graham gave me your name. I am sure he probably told

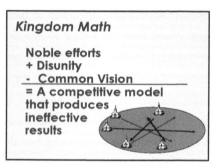

Kingdom Math

Noble efforts
+ Disunity
- Common Vision
= A competitive model
that produces
ineffective
results

you I might be calling you ... I wonder if we could talk?" Sitting down together, Eric told Cole the story of how the pastors of the city were challenged to 'shut everything down' and go away for a 'prayer summit' almost a decade before. Almost sixty pastors responded to that challenge. With almost 400 congregations in the county that was certainly a smaller number than had been hoped for – but it was significant. Together they represented about forty churches from nearly a dozen denominations, a few independent congregations, and a number of para-church organizations. The summits continued for three years, and Eric estimated that about a hundred different pastors and ministry leaders attended in those years, and out of that came about five different prayer groups.

Only one of them remained now. Almost half the pastors who had attended one of the summits had now moved on to other congregations in other cities and their successors had not joined the prayer effort. About a dozen pastors still prayed together weekly – for one another, for the churches and the city. Most were mid-sized congregations ranging from fifty to a few hundred. None of the pastors of the larger churches attended these prayer meetings. They lived in a world apart, with their own staff and prayer times, which though meaningful, were isolated from the larger Christian community. This handful of pastors was most likely to support prayer and unity efforts in the city.

In the old paradigm, the focus was on the local church. These pastors were discovering a new paradigm, a focus that shifted to the need for a greater identity than one church, than one denomination – the church in the city. In the old paradigm, congregations were isolated. Could they forge a new paradigm in which congregations were learning collaboration? In the old paradigm, the Great Commission was a task to be pursued, but never completed. In the new paradigm, the Great Commission became a goal that could be completed, at least in their county – their Jerusalem and Judea, indeed, the nations that had settled into their cities and towns, quietly, without their notice, whose connections reached around the world daily. In the old paradigm, unity was a theological notion. In the new paradigm, unity is incarnational, pragmatic, and visible. In the old

> In the face of the current wave of change, the church in America has two options. Either it will go about its business as usual – and be swallowed up by obsolescence and die by default. Or the church will choose to die – and thus find life.
> ➤ Mike Regele

paradigm, doctrines divide. In the new paradigm, vision and values unite and differences enrich. In the old paradigm, church was a label, a place and a time. In the new paradigm, it became a dynamic gathering of two or three believers.[6] All this was a radically new way of thinking, but it had promise. It was fresh.

Creating a Circle of Concern

Cole decided to call a meeting – a prayer meeting. Karen would rally leaders of the prayer and Bible study groups with which she was aligned. Megan would urge a group of young people to come. Cole contacted Ellen Goodwin and poured out his heart about his findings. The older woman gleamed. "I might be able to die in peace," she said. "No," Cole responded, "I need you now more than ever." Ellen smiled and agreed to contact a circle of seasoned intercessors. "I'll get them to the meeting," she declared. Frank Graham would get members of his team to attend. Eric would be present, and he would urge pastors in the prayer group to come, as well. Cole called and invited the lead pastor of his own church. And he called Pastor Monson. At a local restaurant, he had run into Lee Casey, a professional colleague who had retired. "Haven't seen you at the Country Club," Lee observed. "You were a Saturday morning regular." Cole loved to golf, but for weeks, he been driven by this burden for his city, and Saturday had become a premium day for connections. He shared his compelling burden, almost tearfully, with Lee, who agreed to gather a few professionals, all deeply Christian, to hear Cole's story.

On the night of the meeting, Cole and Karen sat together, thanking everyone in their crowded family room for attending. He thanked all the current leaders – Frank for annual prayer gathering, Eric and the pastor's prayer group, Ellen and the intercessors, Lee and the professionals who were present. "I have no desire to start something new. Or, to compete with the wonderful things

42

each of you are doing. But I have a sense that all that we are doing is not enough ..." For the next hour, ideas were randomly batted about. Cole was amazed at the prayer activities already happening in the city, as were others in the room. Ellen shared a bit of the history of significant breakthroughs, and beyond that, promises yet to be realized. Pastor Monson, now in his eighties, began to reflect on the spiritual destiny of the city, and often he felt the community had been at the door of a significant spiritual moment that had not materialized. No decisions were made. No great plan had been put forth, except the need to link these divergent prayer efforts. Not to recast them as something they were not intended to be or bend their purpose, but to create a construct of leaders for consistent connection.

About a half-dozen teens sat quietly during the evening. Cole opened the door for their contribution. Megan and her friends shared stories of what was happening as the kids engaged in 'Friday Nite Fire.' It was at this church, and then at that one. It was primarily evangelical and Pentecostal kids praying together and some from no church at all. Once a month, they had done a 24-7 prayer campaign called 'Relentless' – 96 kids each taking fifteen minutes to pray over the 24 hour period. They called it 'twitter-prayer.' Every fifteen minutes, the teen on 'the watch' sent out a tweet, and the teen to follow on 'the watch' was to tweet in return. No tweet, and the circuit lit up Megan explained, "Because no one was on 'the watch.'" Each teen took a 15-minute slot and prayed for a dozen things – one item a minute with three minutes of waiting. "We felt like silence and quiet were important," Megan explained, "But three minutes out of fifteen is a lot of silence for teenagers". Everyone smiled. If they could not get the approximately one hundred kids to cover the 24-hour period, some of them took three or four slots, to make sure each period was covered. One of the features of the prayer time was evangelism praying called FW - 'friend watch.' During that segment, a friend was mentioned who had no relationship with God, some with no interest in God, and others whom they wanted to see developing a meaningful relationship with God. That moment usually occurred five minutes into the prayer time. Friends were mentioned by 'text or tweet' only by first name or initials, discreetly, sometimes by a pseudonym – and everyone who received the message was asked to say the name aloud prayerfully, that they would come to know God. Sometimes others retweeted the name of their friend. Megan recalls one moment, when it seemed the entire city was tuned in – and more the 200 names were mentioned in prayer. At times, the very kids they were praying for, joined the tweets asking their peers for prayer. A second connection point was ten minutes into each segment. The person on the watch was asked to offer a particular focus for prayer in a personal way. "Pray that God will help me be a light to ..." Some would say "a missionary to ..." And what followed was an assortment of mission areas – the homeless, a particular gang, the dealers, my teacher, my parents, my brother, single moms. Poignant messages appeared with the names masked, "I am praying for 'Al*c**n' – she is suicidal. She needs Jesus ... I am praying now for 'N*l**e' – she just found out that she is pregnant ... Pray for me and my Mom, there was another shooting in our neighborhood last night ..." Others would tweet their location, "Praying for drug deal going down now, XYZ parking lot." Some would call for a spontaneous prayer gathering: Meet at the corner of 1st and Main; youth hanging out now; prayer on the corner in ten minutes." Sometimes a dozen or more kids would gather spontaneously. One night, almost fifty showed up. Megan reported that the teen group wanted to make the effort a 24-7 project eventually, and they needed a place to meet – a kind of "prayer center." Around the room, attendees wiped away tears. God was at work. The question now, how do a group of people steward a move of God and not control it? How does a movement grow to become denominationally diverse and span the generations and cultures?

Committing to the Journey

"We have to meet again," everyone in the room, agreed.

Out of the meeting, an informal envisioning team was created – Cole and his wife Karen, their daughter Megan and another teen, Eric of the pastor's prayer group along with Pastor Monson, Frank and Lee with another man from the business community, and of course, Ellen with two other intercessors. The envisioning team agreed to meet again in a month. The cry became, "Don't let the fire go out!"

Cole and his team have no idea at the present moment that God is catching them up in a movement far beyond themselves. They are part of a grass-roots prayer movement that may be the only hope for the nation. They are innocent and non-assuming, humble and non-competitive. They are not sure of their next steps, but they are determined to move forward with God's leading to see a broader, more persistent prayer effort unwrap in their area. One that is diverse enough for a broad base of Christians to connect; one that is flexible enough to allow a variety of prayer styles and models, and specifically accommodating to the diversity of prayer efforts already underway. One that would evaluate where and when prayer was happening, and fan those flames, being the number one cheerleader; and one that would systematically plant prayer fires at times and places prayer is not happening.

STORY

After the Little Rock pastors had returned

from their second citywide prayer summit, they decided to study the city. They hired a professional firm to assess community needs, both the harvest field and the harvest force (church). When they unwrapped the primary findings of the costly study, no one was particularly shocked by the top ten list of needs in the city – housing/homelessness, racism, poverty, family stability, teen violence (gangs), abortion – those plague most urban communities. The overview of the study went on to highlight positive outreach efforts of the churches of Little Rock to meet those needs. Then the study became very insightful. Of the ten great social-moral-spiritual needs of the city, the researchers could identify programs in only five of the needy areas. The other five were unaddressed, in fact, largely off the radar screen of the church as something they had a need to address, could or should address. The telling moment was when the research concluded that while the programs operated by the churches that interfaced with five of the needs was significant to the Christians involved, fulfilling, satisfying, rewarding, gratifying, enjoyable – the efforts of the churches were not solving the problem. Personally gratifying. Significant to the participants – but not making a dent in the overall problem. In fact, the high levels of satisfaction for the churches and their members who did have outreaches was masking the larger problem – the lack of unity and strategic plan. Around the room,

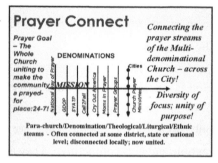

there was silence. A tear streamed down the face of a veteran pastor, as if he had been stunned. "We are the problem." To a man, it was clear; the task could not be accomplished by the independent, isolationist model in place. A greater unity was necessary.

2   One report notes that the most catalyzing religious event in a community in the last half-century has been a Billy Graham Crusade, but even that only achieves the functional engagement of about half the churches or less. Barna reported on some fronts, that less than 3% of the churches in a community ever aligned for a single cause. Mega churches constitute less than .5% of American congregations, and some 1600 of them exist across the nation. Fifty percent of all church attenders crowd into the largest 10% of our congregations. Almost 60% (59) of churches draw less than a hundred for Sunday worship. Another 35% draw less than 500. That means that 94% of the churches are smaller than 500 attenders. The growth trend has been toward the mega-churches that often function as world to itself, sometimes

creating a fellowship of churches beyond the community and their denominational family, if indeed, it is a part of such a theological accord; and even if it is, such churches tend to march to their own drum. (See: http://hirr. hartsem.edu/bookshelf/thumma_article2.html. Also: MegaChurchTrends).

3   About 46% of Christian adults tune in to Christian radio; 91% tune into general radio. Nearly two-thirds of those who listen (of the 46% above, thus around 30%), do so at least several times per week. One third, 15%, tune in to Christian radio each day (about 20 million), significant, but less than 7% of the US population. Listeners are predominantly women 45-54 years of age, frequent churchgoers, Pentecostal/Charismatic, residents of the South, politically conservative, and self-described activists. One in four (23%) of those who listen, don't tune in for Christian programs, they say they are not interested in 'Christian content' (listen mostly for the music); One in five (20%) prefer other content such as news and sports. Eleven percent prefer to get their Christian content elsewhere. Read more at http://www.christianpost.com/news/survey-only-3-in-5-christian-radio-listeners-tune-in-for-music-33305/#2VLDsygpksSaXoR7.99 Read: at http://www.christianpost.com/news/survey-only-3-in-5-christian-radio-listeners-tune-in-for-music-33305/#2VLDsygpksSaXoR7.99

Sixteen percent of adults spend time on faith-oriented websites monthly. Evangelicals: 41%; compared to 18% - other born again Christians; and 10% of non-born again Americans. The younger a person is, the more likely they are to visit a faith-oriented site. Western states and African-Americans are the groups most likely to check out these resources. The same people groups that resisted faith-based radio and television - mainline Protestants, Catholics, Asian-Americans, and the unchurched - were also the least likely visitors to these locations on the worldwide web. See: http://www.barna.org/barna-update/article/5-barna-update/183-more-people-use-christian-media-than-attend-church.

5   The percentage of adults who watch Christian television programming has remained unchanged since 1992 (An estimated 45% tune into a Christian program in a typical month). About 7% watch Christian television daily. Forty-one percent 'never' watch such programming. Christian television draws its strength from people in their 60s and older, females, residents of the South, African-Americans, people with limited education and income and 'born again' Christians. Two-thirds of the 'born again' population views Christian programming monthly, more than double the proportion of non-born again adults (30%). Those most likely to watch include mainline Protestants, Catholics, unchurched people, Asian-Americans and college graduates. More unchurched people watch Christian television than listen to Christian radio, although the margin of difference is small. Slightly more than one-fourth of the unchurched - about 20 million adults - tune in to these shows each month. See: http://www.barna.org/barna-update/article/5-barna-update/183-more-people-use-christian-media-than-attend-church.

6   Bob Waymire and Carl Townsend, *Discovering Your City: Bringing Light to the Task of Community Transformation* (Light International: Aetna California, 2000), Intro – 1.

CHAPTER 3
From the Nation to the City

Meet the Threads and Stands of our Story

Albert – *Albert is a believer, a conscientious one. He has worked a variety of jobs over the years, most in sales. He has traveled a good bit, but nothing charms him more than his mid-western hometown, lovingly called 'Cowtown,' a city of some 100,000 residents. For the west, it is good-size city! For Albert, it is a bit like heaven. Coming back from a national Christian conference, he was swept out of his comfort zone and moved to survey the need for unity and prayer in the city!*

Beth – *A young woman, whose connection with Albert is only that she and he attended the same conference in a city, miles away from each of their homes. They never met. They do not know each other, and yet each will become a catalyst for change. We will pick up Beth's story later.*

Joe – *Another 'regular' guy who listens to Albert share and catches the vision, eventually becomes a catalyst for spreading the movement of prayer to other cities.*

Ed and Patti – Ed is a businessman with considerable influence in the city. He and his wife Patti are moved to partner with Albert in seeing prayer embedded in the marketplace by the proliferation of small groups of praying believers.

Pastor Sam – A local pastor who serves the church at which Ed and his former wife, now deceased, once attended, who watches the prayer movement development with Ed's involvement and voices that raise discomforting questions.

Pastor Jones – A well-known and widely respected pastor in Cow Town that folks lobbied for as a member of the Pastoral Advisory Committee.

Vickie – A local church prayer coordinator who immediately saw the value of the community prayer leadership network and whose faithfulness and volunteerism commended her to a role on the PC²LN leadership team.

Jack Terry – A leader in a small town a few miles outside of Cow Town, who learned about the PC²LN movement and wanted help in organizing something in his community that would link to the larger movement.

Travel with me to a fictitious conference with a couple imaginary characters – Albert and Beth. Albert lives in the mid-western city that has a population of a hundred-thousand or so folks. For that part of the country, it is a good size city. Beth lives in the east in a spreading network of cities, a multi-county area that consists of a collage of sprawling communities, with one municipality running into another. Wide-open spaces are rare. Both Albert and Beth carry a deep concern for the communities in which they live. Neither is a pastor or a Christian professional. Neither has ever worked on a church staff. Albert was raised in a church, but Beth has been a believer for less than a decade. Both are alarmed about the direction in which the nation is headed; Albert for his grand-children, Beth for the three little ones she and her husband Larry are still raising.

It only takes a Spark

Beth and Albert recently attended the same Christian Confer-ence. So did 2500 others. They never met while there, in fact, they do not know one another. Nor do they share mutual acquaintances. However, they have a great deal in common. They care about the spiritual and moral foundations of the nation, and they often feel helpless in terms of their ability to make a difference. The prayer services they attend, the prayer groups in which both participate are quite diverse, and though they are inspirational to each of them in different ways, neither think the efforts are far reaching enough to change the nation – or their communities.

Beth, for the first time last year, went to her community's an-nual prayer breakfast. It was an anticipated highlight. Although she had been a believer for some time, this was the first she had heard of the event. The speaker was engaging. The moments of prayer at her table were inspiring, but it was quite different than she had anticipated. It was sadly, a very politically correct event. Everyone took great care to see that no one was offended; that is, no one but God. Deep inside, Beth left a bit disappointed. Grateful that such events take place, she left with a sense that the commu-nity needed a more unpretentious and authentic encounter with God – and more than once a year. She was surprised that only a few hundred attended the event. Her own pastor was not present. Miles away, Albert has been a part of prayer gatherings for de-cades in his town. They ebb and flow. The meetings tend to be more reflective of the conservative hue of his Midwestern culture, but he also sensed that the community needs more than a handful of annual prayer events attended by far too few of its pastors and people.

Is there a Logical Beginning Point

Returning home, after the recent conference, both Albert and Beth are considering what they can do to make a difference in their cities. Neither of them is convinced that they are 'the' leader for some new effort – both are too humble for such a lofty assumption. Both intentionally looked for other believers at the conference who were from their area, but as far each could tell, none was present. Beth's sister joined her there, but she lives in another town. An

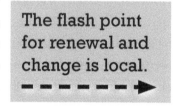

The flash point for renewal and change is local.

ex-pastor invited Albert, but he too, is half-way across the country. So Albert and Beth have been equipped, thoroughly challenged, in some ways shaken – but what do they do now? Where do they go with their passion; their new insights and information? To their pastor? To their prayer group? To some existing Christian organization? Do they hand off the baton of Christian concern stirring within them to someone else?

Who knows how many Christian conferences occur in the US each year? With multiplied thousands of congregations – more than 330,000; all the different denominations and independent churches; Christian and home-school conferences; Christian colleges; Christian Publishers; singles and seniors; pastors and youth leaders; music and children's conferences; 'this' model and 'that' new one; then para-church organizations besides – the number is probably easily in excess of a million. The largest of these conferences number in the tens-of-thousands. Most are sincere efforts to help some slice of the Christian cause. Many are significant conferences for those who attend. In some cases, a conference can be life changing. This conference was certainly life jolting for Albert and Beth.

The synergy of passionate speakers, the exhibit halls full of resource ideas and materials, the moments of impact by multi-media images, all coupled with a heart-felt and compelling concern about common issues, move people to resolve to make changes in their lives and that of their church or community. Days later, back home, Albert and Beth unpacked from their trip and picked up the life-reins they laid down days earlier to slip away for the conference. Settled back into their older routines, playing catch-up with life, the ideas lost steam. The intent of both Albert and Beth is sincere, and the need is no less compelling, but they are now alone. A week ago, in the crowded hall with thousands of other Christians, they felt that a change should come to the country, indeed, that it could come. Christian change is certainly needed, but now, back home, the dynamic seemed different. They struggled with starting points. They thought about all the existing structures and organizations, surely they could do something. They were in a position to bring change. Maybe these fresh ideas could be poured into older wineskins and the existing organizations could adapt their mission. She knew the answer before the thought ran its course in her head – old wineskins usually fail at holding new wine, at least according to Jesus, and he usually knew what he was talking about!

The Solution is Local – Not National

This scenario is repeated hundreds of times each week. Hundreds of others, just like Albert and Beth, sometimes as individuals, perhaps as a small group

Cities lead nations. ▬ ▬ ➤

from a given community, go to a regional or national conference, where the meeting venue is crowded, the excitement is high and the ideas are almost tangible. However, when they return – there is no platform onto which the idea can be easily unwrapped, no organization that can be a delivery system for the concept. Great conferences pull people together from across the country – first here, then there; next week yonder and the following week in that distant place. But when the conference ends, all are dispersed to only a handful of the 35,000 communities in the US – the diluted impact is marginal. By sheer numbers, they are too few to effect systemic national change. Their impact, but for a miraculous intervention of God, is far too marginal, too diminished.

What we are doing – is upside down! Our energy and volume are 'at the top' of our efforts, when it needs to be 'at the bottom.' Even then, it is divided into a thousand different slices with each national organization or denomination, unwrapping its programs and goals on different cities across

> **What we are doing – is upside down! ▪▶**

the nation – often competitively. The flash point for renewal and change is local. Cities lead nations – not the other way around. State and national organizations as well as movements need a sound and broad base - that is without dispute. Let's just consider prayer.

Prayer organizations gather their people – in national and regional conferences. Plans for this prayer effort; that 'day' of prayer; that 'event' is unwrapped. Hundreds return and pass the information down through their chain, but almost always to single individuals working alone to pull off the prayer event in their community. The time for the annual prayer event takes place, and a few gather, perhaps hundreds and in rare cases thousands. Then the event is over – until next year. A few months down the road, another prayer effort takes place sponsored by another prayer organization working in the city. Most Christians in any given community do not even know that such events take place. Great prayer efforts and resources go unheralded – because there is not a grass roots, national delivery system in place; no relational construct of prayer leaders in different communities who are stewarding prayer; not merely prayer for an event or a day, but prayer in the whole of the region and throughout the year.

Not a new organization! Rather, we need our existing organizations reorganized to collaborate, not compete. ━ ━ ➤

Cole and his team were discovering the same need, in their city, miles away from Albert and Beth, what was needed was a new construct, a prayer-connect network to steward prayer in our communities. Not a new organization! Rather, we need our existing organizations reorganized to collaborate, not compete; to transform events into process; to champion not one prayer cause, but all prayer causes, a diversity of prayer options. We need a community prayer leadership team that operates beyond the boundaries of our congregations and denominations; one that reaches further than any single-interest prayer endeavor. We need a model that honors the different congregations, pastoral leaders and the expressions of Christian life, and yet, one that transcends the differences that so easily divide us denominationally, in terms of style and emphasis, liturgy and distinctive traditions. The one thing we should be able to do together – is pray. Now, the country needs prayer as it may have never needed it before. We need a community-based, yet nation-wide network of prayer leaders and intercessors, based in neighborhoods and the marketplace, functioning Monday-through-Friday, when churches are closed.

STORY

In Bridgeport, the pastors had been gathering for a citywide monthly prayer meeting and
their attendance was in the range of 40-60 pastors. The meetings were spirited, and typically
utilized a 'prayer summit' model. Three pastors,
none of whom served large churches, but were
gifted at leading the relational prayer gatherings
were chosen as facilitators. The meetings began
promptly and pastors where asked to arrive on
time since the prayer time was limited to one-
hour. Fifteen minutes was provided at the end for
announcements, but no promotions. Promotional
materials were allowed on a table in the back of
the room, but the meetings were not allowed to
be commercialized. Month after the month, the
gatherings consistently provided times to seek
God. But on occasion, and with growing frequency, some pastor's bruising experience became the
center of the prayer gathering. "That was good,"
explained John Letchner, one of the facilitators,
"Where does a pastor go with his pain?" The
other pastors gathered around and prayed, some
cried, most knew personally some similar experience. "That was bad," John continued, without taking a breath, "Because suddenly, almost
imperceptibly, the prayer gatherings were again
about us and our pain." With that realization
in mind, they switched their model. Instead of
a comfortable time on Tuesday morning for the
one-hour-and-fifteen minute meeting, they chose
an unreasonable time, 6:15 AM. And they did so
in order to reach out and invite community lead-

ers – the mayor, the school superintendent, the head of the chamber of commerce, and a news anchor for a local TV station who was a Christian, a judge, the police chief – on and on. Their goal was a community leader a month. Their invitation went something like this, "We are a group of pastors who are concerned about our community. We meet together once a month for prayer, and we would like to invite you, in view of your role in the city, as the focus of our next prayer gathering. We want the opportunity to give you the 'gift of prayer.'" They made it clear, their goal was not political. This was not a time for information exchange. While there would be a brief moment in the beginning for the invited guest to share how they felt the group might best pray for them, the time would be spent mainly in prayer. When their guest arrived, they welcomed them warmly, invited them to briefly share so their intercession could be informed. Then, they promptly seated them in the center of the room, and gathered around them for prayer. For some, it was the most unique prayer experience that had ever encountered. The pastors prayed one-by-one. At times, they read a Bible passage. Only the briefest of questions were allowed, and then only to refocus prayer. There were often tears. Every guest felt the sincere warmth and concern of the pastors. The fruit was open channels of dialogue, connections with leaders that many pastors might never have experienced, a deeper appreciation among community leaders for pastors, doors opened for collaborative action – and answers to prayer.

CHAPTER 4
Suddenly Moments

Meet the Threads and Stands of our Story

<u>Beth and Larry</u> – Beth, like Albert, was exposed at a national conference, to ideas about prayer mobilization in her community. She came home hoping to dismiss the idea, but soon found herself exposed to community concerns that were not being addressed and increasingly, she felt that she was a part of a sleeping Christian culture. She was moved to act beyond herself, and in humility gather leaders of prayer movements and other believers and forge a union for spiritual renewal.

<u>Genny</u> – A veteran intercessor with an informal group of interconnected people of prayer who had persisted in pleading with heaven for revival – through this movement and that one, this effort and then another. When the smoke cleared, Genny was still praying.

<u>Martha</u> - The Prayer Coordinator for a local congregation that has taken prayer very seriously. Martha is thrilled to see

the Community Prayer Leadership Team. She feels that she has been alone – for a long time! She welcomes the opportunity to dialogue, to share and learn. Moreover, to see a broader prayer movement emerge than could ever be released in her congregation.

Jackson - A former missionary, Jackson, settled in the area. He has sponsored prayer events for businessmen in the city over the years and is well known and respected. He is a man of prayer. His experience in both the church and the marketplace, in the states and abroad, offers a unique perspective.

Liz and Mark - Liz and Mark put together an innovative Christian Celebration a few years ago. It is part entertainment and partly a prayer and American heritage experience, a kind of festival, and it draws thousands annually, not only from the region, but also from a multi-state area. Christian artists perform. Nationally known speakers address the crowds. It is a premier annual Christian event.

Reading the newspaper one morning, Beth noticed a statistic, a wave of youth crimes in a financially distressed sector of the community near her. On investigation, she found alarming discoveries about drug activities, a new 'adult club' in a somewhat upscale area far too close to home. Rumbles about the Harry Potter games played at the middle school that in-

> *I have posted watchmen on your walls; they will pray day and night ... a constant watch ...* ━ ━ ━ ➤ Isa. 62:6

volved a family friend also concerned her. Suddenly, it was clear – she knew the street names and the location of shopping malls. She knew how to navigate the major thoroughfares of the city, but she did not really know the spiritual trends of the city, the moral moods, or the level of appetite for disturbing behaviors that she felt were threats to her family, and to the very pillars of principle on which a healthy community rested.

What difference would it mean to the city, she began to ask, if there were constant, ceaseless prayer? If there were never a time when an intercessor was not praying? If there were not a business or building in the city that did not have an intercessor's attention? A city covered in prayer? If there were growing numbers of Christians who were no longer sleeping, but beginning to cry out to God for intervention in their community?

> **What difference would it mean to the city, she began to ask, if there were constant, ceaseless prayer?** ▬ ▬ ▬ ➤

Would it make a difference for God see a steady stream of incense rising from the community – first here, and then there? The prayer lamp always burning, being passed from one to another; moving from evangelicals to Pentecostals; from Baptists to Methodists; from liturgical churches to non-liturgical congregations; from blacks to whites to Hispanics and beyond that among an array of cultures and generations. Would it make a difference? Does community-based prayer make a difference? Could it actually change a community? Or even a nation? The idea was more than intriguing. It haunted Beth, and it was at the same time overwhelming.

A dozen states away, Albert found a list of churches on which he had been asked to call a few years before for a special city-wide community evangelism effort. It was quite an undertaking. He sensed God saying to him that the discovery of the list was not an accident. Albert remembered the number; there were about 129 churches and missions, Christian organizations and agencies. He wondered - how many of them had an organized prayer effort? He decided the start the process of finding out. He contacted the organization that had provided him the list, and gained permission to reconnect with the churches for the new cause.

Beth soon found five different prayer organizations in her area. She knew there were probably more, but she had a starting place. She invited each leader to coffee, talking about prayer's bigger picture – and the need for a prayed-for community. She claimed to be no expert, she simply shared what was happening to her and how she sensed God's leading – and her plea was for guidance from these more veteran prayer leaders. All sensed her lack of a personal agenda. And she secretly hoped that one of them would pick up the torch for the mission, but none did so. Albert called two friends and shared his burden for the area. Each took a third of the list; one recruited another partner, and together they started contacting pastors.

An Inescapable Call

Beth and Albert have now become the 'catalyst' their community needed to see movement in the area of citywide, on-going, relentless prayer. Every movement has to have a catalyst; someone with fire in their belly, an unshakable sense of mission, and a clear compelling view of the need. The path may not be clear, but there is enough light and adequate vision to propel such a 'John Knoxer' forward.

In other cities, there are dozens more like these two who are shaken by the paralysis of the Christian community and its divisions, and yet they realize that a mere Christian-based political process unwrapped on their city is not the answer – only an intervention by God can help us. These folks, like Albert and Beth, are searching for ways to bring people together in broader local coalitions than a local congregation can do, or even a cluster of denominational churches; something more sustainable than the mobilization of prayer for an event. They have not conceptualized a PC^2LN, but it is that type of configuration that they need. In other places, the process is well underway and a variety of models exists. However, they are isolated and unique to a given locale and would benefit from a connection to a national network.

Albert's plan was to find a pastor or prayer leader, share the information he had gained at the conference, and stand back and watch the process unwrap. Beth was confident that one of the prayer organizers she did coffee with or a godly leader with name recognition and community credibility should lead the process. But, that is not how God always works. Genny is a veteran intercessor whom deeply senses the need for Christian unity and collaborative prayer. She has carried the burden to see the community bathed in prayer for more than four decades. Hearing about her, Beth was sure she had discovered the right leader, one she would be glad to help. But while Genny had a burden for prayer, she did not have the gifting to lead a movement. Nor, in her mid'80s, did she have the strength. However, her deep roots and wide connections offered much needed relational collateral for Beth. That was a gift that Genny was willing to give - influence. Just her name seemed to open doors that Beth might not have readily accessed. Suddenly, Beth was in a room with a couple dozen folks that Genny had called together – pastors, prayer leaders and other intercessors – all of whom knew and respected Genny. The veteran intercessor set the stage as she introduced Beth. "I recently met a friend, and as she shared, I felt she had something all of you should hear – an idea whose time has come!"

The Message of the Catalyst

Beth took a deep breath, and humbly began. She briefly shared a slice of her own journey. Then she talked about both the conference she had attended, that had awakened in her a growing sense of awareness for the need for spiritual renewal in the community. "We are better when we are together!" And, "What we are attempting to do individually, we can do more

We are better when we are together! ⇒ ⇒ ➤

effectively in collaboration and unity. Prayer and unity have to be partnered. Some things may separate us as believers, but in the very least, we can pray together! And God promises a blessing when his people pray together (Psalm 133). Jesus wanted us to be one – it was the centerpiece of his last prayer (John 17). We have numerous prayer efforts already going in our community. How can we connect these? How can we support one another in a unified prayer effort?"

"That is the simple goal," she stated – "to collaborate, to co-operate, to synergize, to translate prayer events into a process, to create community-wide construct of collaborating pastors, prayer leaders, congregations, para-church organizations and intercessors, respecting diversity, learning from one another."

STORY

The inner city school was on lock down. It was chaotic. Over half the students were in the halls, the gym or the front lawn and not in class. Despite the use of the loudspeaker, the principal's best efforts, even threats, the problem grew worse. It escalated day after day. These kids did not need another encounter with the police. There were only two weeks left before summer vacation. In after-hours meetings, school administrators considered the alternatives. There seemed to be few. The students came to school daily, but by mid-morning break, they were out of control.

They refused to follow their class schedule. Daily, the disorder seemed to intensify.

A local youth pastor first heard about the issue from members of his own youth group. The Holy Spirit, he recalled, nudged him, to offer to the school a unique solution. Soon, he was in front of the principal. What he suggested did not seem to be a solution at all, "Trust me", he pleaded with the principal. The administrator knew the young man to be a leader with integrity. Having established relationships is critical to open doors. "I will bring a dozen youth pastors. You can orient us on 'dos and don'ts'. We know we are not coming to preach, just to bring peace. We'll walk the halls, chat with the kids, urge them to return to class, and try to restore order." The principal shook his head, "It's crazy. Why do you think you can bring order, when thirty educational professionals, the whole school faculty and staff, cannot?" The youth pastor smiled, "It is a spiritual thing! What you are dealing with is not just restless adolescents; you are dealing with a spiritual problem." Facing near pandemonium in his school, the principal still was resolute against religious activity. "You can't pray!" Strange isn't it? We worry more about keeping prayer out, even if it means affirming behaviors about which we all disapprove! "I know," the youth pastor responded, "I know – and you will not hear us praying!"

Wherever the kids assembled, youth pastors moved in among them and struck up a conversation. Kids who were churched seemed empowered by the presence of their youth pastor, and a new level of peer pressure kicked in – a positive kind of peer pressure. "Do the right thing!" the

Christian kids told their rowdy peers. And a good number of them were motivated to shape up as well. Within three days, everything was back to normal. Over 200 kids had been in the suspension room at one point, now there were less than twenty. The school finished its year. Exams went on as usual. The principal and teachers gained a new respect for the youth pastors, not only for their willingness to enter the fray, but also for their respect of boundaries that could create a legal issue for them by the radical anti-Christian crusaders. That would pay dividends in the coming year in terms of legal Bible Clubs, See-You-At-the-Pole, and other efforts.

▬ ▬ ▬ ➤ PC²LN creates a connection that also allows for learning from other communities. If you feel God calling you to start the process of creating a PC²LN in your community, we want to help - and of course, we need your help. Register your effort by a simple email via the web-site. Or give us a call. We'll help you determine whether or not an effort has already been launched in your community.

Register Your City Wide Prayer Network Now

1. Register their name – as a catalyst.
2. Provide contact information ... City, County, State, Zip ... Phone ... email.
3. Provide any credentials, connections – do you work with a national prayer organization (Helpful, but not necessary)? Are you a prayer leader for a local congregation? Info box ...
4. Provide references! Name ... phone ... email ... relationship to this person ... their title/role ...

CHAPTER 5
Navigating Resistance

Albert and his friends finished their calling. They learned about a movement of pastors who were convening to consider next steps for collaborative efforts in the region. Albert arranged to meet the leader and share what was stirring in his heart and then was invited to talk with the group of pastors. Fourteen pastors and a few leaders of para-church organizations were at the table. After three-or-four ideas had been discussed, Albert shared the concept of a communitywide, prayer leadership network – an idea being set forth by the Mission America Coalition and the National Prayer Committee, but one that the community itself would steward. Albert had not prepared a formal presentation. He had no Power Point to unwrap. He knew he was not a polished speaker, but he shared from his heart. He reminded the pastors that he had grown up in the area and that he had been a part of a number of collaborative events. "We come together for this, then that … but we don't 'stay' together," he urged. "The one thing we can do together; and we must do together", is pray. The pastor of 'First Church' suddenly stopped him. It was the largest church in the city, perhaps the most influential, "You're too late with your plan. We are already doing that. We have intensive prayer rather consistently. We also have teams that pray throughout the city once a year. Great idea – but we are already doing it!"

It was a moment of cold water. It seemed to stop the discussion. Albert did not know what to do. He certainly wanted to be respectful, not only to the pastor of First Church but also to his host who had opened the door for his presentation. Suddenly he was inspired. "Even if such a task could be accomplished by one congregation," he gently responded, "it would be a mistake for that single congregation to walk alone in such an endeavor. This cannot be the task of one congregation, but the call of the church-of-the-city, a mission for the people of God united." He said it humbly, but forthrightly. "The one thing we can do together – is pray! We may not agree on various action strategies, but we can agree that our cities

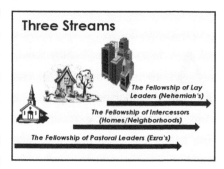

desperately need prayer. The nation needs God, and nations turn only as cities turn. Cities lead nations. In joining in unified prayer, we move toward the fulfillment of John 17; and Psalm 133. If there is power in prayer; there is explosive power through unity in prayer." He made his case that prayer should be a platform for beginning the process of unifying congregations together in community changing mission. He secretly wondered if the reason this pastor had operated so independently of other churches was his commitment to a particular prayer style and theology, and an aversion to others who differed. Albert looked around the room, "In the past, we have attempted to come together minimizing our differences, even ignoring or denying them. The best approach may be the up-front recognition of the significant differences between us – and simultaneously, a commitment to the central and most cohesive element in our theology, the supremacy of Christ. If we can agree – that Jesus Christ, the Lord of Glory, is indeed, our Lord; and that nothing is more important than our living in ways that honor him and tell his story, that is a good beginning point." No one said anything. But no one disagreed. How could they? "Our differences will not disappear. But under the banner of Christ's Lordship, around 'the essential core' of theology and driven by 'task theology' – we can move forward to engage our community."

It was clear now, he was talking about more than prayer. He was calling for a prayer platform, a connection point, shared mutuality in terms of concern for the community, and then finding ways to collaborate for the fulfillment of the mission. "How would we do that?" a pastor of a smaller, but significant congregation asked sincerely. "How would we move forward?"

"First," Albert noted, "by making our county a 'prayed for' place" and then offering a kind, respectful smile to the pastor of First Church "... by joining all our efforts with what God is already doing. You see; God is obviously at work in the city – He is racing ahead of us and we need to join Him. We need to talk with the prayer team at First Church and learn from their efforts, and find ways to strengthen and replicate

Our current model is on-and-off. We need relentless, passionate, united prayer. ------▶

that effort, add new layers of prayer to what is already taking place. And then, we need to find common ways to express the love of Christ together, making our city a 'cared for' place. Finally, we want to develop a comprehensive strategy to engage every home in the community, every person with a fresh personal witness of Christ and do so by a given date, and then relentlessly – praying, caring, sharing – until there are a great harvest and a spiritual awakening."

Albert suddenly realized; he had at least won another opportunity to go to the next level. He had the ear of a group of key pastors in the city.

Begin with a Relational Prayer Construct

Weeks had passed, and now Beth was in front of another group – and this time, the presentation was more formal. Those who sat in Genny's front room had agreed to return, and bring others with them. Additional prayer group leaders were in the room, as were a handful of pastors along with some intercessors.

Beth began, "In our current model, prayer is hit-and-miss. It is seasonal. It is 'days' of prayer. It is this group and then that one

> ▬ ▬ ▬ ➤ What we are calling PC²LN from the national stage might be called something else in your community – the brand is not important; and in fact, the process may have already begun. Unified prayer is clearly on the heart of God. The goal of the movement, now being encouraged by the National Prayer Committee and the Mission America Coalition is to nurture, at a national level, what God is doing in pockets across the nation; and to prevent, to whatever degree we can, from allowing those movements to be silos, functioning in isolation. We want to spread the word, to champion the movement, to fan the flames and connect the leaders of such local movements across the nation.

– but rarely is it the whole community together. We need relentless, passionate, united prayer. And we need to develop a rhythm of prayer. The purpose of the Prayer-Connect Community Leadership Network (PC²LN) will be to call together leaders of existing prayer ministries, para-church organizations, and congregational prayer coordinators – and invite them to the same table. Some are in the room

> How do we translate independent prayer events into a seamless movement, a process in which one event flows into the next? ━ ━ ➤

today – but we want to keep beating the drum until we reach as many of them as we can, and connect them. We don't want to leave any prayer effort out." She took a moment, and asked for the spontaneous naming of existing streams of prayer that others might know about and then she passed around a sheet for names and contact information.

"Throughout the community, during the course of the year, there are often numerous and diverse, but typically sparsely attended prayer events." She had a list of such events on the calendar that was distributed. "These are certainly not all the events. They do not even attempt to list prayer specifically sponsored by individual congregations – these are community prayer events. Look over the list", she encouraged. Then she invited others to post their community prayer events or groups to the calendar, and to note events that were not listed or represented in the room. "Our goal," she explained, "is to explore the extent to which we already have prayer activities during the course of any year, and the 'who,' 'what,' 'when,' and 'where' of these events. No one," she offered, "doubts that the organizers of these prayer efforts are sincere. The support materials of national organizations are often superb. The cause and focus of the various prayer efforts are noble – but the numbers of people that respond are less than marginal – dozens, rarely hundreds." She paused and took a deep breath. "What would happen, if the numbers participating in these prayer gatherings were not dozens or hundreds, but thousands?" The looks she received ranged from incredulous to suspicious; from dismissive to a settled and unmoved embrace of apathy. "Really," she urged, "What if they received broad Christian community support?" They had all dreamed of better-attended community prayer efforts, and many could remember when they had the kind of fresh optimism that Beth was evidencing. She asked two more questions, "Are we content with the current level of community response and participation to our prayer efforts?" The answer was obviously, 'No!' "Are we content with only decorating our calendar with a handful of annual prayer events?" Eyebrows were raised. Questioning looks surfaced. "We should not only be asking, 'How do we strengthen these events?' But more importantly, 'How do we translate these events into a seamless prayer process, a 24-7, 365 prayer effort, a movement in which one event flows into another?'"

Going it Alone - Together

The help that Albert and Beth need will not be found in larger national conferences. We cannot convene the entire nation of believers as Israel attempted to do in their feast days – even if that is needed. Nor will success be found in the triumph of one prayer organization over another or one denomination or para-church prayer plan. It is precisely the opposite that is needed. The solution is a grassroots, broad-based, one-for-all and all-for-one prayer movement that champions multiple and diverse on-going prayer efforts with a goal toward 'great awakening.' An effort that utilizes the existing resources of national prayer organizations and denominations honors their distinct purpose and mission strengthens the focus of each national prayer representative working lo-

▬ ▬ ▬ ➤ The Catalyst engages other significant prayer leaders and pastors with the idea of
the creating of a PC²LN. In some cases, an informal construct of prayer leaders may already exist,
but no opportunity has been available to connect
the local team with a national network.

Using support materials, provided by the National Facilitator, the catalyst persistently shares
the vision, beating the drum for the formation of
a PC²LN. This vision sharing may be one-on-one.
Or with small groups. The catalyst pursues potential conveners, men and women of prayer, along
with him/herself, who have the relational collateral necessary to call a larger envisioning meeting, and subsequently, a constituting meeting to
launch the PC²LN.

cally, and yet, does so in tandem with other prayer efforts in the
community, and for the good of that community. In this way, national prayer organizations more effectively serve the city, have
a broader base of support for their prayer efforts; and simultaneously, local prayer leadership teams emerge with greater influence
in the community. In the same way, at the same table replicated
in thousands of cities, denominational prayer plans and resources
are shared at the table – and churches from a variety of streams
embrace, perhaps modify, but adopt different prayer resources,
contextualizing them not only for their congregation, but doing so
collaboratively across the city.

▬ ▬ ▬ ▬ ▬ ▬ ▬ ▬ ▬ ▬ ▬ ▬ ▬ ▬ ▬ ▬ ▬ ▬ ▬ ▬

STORY

Brawleyville is a wide-open town. It is a bor-
der town. The influx of immigrants changed the

*city dramatically. While it has its share of estab-
lished churches, the immigrants, as is often the
case, brought their religion with them, even their
version of Christianity. They want a church like
they had it at home. That led to a proliferation of
storefront, shopping strip churches. They popped
up like mushrooms. At one point, 20% of Brawleyville's churches were storefront varieties. That
is not surprising, since 40% of the population is
recent or generational immigrant groups.*

*The city fathers could not stop the tide of im-
migration, but they did take action against immigrant churches – just not on that basis. They knew
such a direct assault on faith would fail. They
chose to act on the basis of the churches being in
violation of zoning ordinances. Inspectors toured
the city and gathered data, and in one mass action, the city sent letters informing the churches
that they had thirty days to vacate the strip-malls.
Never mind the obligation of the churches to legal contracts as lessee, which was not the concern of the city. Never mind that thirty days are
an inadequate amount of time to find a place to
relocate a congregation. Never mind that the city
knew the churches had no place to go. They were,
using a legal technique, closing almost 20% of
the churches of the city.*

*Pastors who did not know each other were
suddenly standing shoulder to shoulder in city
hall asking why and what this all meant. They
gathered for prayer. Fortunately, a Christian legal team came to their rescue, and the city relent-
ed, but not before a great deal of confusion had
been created and a good bit of funds invested to
defend their right to exist.*

Across the country, home Bible studies, store-

front churches, Christian schools using church facilities, churches that bake pies and sell dinners or even feed the poor, are coming under legal attack by cities who fail to see the church as a community asset. The only prescription is to stand together. "First they came for the Communists, but I was not a Communist, so I did not speak out. Then they came for the Socialists and the Trade Unionists, but I was neither, so I did not speak out. Then they came for the Jews, but I was not a Jew, so I did not speak out. And when they came for me, there was no one left to speak out for me" (Dietrich Bonhoeffer).

CHAPTER 6
Convening Leaders in a City

The Role of the Catalyst

Beth has now shared the vision for a PC²LN in her area several times. She has already had more coffee and telephone conversations than she can remember. She has been enthusiastically embraced and politely, but cautiously received. On at least one occasion, she was hurried through a presentation that was not comfortable – but even there, some sought her out and ended up listening to more details and loving the idea. It has been more than six months since she first reached out after returning from her conference and having her jolting morning over an open newspaper, God stirring her to be a catalyst for change. Her husband, Larry, doesn't quite have the same passion, but he has been supportive, attending meetings with her, watching the kids, reaching out in his own way.

Beth has not stopped connecting with people of prayer or pastors. She printed some cards that simply carried her name, cell phone number and email address with the line, "I'm all about a 'prayed for' community. Wanna help? Call me." Now, she is not alone. A pastor, though not her own, has joined her cause. His church is quite different from the tradition she knows, and this pastor has shown no interest in proselyting her and Larry, rather he seems to be genuinely, kingdom minded. He has opened numerous doors for additional contacts. Besides Genny, she has other people who now meet and share the idea of a community prayer network with others. Ann is the leader of a small network of praying women. Another, Martha, is the prayer coordinator of a church that has taken prayer very seriously. The final member of the team is a man, Jackson, who has

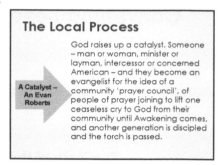

The Local Process

God raises up a catalyst. Someone – man or woman, minister or layman, intercessor or concerned American – and they become an evangelist for the idea of a community 'prayer council', of people of prayer joining to lift one ceaseless cry to God from their community until Awakening comes, and another generation is discipled and the torch is passed.

A Catalyst – An Evan Roberts

sponsored prayer events for businessmen in the city over the years, at one time, he was himself a missionary, and he remains a man of prayer. Each of them came to Beth with assorted backgrounds and connections to various streams of church life. Together Beth and the others sensed that they had the relational collateral to convene a more formal envisioning meeting to consider the establishment of a PC^{2}LN in the community. Through the highs and lows, the one constant has been a bi-weekly prayer gathering for the effort led by Genny. Beth recalls, "I go to the prayer meeting energy depleted and feeling like this is an impossible task, and I leave convinced God is in it, and it is doable". Genny keeps reminding everyone, "Nothing needs more prayer than a prayer effort". So the prayer meeting, with a small but consistent number has been the constant anchor in the months of vision casting.

Albert had his earliest success with pastors. Next, he began to connect with prayer leaders and local church prayer coordinators, even with intercessors. He connected with Christian businessmen whom he felt had a heart both for the community and an appreciation for prayer. At each meeting, he would share his vision for PC^{2}LN. And he would ask, "Who else should I talk with about this?" It was slow and deliberate process. In some cases, he would ask, "Would you call him and make the introduction?" Gradually, his circle was expanding from pastors to prayer leaders, from intercessors to praying people in almost every sector of the marketplace. It was Joe who began to help Albert tip the scales. He met Joe through a mutual friend and immediately, Joe's heart was turned on to the vision. At first, Joe seemed to show

> This is an interesting idea. Impractical, against the grain of our independence, a thankless uphill journey, but just crazy enough to be a 'God-sized' idea.
>
> ━ ━ ━ ━ ━ ➤

up and listen quietly as Albert shared the vision, first with one and then with another. "I thought," Joe recalled, "this is an interesting idea this guy has come up with! It's impractical, against the grain of our independence, a thankless uphill journey, but just crazy enough to be a 'God-sized' idea." When Joe found out it was part of a national movement, he had even greater hope that this could succeed. He began to line up other appointments for Albert. "Tell them about ..." Joe had Albert's lines memorized. Soon, he was spreading the news with equal passion.

Ed and his wife, Patti, heard about PC^{2}LN from their pastor who suggested they contact Albert. They did, and through their connections, Albert and Joe were soon sharing with a room full of diverse believers from more than dozen different congregations, all friends of friends of Ed and Patti. Now, the diversity Albert had sensed he needed at the lay level was developing. A consensus emerged, concluding that it was time for a formal sharing of the PC^{2}LN vision.

━ ━ ━ ▶ PC²LN Convening Team

General Role Description

The Convening Team is a group of leaders, drawn together with or by the Catalyst, the John Knoxer, who carried a vision to them for the creation of a PC²LN in their community.

The Identity

The Convening Team consists of a group of three-to-five Christian leaders, perhaps more, who have concern for prayer in their community. Together, they have the credibility and relational collateral to convene one or more envisioning sessions.

This Convening Team may be prayer leaders, pastors or other. They should represent some level of diversity. Ideally, they are ethnically diverse and from different streams of the Christian community. The prayer effort you want to mobilize should be broad enough for all Bible reading believers in the community and the churches they attend. It should embrace a variety of prayer styles and expressions, prayer focus areas and interests.

Vision Casting Stage

The Convening Team senses the strategic relevance of the PC²LN to the city/county. They join their voices with the Catalyst, engaging other leaders and people of prayer.

Representatives of various prayer ministries in the identified geographic area are contacted. Vision is cast – informally. Congregations that have prayer ministry leaders are likewise envisioned.

These sessions may be an informal meeting over a cup of coffee or formal vision-casting sessions complete with power-point. A systematic effort should be made to connect with all the divergent streams of the Bible-reading believers in the area so that when a formal envisioning meeting occurs, it is a constituting diversity that is genuinely representative of the community. And still, that may be the first of several envisioning meetings in different venues, with different sectors of the prayer leadership constituency.

The informal sharing escalates to formal vision-casting sessions – some in small groups, others in large groups, some in this stream and others in that stream. It will be very important to have endorsers early in the process, who echo the need for the PC^2LN – among various denominational streams, ethnic streams, prayer ministry efforts, etc.

The convening team that both Albert and Beth had gathered in their respective counties was informal but committed to seeing the project through to the constituting meeting of the PC^2LN. In both cases, the others realized that Albert and Beth had been called by God to provide initial leadership – and there was no wrestling over the leadership mantle. Mutual dependence on one another and the Spirit developed in the context of prayer. They decided to do one more vision evening in which they tried to get as many prayer leaders as possible in the room along with key pastors and key Christian leaders.

As the larger vision meeting approached, Albert and Beth, along with their convening team, emphasized the importance of yielding to the Holy Spirit and the will of the larger group. Neither Albert nor Beth presumed a leadership role for themselves. Those who helped them also retained a servant-heart and refused to manipulate the process. Albert and Ed chaired the meeting in their mid-western town, and Beth asked Jackson and Genny to sit with her in the formal envisioning evening she hosted miles away.

The convening teams, led by Beth and Albert in their respective cities, engaged others with passion and yet with tenderness. They let God guide and direct the process. They exhibited patience, waiting for God's timing. Albert knew he might have to live through the death and rebirth of the vision, but he was now committed to see a PC^{2}LN established.

Beth welcomed everyone with Jackson and Genny seated next to her, and then she invited Jackson to open the meeting in prayer. She really wanted Genny to do so, but Genny had a way of 'getting lost in prayer.' Beth had never encountered anyone that prayed like Genny, and she had come to both understand her passion and appreciate it. Nevertheless, on this occasion, even Genny felt that the decision for Jackson to begin was a sound one. After prayer and some brief introductions, Beth explained what some had heard her say a dozen times, "What we are attempting to do individually, we can do more effectively together. Prayer and unity are partners. Some things may separate us as believers, but we can pray together! God promises a blessing when his people pray together (Psalm 133). Jesus wanted us to be one – it was the centerpiece of his last prayer (John 17). We have numerous prayer efforts already going in our community. How can we link these? How can we support

The Local Process

Around the catalyst, a small team forms who join their voice in the plea to people of faith, to come together to pray. This informal team, with the favor of God, heart-felt passion, personal credibility and persistence, engage leaders in vision casting sessions, formal and informal, until they can convene a constituting meeting to launch the prayer council.

A Catalyst – An Evan Roberts ► A Convening Team

one another in a unified prayer effort?"

A few questions followed. Beth had the larger group break up into small discussion teams, and each team was led by a member of the convening team or someone who had been in previous vision casting sessions and had a grasp on where the idea was going. She showed a brief video (Available at www.pc2ln.org). She reviewed the highlights of a power point presentation (also on the website). She explained, "We will have complete control. This is our project, a prayer leadership team for our community, but we will not be alone. We are part of a national, grass-roots movement. Honorable and tried organizations are helping us with this endeavor – the Mission America Coalition and the National Prayer Committee." She distributed basic written information gleaned from the web site. She noted the names of those endorsing the movement.

At the end of the meeting, after reviewing the 'imagine' section of the power point presentation, she asked for spontaneous 'imagine' prayers focused on the local community. One by one, voices were raised. "Imagine every school adopted by an intercessor ... imagine a map displaying the locations of intercessory prayer coverings in the city ... imagine teams regularly prayer walking ... imagine prayer evangelism efforts ... imagine a prayer team for the mayor ... the school board ... one praying over zoning decisions ... imagine prayer for the downtrodden ... imagine a 24-7 prayer hot-line for the city ... imagine pastoral prayer teams ... imagine triads of prayer during the week throughout the city ... imagine gatherings of men for prayer ... and women ... and teens ... and even children ... imagine ... imagine prayer ... imagine a prayed-for city ... imagine a great awakening!"

Beth was sure – it was a done deal! The date for the constituting meeting was then announced along with the location.

STORY

Their downtown hotel covered a block. In the '50's, it had been a proud establishment, but now it was sad in appearance, and a breeding ground for corruption. It became the center of prostitution and drugs. Police were pressured to 'clean it up' to no avail. An occasional drug related arrest occurred, but the eyesore and moral blight of the downtown area only seemed to grow worse. Attempts to correct the situation through zoning or business regulations seemed to meet resistance, as well. Belinda Keller concluded one day while passing the place, "There is nothing left to do, but pray!" She began to share with her friends the possibility of targeting the area for prayer, for an entire week. Finally, a small team of intercessors committed to the wild notion. They marked their calendar. The first day, only a handful showed up. Belinda was not discouraged; she knew victory was not in numbers alone. They gathered. They prayed. And they marched around the entire block. A few 'residents' looked them over as they sang and prayed their way around the complex. They concluded their prayer walk with another prayer, and agreed to do the same thing the next day. Each day their numbers grew, until near the end of the week, more than a hundred gathered. The last day, they marched around the building seven times. A crowd also gathered to watch – and chuckle. The media covered their march. When the crowds dispersed, the media told their story; the owners continued their nefarious deeds, and nothing seemed to have changed. Belinda felt dif-

ferent. "The Lord put this on my heart. We had tried everything – political pressure, political process, police action – and we cried out to the Lord, and I knew he would hear us." As they say, "God works in mysterious ways." In one of the rooms on the backside of the sprawling motel, a fire broke out in one of the rooms and did significant damage to the establishment. For weeks, it sat as the sad spectacle it was, and then a miracle happened. The owner was not able to raise the money to repair the facility – not with all the fire code regulations he now had to meet. Suddenly the drug dealers and the prostitutes were gone. The building changed hands, and a new investor restored the facility to its 1950's persona. "It is now a cute establishment in the heart of our city, bright and clean, what a change – and prayer, united prayer, bold prayer, was the key."

CHAPTER 7
The Monkey Wrench Moment

A lbert had completed his final vision-casting session. To the best of his knowledge, all the prayer leaders and ministries willing to hear him out had been envisioned. Cities as far as a hundred miles away had sent folks to observe so that they could launch a similar process. In fact, Albert and Joe, while trying to focus on their own community, had made a couple trips to share with pastors and prayer leaders in other cities.

In the next few days, Albert became aware of an issue that was gaining a good deal of attention among those involved in the process and beyond it. There was an unseemly chatter and a growing restlessness that threatened unity. Ed, who had been so instrumental in bridging the gap to the business sector, had been an elder at a significant church in the city and had left to attend another church. Albert didn't know the details, but there were wounds that seemed far too fresh. Albert addressed the issue with Ed, who agreed to step-aside from the informal convening team. Albert knew, that without Ed's involvement, the prayer component they had already envisioned for the marketplace would suffer a setback. He asked for permission to set up a meeting with the parties involved. Ed cautiously agreed, revealing his perspective of the very personal issues to Albert. His first wife had died, and while the church had been their spiritual home for more than a decade, in the process of grieving, he felt he needed a change. At first, he visited a few other churches always coming back to this home church. Then, he joined a single's grief group at another church, and finally made the switch permanent. He had no intention, he asserted, of hurting those with whom he had worshiped for so long. However, some of them obviously still carried a hurt, feeling they had invested in him, and he had walked away. As Albert sat in the room with Ed and

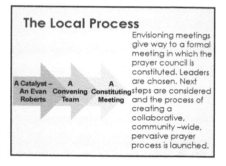

The Local Process
Envisioning meetings give way to a formal meeting in which the prayer council is constituted. Leaders are chosen. Next steps are considered and the process of creating a collaborative, community –wide, pervasive prayer process is launched.

A Catalyst – An Evan Roberts   A Convening Team   A Constituting Meeting

his wife, his pastor and the new pastor of Ed's former church, two other friends, both elders of his former church joined the meeting. It was Albert who had called Dr. Sam Welch, the pastor of Ed's former church, and suggested a meeting. Pastor Sam explained that he had heard no rumbles and knew nothing about the situation. Whatever had occurred had taken place prior to his coming over three years ago. Albert persisted, believing the meeting was critical to the process going on in the community.

Ed shared his confusion and personal pain in the loss of his first wife. The former fellow elders shared their grief over his loss to them in leaving the church. Tears flowed. Understanding grew. Forgiveness flourished. It was a poignant moment. A powerful reconciliation was affected, and had it not happened, it would have set back the movement, deepened existing divisions, and dispersed malignant information. Instead, two pastors and churches now seemed closer. Old friends whose relations had been severed in a time of personal confusion were friends again. As painful as the meeting had been, Ed agreed – it was a good kind of pain. "I never knew my leaving hurt them so deeply," he noted. "They love me, I have always known that. I don't how I missed the fact that my leaving might have wounded them so severely. I was hurting so desperately over the death of my wife. I was blind to others. Wow!" Pastor Sam suggested that Ed tell the whole congregation this part of his journey. "It would be good for those who are now dealing with loss. It would also be great for old friends to understand why you left, even if it had been almost five years ago! It would allow us to release you with a blessing into what God is calling you to do in the city."

━ ━ ━ ━ ━ ━ ━ ━ ━ ━ ━ ━ ━ ━ ━ ━ ━ ━ ━ ━

STORY

The meeting had started at 9 AM. All day long, pastors had prayed together. When 9 PM came, the prayers persisted. Past ten o'clock, the facilitator suggested, we need to wrap this up; we have a full day tomorrow. In the circle of some fifty pastors from diverse backgrounds, one pastor asked, "Can I say something?" Men who had begun to move settled back down. Restlessness gave way to quiet. The atmosphere shifted. "My elders asked me to come to this meeting to represent them and our congregation. As you know, we have had quite a high profile over the years. And we have been the subject of a good bit of controversy and misunderstanding. Some of you are pastoring people who at one time were part of our congregation. A few of you were at one time, part of our ministry, and now you are serving as pastors, and you know more than the others the painful side of our journey. I want to ask for your

91

forgiveness for those who have been hurt by our attempts to find an alternative model to discipleship. And our elders want me to ask you to admit us again to the circle of Christian fellowship in the city." There was in the room the sound of quiet weeping. On the faces of many, perhaps most, tears were seen. It was a profound moment. Suddenly, every man in the room was on his feet. The pastor who had been speaking was now seated in the middle of the room, and pastors pressed closer to touch him, to pray for him, to bless him. In a few brief moments, the cords of reconciliation were offered, and a healing begun for a city in which church strife had been a major challenge.

Beth had arranged for the Constituting meeting. But what area would it cover? The Metropolitan area encompassed sixteen counties with a 164 municipalities. The city in which Beth lived was not even the county seat. Her envisioning team was from three different cities – although almost everyone thought of them as one encompassing region. The team wrestled with the issue of boundaries and concluded that it would be presumptuous to assume responsibility for sixteen counties. And since they were not central to the region, they concluded they would focus on the county south of the metropolitan center. They

> What could be worse than being born without sight? Being born with sight but no vision.
>
> ■ ■ ➤ Helen Keller

would invite others, in fact, anyone from the entire area, but their focus would be on South County. And from that area, they would hope to replicate similar leadership teams in other cities and counties, all graciously networked.

The meeting would be primarily about vision, and it would take place over the better part of a full day. It would not merely be a political event, to vote in a slate of leaders. Rather, it would creatively tell the story of what was already happening in the community in terms of prayer efforts and perhaps across the nation. It would be an experience designed to show the unseen, but valiant prayer efforts by individuals, organizations, and congregations already happening in quiet disconnected ways. The day would be sprinkled with video segments, visuals, and stories. All these vari-

━ ━ ━ ➤ Using support materials, available on-line, the envisioning and constituting meetings move the process of community prayer and unity forward. It must be remembered that the members of the PC²LN are in their positions due to their appointment by national prayer organizations, local congregations and church agencies, or para-church entities. In some rare communities, there may be no formal national prayer effort – no National Day of Prayer representative, no Moms-in-Prayer group, no SYTP effort, etc. In such a case, the PC²LN will become very strategic in starting those efforts. Where such representatives do exist, every effort should be employed to get them to the table.

The group may need several sessions beyond this initial council gathering in order to approve a working organizational document. Samples are provided, both simple and complex. Some groups may choose to work informally, at least for a season, without a formal organizational constitution or set of by-laws. In some cases, a small team may be appointed to bring back originating articles.

ant pieces constitute the patchwork, which they believed, when knitted together, had the potential to blanket the city in prayer. Throughout the day, they would also take time to pray.

This launch meeting would also include the commissioning of a leadership team, agreement on some primary goals, and a preview of a simple structural model with the flexibility for expansion.

Beth and her team had made a list of critical attenders. Almost all of them had been in at least one envisioning session, and the great majority were planning to attend the constituting meeting, seeing PC²LN as a win-win for all their prayer efforts. Then, Beth learned that Liz was not coming. Liz and her husband, Mark, are leaders of a local prayer celebration event that annually draws thousands on Memorial Day. The event is unique to the area, but it draws folks from five states. The day of celebration was laced with prayer

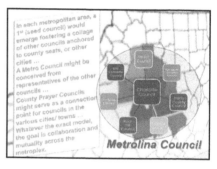

and music. In the months prior to the event, prayer walks and gatherings occurred all over the metropolitan area. Without the involvement of Liz and Mark, and the major prayer organization they represent, Beth felt that the Community Prayer Team would not be as effective; it would be missing a significant portion of the existing prayer effort. So Beth repeatedly called Liz but could not make contact. She attempted to connect with her through mutual friends, again to no avail. She learned that Liz apparently felt that the PC²LN would force her to surrender the autonomy and control of her event. Further, she seemed certain that the emerging team would add little to their effort. She already had significant contacts and influence with churches; in fact, as Liz noted, she would be giving more than she was getting. Her other concern was that prayer throughout the year would minimize the impact of her once a year event. Beth was exasperated. There was little she could do, except to assure Liz that she and the team were committed to be as passionate about promoting the event as they would if Liz were a part of the council. Shockingly, Liz sent word back, that their support or endorsement was not necessary. In the coming years, Liz would come to see the sincerity of Beth and importance of the PC²LN. But it was a longer journey than Beth had desired.

When the day arrived from the constituting meeting, Beth walked from the prayer circle with her hands a bit moist from anxiety. She had already made the rounds in the room attempting to greet and welcome all personally. A few more had slipped in during the last few minutes. Beth was designated and best suited to lead the discussion about next steps, but the small leadership team advised that she not stand alone in the opening moments. Genny would welcome all. Jackson would make brief comments, pray an invocation, indeed, lead a segment in prayer along with

━ ━ ━ ➤ At the Constituting Council, a Servant Leadership Team is chosen. Among them, a 'Moderator' for the leadership team, the cabinet and council gatherings is chosen. This leader will guide the general process, provide leadership at most meetings. It is important to find someone with a broad perspective, a person of prayer who also has huge leadership gifts. With the 'Moderator', a Vice-Moderator/Executive Assistant is found along with a Recording Secretary-Treasurer and three-to-five at-large members. Together, they constitute the Servant Leader Team for the PC²LN. The PC²LN may also create an advisory team of three-to-five individuals.

Genny and provide the 'how did we get to this moment', and introduce Beth.

Now front and center, Beth received a warm applause – all knew it was her passion, at some personal expense, that had created a gathering of over two-hundred pastors, intercessors and community Christian leaders. She acknowledged them. She welcomed all, and then shared pieces of her own story. This was, she noted, a historic moment. Without an attempt to dictate, and yet with a clear sense of where she felt the meeting needed to go, she unwrapped the process. Most had now visited the PC²LN website. Most had reviewed the proposed constitution. Most had read the vision document. Most understood that the Servant Leadership Team would strive to meet monthly and

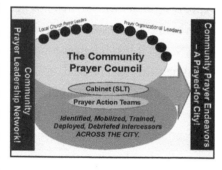

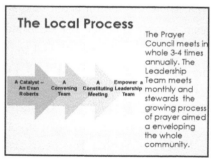

that the larger network would gather quarterly – open to all prayer leaders. Other special focus groups and action teams would meet as needed.

It had been agreed that Beth would moderate the Constituting Meeting, and in the end, hand off the gavel to whoever was chosen as the 'Moderator' for both the Network and the Leadership Team. Across the country, Albert and his group gathered in a similar meeting. "The proposed configuration of the Servant Leadership Team," Albert noted, "is for a 'Moderator' who will guide the overall process, and provide leadership at most meetings." Albert explained that it was important to find someone with a broad perspective, a person of prayer who also has huge leadership gifts. "That's you!" someone shouted from the back of the room. And by an almost unanimous vote, it would be Albert, but not without his diligently pointing out the talents of Joe, and the special leadership gifting of Ed. "Let's pray", he demanded. His humility was genuine. His willingness to release what he had started was authentic. However, in the end, the group chose him to provide leadership, at least for the first year. Ed was chosen as Vice-Moderator/Executive Assistant. Vickie, a local church prayer coordinator, was chosen as the Recording Secretary-Treasurer. Next, the group selected three at-large members for the leadership team – one was the leader of a youth prayer initiative, another of the women's prayer network, and the final one, a prayer leader for a para-church organization.

Albert explained that because the model of PC^{2}LN is designed to be dynamic, not static, that the template calls for the appointment of additional advisors and at-large members. He asked the larger group for the privilege of having an advisory team (three are recommended), not based on a vote or popularity, but a team with whom the leaders felt comfortable in confiding. The network agreed to allow the leadership team to appoint its own advisors, but make the choice known to all. From the back of the room, a voice called out, "Make sure Pastor Jones is one of them!" Every-

━ ━ ━ ▶ In any concentrated metropolitan area, a collage of PC^{2}LNs working collaboratively would allow for specific township/city/county attention, and then by connection, multi-county, broad coalition efforts. The possibilities of such unity are almost unimaginable. No such prayer construct now exist in most cities.

one laughed. Everybody knew Pastor Jones, and indeed, he would make a great advisor.

AMBASSADORS – Lateral Connections

Once the first team in any geographic region is chosen, they have the wonderful privilege of replicating their effort by assisting the establishment of PC²LNs in adjacent communities. The more these efforts are conjoined, networked, the more synergy is possible. Albert wasted no time in appointing Joe as the lead Ambassador. He and Joe had already made a number of PC²LN missionary trips, even before they had been formally organized. Now, with the leadership team named, and the community prayer leaders having adopted the model, he felt they could make a difference across the state. If a city network could be effective, how much more could a statewide network be effective?

Albert had confidence in Joe. He knew he could envision catalysts and conveners in adjacent communities. He would use the strength of relational connections to further the PC²LN. Ed had a ton of contacts across the region. He and Joe quickly made a list of the most likely cities and conveners. The opportunity came sooner than later. Jack Terry called Albert two days after the constituting meeting with a proposal. "Albert, I am calling for a group of about five people who were at the PC²LN constituting meeting," Jack explained, "and we want to be a part of what is happening, but we live in XYZ Township. It's about twelve miles outside the city-limits, and it is actually in the neighboring county." Albert knew exactly where it was. "You see," Jack observed, "most of what happens there affects us, but a lot of what happens in our little town isn't on your radar screen. We want to champion unity, but we wonder if you would mind if we created our own little PC²LN for our town, and still stayed connected to you?" Albert was listening, but his mind was racing over the area map. Within fifty miles of the city limits, he could count two dozen more towns, any one of which might want to connect their smaller prayer effort to the larger emphasis. Each had unique needs in their smaller community but needed the connection to something larger. "I think that is a great idea. Tell me what, if anything, we need to do to help you; and then let's figure out how we connect with smaller network teams in the cities around us." It would be a win-win. The small towns would get the benefit of the greater effort, and retain a sense of autonomy, with a focus on the unique needs of their own communities.

STORY

When Pastor James was considering a mission project in the neighborhood, he never thought about the school next door, until one day, passing it and watching a teacher plead with an upset student who seemed to be attempting to escape the campus, probably with nowhere to go, given the number of broken homes in the neighborhood, he found himself captivated, and thought, "Here is our mission field, next door".

He shared with his leaders, a vision for adopting the school. It was novel. It was not a typical mission project. And it would not be fulfilled in a typical way. The neighborhood around both the church and the school had drastically changed, becoming a low-income community with a lot of crime, a lot of single moms and latchkey kids, a lot of gang activity and drugs. He learned that the middle school, next to the church he now led, had been there for over thirty years. And that it was the lowest performing school in the district academically with some of the greatest instances of poverty.

With an expression of openness from his leaders, he went next door to have a chat with the principal. In the eight years he had pastored the church, this was his first trip onto the campus and into the building. O, there had been a few exchanges. When the school asked permission to use the church parking lot for special events, the church had always agreed. Then, many years before, there had been a storm shelter arrangement due to a secure basement of the church facility, but that was no longer in place. To his knowledge, only five students from his church attended Collins Middle School.

He was greeted warmly by the principal, and when he introduced himself as the pastor from next door, the principal quickly asked, "Is there a problem?" He smiled, "No, on the contrary. There is a possibility! We want to adopt your school as a kind of church project." He could see her eyebrows arch. "I know there are church-state, church-school issues, but we are thinking about how you might need volunteer support. How you might need assistance that we could offer that is not in your budget – we are not a rich church, but we are a giving church. And we are a praying church. I think the greatest gift we could give you would be to have our congregation, each Sunday, turn toward this school and ask God to bless it, you and all the teachers and staff." With that, the principal offered a doubting half-grin, "That may not be legal you know!" The pastor smiled back, "In your world it may be a prohibition, but in our world it is an admonition. What could you lose?" He winked, "Good things are going to happen this year at Collins Middle."

In the next few weeks, the pastor carefully considered what could be done without creating problems for the school. First, they could pray! Asking for the blessing of God on the children, the teachers and the staff, the learning process and the families. Second, the school needed volunteer readers for the reading program, and three seniors in the church offered three afternoons a week for that chore. Third, the school needed occasional volunteer help for special programs. It all seemed doable, but the priority became prayer support for the school, and yet, not without legs on the prayers. The pastor dropped in regularly to see the principal and asked, "Is there anything we can do to help?" The weekly "Bless Collins Middle" prayer time on Sunday morning, at the church, caught on and one member launched a campaign, determined to make sure underprivileged kids got a thanksgiving dinner, and then a Christmas toy drive was conceptualized. Suddenly, it was not just a single church helping, others joined the effort. A small group of Christian teachers at the school shared classroom needs with the pastor and a group of business leaders in the community were soon pouring help into the school that it did not have before.

From out of the blue, the school principal received a call one day from a computer firm. "We heard that your school might be in need of equipment for your computer lab!" That was a surprise. The school didn't have a computer lab. Trying to be kind, the principal replied, "Thanks for your interest, but funds for a computer lab are just not in our budget this year". What followed made her almost a believer in the pastor's prayers. "We are not trying to sell anything, we have computer equipment from a company that is upgrading, but the equipment is still very functional. We want to give it to you." It was like getting a bicycle the day you broke your leg. "Even if you gave us the equipment," she confided, "We neither have the capable staff or the budget to set it up!" So close. So far away. "No, you don't understand. We'll give you the equipment. We will set it up and train your teachers to teach the children. All we need is a room that will serve as a computer lab." She was almost breathless. She could hear the pastor's words. "Good things are going to happen this year at Collins Middle." She didn't dare tell him about this. Before the Christmas break, the computer lab was functioning. Kids were returning from Thanksgiving break with stories about provision. A new spirit was sweeping the school. Even those who were usually vigil about church-state divisions could not help but sense that somehow all the good had to do with goodwill generated from the pastor across the street - and maybe even God. By the end of the year, student scores had soared making Collins Middle, the most improved school in the district. The superintendent of schools asked the principal, "To what do you attribute such positive change?" She almost surprised herself and said, "Prayer!" Instead, she smiled and said, "Inspired leaders and neighborhood friends." She knew better. The next year, the partnership continued. And the school continued to improve.

CHAPTER 8
Christian Family, USA!

Meet the Threads and Stands of our Story

Jarret and Jan Thompson – *Jarret is father whose concern about the lack of faith support in the community for his children, led to surprise opposition, and a public outcry. He is an advertising executive. Jan works at the County Building as a receptionist. They are both strong Christians who are concerned about their children.*

Anna and Kaitlan – *Anna and Kaitlan are the children of Jarret and Jan Thompson.*

Jake and Sharon – *Unsaved neighbors of Jarret and Jan. Their daughter, Sheila, was a playmate to Anna, until Anna's innocent references to love for Christ became offensive to Sharon, Sheila's mother.*

Lois - *Organizer of the annual National Day of Prayer event.*

Ed Black – *Pastor to Jarret and Jan, who became involved as an agent of reconciliation in the city. He used the negative experiences to launch a movement of prayer and unity across the city.*

<u>Mills Pearce</u> – *Attorney with a national legal group concerned about the rights of Christians.*

<u>Glenn</u> – *Neighbor who is a fervent advocate of environmentalism.*

<u>Allen Hampton</u> – *Senior Partner at the law firm at which Jake is employed, a devout Christian, and eventually a leader in the city process.*

Jarret Thompson is old enough to have seen the national shift from traditional values, from our being primarily a Christian culture to rabid pluralism and a growing anti-Christian ethos. He married late and considers himself the old man in a neighborhood of young couples. Praying with his children one night, his middle child remarked, "Sheila doesn't pray!" That was his daughter Anna's closest neighbor friend. What followed was a disclosure by Anna about how she had engaged Sheila in playing church! Sheila's mother stopped them, explaining that such actions were not a part of their family practices, and she suggested that the two girls play another game. Jarret conferred with his wife Jan, and both were a bit dismayed. The neighbors, Sharon and Jake, seemed to be a wonderful young couple. Certainly, they knew about Jarret and Jan's faith commitment. But Anna was troubled by the experience. Was praying not okay? Was she that different from Sheila? Would she get into trouble if she prayed with someone else? Was going to church and being a Christian a bad thing?

Becoming Engaged

Jarret was shaken, personally, and for the sake of his kids. He was disturbed about how careless he had been about his assumptions regarding his neighbors and his failure to be a clearer Christian light to them. He talked with one of the pastors at the congregation where he worshipped. And he talked to an uncle who was a minister. Then Jarret entered into a quest – to discover how much prayer was accepted in the community, and how much it was resisted.

He discovered that the National Day of Prayer was the largest community prayer event held annually, and it drew only a few hundred at best, for an hour or so. He had never been to the event, sadly. He connected with the organizer, Lois, and he and his wife Jan, met her for coffee. He was loaded with questions. She readily agreed to pass along his name to other prayer leaders, and other community prayer initiatives. In addition, she sent a couple emails to strategic people, copying Jarret, and that opened some huge connections.

Jarret was not a stranger to prayer! He was part of the men's prayer group at his church. For almost a decade, he had led the pastor's prayer team. He was one of the volunteers on the church prayer line. He and Jan had sponsored a number of prayer weekends for couples. However, he had never seen prayer as so essential for the spiritual well-being of the community or the nation as he did now.

For more than three months, he read and researched. He met with one person who then led him to another. After about six weeks, when he called someone new, it was as if they anticipated his call, "Yes, I know so-and-so, and they have spoken with me about you, and told me that you might be calling". Jarret had no plan, just a driving desire to see a spiritual awakening. He had no experience in citywide prayer. He had no idea that other cities were developing networks of prayer. He just knew the burden would not go away, and each night when he said bedtime prayers with his children, the sense of what the culture would look like when they were adults, a culture hostile to Christ, prayer and God, troubled him.

Jarret had no intention of becoming headlines when he visited the local elementary school in which his children were enrolled. He was innocent and later he confessed, far too naïve. He made an appointment with the principal to discuss faith practices in the school. When he stated his concern, she enlarged the meeting to include the curriculum coordinator and the school counselor. When they were seated, the principal firmly declared to Jarret that the separation of church and state probably disallowed the conversation itself, based on what he revealed to the receptionist. He told them he was no preacher – just a parent. He was not asking them to commence prayer and Bible reading, he was simply trying to assess the degree to which environments in which his own daughter trafficked were friendly or hostile to her faith. At this point, he needed no words to confirm his suspicions. "I did notice, when I arrived that the school is decorated in Halloween themes." He paused to gather in the silent exchanges in the room. He knew now that his values did not make him a welcome guest, even as a parent. "Isn't that faith? It is certainly the dark side of faith. Why is that admitted and not the positive?" It had not been his intention to be so blunt, but he persisted, "I know, come Christmas, such themes as the winter solstice, 'Frosty the Snowman', 'Santa Claus', will be publicly celebrated, but Jesus will probably not be mentioned. Christmas Carols will not be sung." He had not intended to be argumentative. He became earnest, humble, attempting to alter the atmosphere. "I came here with no agenda, except a concern for my own daughter. Do you not feel any obligation to honor my role as a Christian parent? He knew the answer before he asked the question. Do you not see yourself as a partner to me and my wife, to our home? Should my faith and values, and those of my child not be honored?" For a moment there was silence. Then came the firm response, "That", Mr. Thompson "is not our role." With that the principal rose, as did her two assistants. The meeting was over.

Jarret left the building, and he recalls, "I was shaking. It was not what was said, but the manner in which I was treated. My child, they believe, belongs to them. I am an obstacle in the training they want to provide to her." Suddenly, he realized, he could not leave. Two of his children attended that school. One was away with his wife, but Anna was in her classroom. He turned on his heels. Went directly to the classroom. And from the door, he signaled to his daughter – and took her home! He did not have the money for tuition for his children in a private school. His wife worked, so homeschooling was not an option. "I over-reacted," he recalled. I just did not want her there another hour, at least on that day. A parent's right to remove a child from objectionable classroom instruction and activity is grounded in three constitutional provisions: the Fourteenth Amendment's Due Process Clause and the First Amendment's Free Speech and Free Exercise Clauses. By the time Jarret reached the parking lot, the school security officer was present. "You can't remove the child," he insisted. "You must check the child out of school properly." It was as if the whole world was claiming ownership of his own child. He knew, under any normal circumstances, that such rules had logic about them, protection for the child and the parent. Now the rule seemed to exist for power purposes, for control, to show his subordination as a parent to the authority of the school, not the original intent, to protect a child by the school in behalf of the parent. Suddenly, he had to check his child out, as if the child were the property of the state, only on loan to him for the evening. The school, not he as a parent, was the ultimate authority. He said nothing. He climbed into his car with his daughter and drove away, still trembling.

At dinner, he rehearsed his bizarre day with his wife Jan, expressing regrets for overreacting, and yet concerns about the presuppositions that seemed to be confirmed – they were viewed suspiciously, just for raising their children as Christians. It had never been so clear to him or confusing.

What came next was shocking! Around six o'clock, there was a knock on his door. A local police officer asked him to step outside and immediately handcuffed him. A paper was waved in his face, and suddenly his home was filled with strangers. A flash went off in the excitement; a photojournalist for a local newspaper had trailed the police to his home. The next day, he was front-page news. But the greater concern was that Anna, his daughter, was taken from the home along with her older sister Kailan. Their oldest child, Josh, was away. Jarret was charged with bullying school officials, and abducting his own child. His children were carried away over the protest of his wife Jan's pleas and sobs. It was a nightmare. Jarret was hauled away handcuffed in the back of a police car with the neighbors watching, including Sharon and Jake. Jan was informed that a court date would be announced and that the children would be in foster care to determine what would be best for them after appropriate hearings. Jan had no idea that Jake was a young attorney. He quickly acted to get Jarret released on his own recognizance and the children placed with Jan's Mom and Dad, their grandparents. Though he was not a practicing Christian, he knew that the school had overreacted and that such a matter could have been handled more sensitively.

By ten o'clock, Jarret and Jan were together again with friends, in their own quiet home. Fearing for Josh, they arranged for him to stay with friends. Jan had called their pastor, Ed Black, and he and his wife immediately came over. Ed, that night, called a Christian legal action group. "Ed," his long-time friend told him. "I am glad you woke even if it is late. We have an associate a few miles from you, scheduled to start home tomorrow. I am going to call and wake him up!" With that, the two laughed. However, an hour later, Jarret's phone rang again. It was Mills Pearce,

Ed Black's indirect connection. By mid-morning, the next day, the wheels had started turning. Mills systematically gathered the facts. The next day, very early, he connected with the District Attorney and the with the School District's attorney. He informed them that Jarret had no desire to engage in counter legal action and suggested that while he had acted impetuously, and the school administration had viewed his inquiries as 'bullish' that was not his intent. At least one of the participants in the room, at some vocational risk, acknowledged that his questions were sincere. And that the conversation on the past of the school could have been more amiable and without consequences.

In a small town, Jarret was a big story. A news camera crew set up on his lawn for a late news story. Pastor Ed Black offered a brief statement, attempting to ameliorate the problem, saving face for the school and protecting the character of Jarret. Shortly after midnight, local Facebook connections in the area lit up – kids learning the news told their Moms and Dads. A local intercessor's network picked up the theme for prayer, asking God for guidance, for the children to be restored. Jarret and Jan had sterling reputations. Neither had as much as a traffic ticket. Jarret had been with the company for which he worked, an advertising agency, for more than fifteen years, and Jan had worked at the County Administration office as a receptionist for almost a decade. When Jan called in the next morning and reported that she needed a day off, her boss, the chair of the Supervisor's Board, immediately called her back. By mid-day, the charges against Jarret had been dropped. By evening, their children were returned to them. That reunion was televised by two local TV stations. The story again became front page in the local news and on TV. Jarret's attorney, Mills Pearce, proposed a joint news conference with the school and Jarret, but it was not to be. Mills, Jarret and Pastor Black did news briefing without school officials' involvement trying to touch the critical issues without inflaming the situation.

Turning a Problem into a Possibility

It was apparent, the matter was not about to be over! A group of concerned parents met with school administrators to press the issue of parental rights and greater sensitivity to the school-parent relationship. They were stonewalled with the phrase, "It is the law of the land, get over it". Pastor Ed Black called for a parent-child prayer gathering across the city that blessed the schools and prayed for God's hand to be on both the children and the schools, and evident in them. A number administrators and teachers were present and joined in open prayers. A local Christian school called Jarret and Jan and offered free tuition for the remainder of the school year for all their children. In the end, they decided to leave their children in the public school system and attempt to be more vigilant parents.

The prayer gathering became a catalyst for a new movement, 'Parents and Teachers Praying for our Schools.' Prayer triads and quads formed that consisted of parents and teachers with administrators – all Christians – who agreed to connect at least twice monthly in prayer for their community's schools. A group of local Christian businesses determined to discover the needs of the schools and find ways to bless them in concrete ways. A number of youth pastors banded together to offer to volunteer to assist the schools in mentoring – training kids to be a member of a band, running sound-boards, lighting and stage props, mime and drama coaching. Intercessors across the city committed to form teams to adopt each school for prayer. A new emphasis was placed on Bible clubs.

Six months later, the whole incident that seemed to have been resolved was resurrected. Someone who had been a part of the original meeting in Anna's school, along with a non-Christian parent, watching the flurry of Christian activity around the schools, filed a lawsuit to stop the relationships between Christians and the schools, arguing that they were all a violation of Church-state boundaries. Suddenly, the whole city was divided. Jarret was again the lightning rod along with Pastor Black and the 'Parent and Teacher' prayer group. Anna was the poster-child. For a while, it appeared that the county might join the lawsuit on the side of the school district. Jan recalls, "Things became so tense, I was not sure I would be able to keep my job or endure at my work." Suddenly, all over the city, Christians began to examine their acceptance, as *Christians,* in their workplaces. Jan recalls, "We had a Muslim, who began work as an assistant attorney. He asked for time off to say his prayers, and that was accommodated. One of the Judges is Jewish, and everyone knows he will not hold court on Saturday – and everyone respects him for that. But suddenly, my Christian faith became an issue."

Jarret cannot remember when he first saw the bumper sticker, and he could not figure out whether to laugh or cry. It read: 'Jarret and Jan – Local Hero's!" There was a halo above the 'o' in hero. Jarret knew he wore no halo, and he did not feel like a hero, still, a local men's bible study asked Jarret to share, and Jan began to get invitations, as well. And they did more than tell their story. They began to share their concerns about how the culture was pushing Christianity into the shadows. And with the impending lawsuit in such a small community, it wasn't hard to convince their audience. Yard signs appeared. Prayer groups seemed to form spontaneously across the city.

If Jarret were the lightning rod and Anna the poster child, Pastor Black was the oil on the waters. Moreover, Mills Pearce was the operative behind the scenes. The entire Christian community rallied to pay legal fees; they knew the battle was not about Jarret and Jan or their recent embarrassing episode. Mills met with the County Attorney, and after the meeting, they declined to join the school district in the lawsuit. Pastor Black said on radio and television interviews, and in gatherings of Christians and community leaders, "This is not about a lawsuit, and it is not a movement of Christians against our schools. Many wonderful Christians serve in our public schools. This," he said "is about our need to come together as a community. It is about our need for the clarification of roles and boundaries, rights and respect." And to the Christians, he appealed, "It is about our need to be salt and light in our community".

Peace – Yes; Status Quo - No

In the end, Mills Pearce was not only able to avoid a lawsuit that would have been costly and divisive, he was able to point out to the school attorney, legal guidelines about which he had been unaware regarding the religious rights of parents and students, and of teachers, within boundaries. He assisted in producing guidelines that reflected more clearly the lines of legal authority between faith and the schools.

Pastor Black formed a coalition called 'Christians and Schools.' It was more of a fellowship, but for the first time ever, Christians involved in education, both public and private, were in the same room. In the first meeting, there were almost four-hundred. Some came out of curiosity. Some were not Christians; they came to see what the next move of the Christians might be! A map of the city and county was unwrapped with the location of every school and the location of every church. For every school, there were about three churches.[7] Pastor Black said, "Sadly, there are perceived legal issues with church-state-school connections, some of which are not grounded in sound law, but the prevalent view complicates the matter.. However, nothing prevents Christians from adopting the schools for prayer and providing volunteers. Further, Christian parents whose children attend the schools should get involved. We want to identify some kind of partnership between Christians in each of these schools – volunteers, the church used as an alternate shelter, the youth pastor serving as a mentor, parents or members in the reading program. But the most important aspect is for those of you who are Christians, and work in the public school systems, to be true Christians, salt and light."

What followed was a lively discussion and a season of prayer about what that might look like. Suddenly, Christian teachers, who had never been in the same room, were praying together. Teachers who knew one another, but not as Christians, now were relating at a different level. "Divided," one teacher confessed, "We have felt powerless. United, we are encouraged. The very reason some of us came to be teachers was in part because of our love for Christ and our desire to serve children. It is our ministry, and yet, in the past few years, our hands have been so restricted. This is encouraging. I didn't know there were so many of us." They planned another meeting of Christian teachers and administrators and there, they chose a leadership team for a new organization, the Fellowship of Community Educators (FCE). They struggled about inserting the terms *Christian* or *prayer* into the title, but they knew their heart, and they knew how easily their motives might be misunderstood. Triads and quads of praying teachers and administrators started to develop across the city. Almost immediately, these groups were present in every school district and in half the schools. A small team began to circulate an email, *Daily Bread for Educators!*

Pastor Black began to wonder. What would the effect be if such gatherings took place across other professions? How many Christians were in the social services sector? In the legal community? In law enforcement? In the finance and banking industry? In the various service sectors? In healthcare? In media and arts? In commerce and manufacturing? And what about the pastors? Rarely did more than a dozen attend the local ministerial fellowship. It had taken a bizarre event to catalyze such community openness and Christian unity, but now a completely new paradigm was emerging.

For the annual mission conference at his church, Pastor Black suggested that the church, without ignoring its traditional international missionary support, sponsor a weeklong conference called, "The City is Our Mission." The gym would be filled with displays 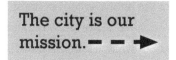 from local mission agencies and para-church organizations, even unique ministries of other churches would be showcased. Every morning would begin with a prayer gathering and service. Each day would offer a tour to some sector of the city. Each evening, he invited a different pastor from the city to serve as the host of the meeting in his church, and a series of speakers – not all of whom were fervent believers. More than thirty churches signed on to cosponsor the event. The attendance was encouraging and grew as the week went on. After the week of learning about their city, and praying, two teams were formed. One in the church. And the other, across the city, composed of pastors who had participated and wanted to walk further in the process, laymen from multiple denominations, each representing some slice of the city, and a growing number of intercessors. They called the group simply, "Mission: Our Town!"

One Person at a Time

It was almost a year later before Jake and Jarret talked about the yearlong ordeal. After the first episode, Anna had little contact with Sheila. The invisible wall between the two side-by-side homes grew in thickness. Standing in the adjoining backyards, the two men chatted. "Faith is not an incidental thing to me," Jarret told Jake. Jake was silent. Jarret thought of another neighbor, Glenn, who lived a few houses further down the street. "Do you know Glenn," he asked. Jake nodded. Jarret's eyes twinkled as he began to share. Making the comparison indirect, he thought, might ease the conversation:

> Glenn drives one of those small uncomfortable hybrid cars. He mulches his leaves. He refuses to use his fireplace, even for ambiance on a winter night. His yard is filled with bird feeders. He has a solar panel on his roof. He works hard to minimize the impact on the local landfill. I have gotten more than one of his tracts on global warming stuck on my door or car windshield. He is an evangelist for environmentalism. I was on the neighborhood email list and after he became the secretary. I started getting so many warnings about the Brown Pelican and other endangered species, as if one of these birds was going to show up in all our backyards – and we were duty bound to be on the alert and save the species, when we are a couple hundred miles from the coast. He is passionate. He believes in saving the animals that are threatened and that it is a duty we all should share. Even though I don't agree with him, at least on some issues, I respect him – he lives by his beliefs. There is a lot of debate about global warming – is it a threat, can we really alter the earth's temperature? With Glenn, it is not a debate. It is a settled issue. He is a downright fanatic. I don't think he should be arrested, seen as a threat or socially marginalized. Last year, at Christmas, we had a neighborhood open house. Here comes Glenn, with a handful of flyers. I just smiled and welcomed him. You know, I want to be as passionate – with a bit more discretion than I have used in the past – for the threat to the globe that I see and for the most en-

dangered species of all, called mankind. As passionate as Glenn is for the brown pelican. I want to be seen living by my beliefs in the neighborhood, just as Glenn does. Yet, I do not want, nor do I believe he does, to be a nuisance, but to be an example and a voice, and a part of a movement that calls others to make a difference. The problem is that his movement, environmentalism, endangered species, is an acceptable passion; and mine, Christianity, concern for men, is not.

For a moment, both men were quiet. Suddenly Sharon popped out onto the back porch and quickly disappeared. "I am grateful for the help you gave me a year ago when my life took this suddenly 'public' turn. I learned that when news reporters showed up that you, along with Ed Black, met them on my lawn and encouraged them give us some space. I am so grateful. And I am sorry for the emotional stress that we might have caused you. I am sorry most of all that Sheila and Anna can no longer play together because of our Christian faith."

What followed was a sensitive and exploratory discussion over weeks between two men, and eventually their wives. Jarret prayed with Jake. He learned that Sharon had grown up in a very harsh Christian home, and then her father died. Her mother then married a man who was increasingly agnostic and very intellectual, and into a heart wounded by an aberrant form of Christianity, he had poured his skepticism and disbelief. Jake and Jarret began a weekly coffee-shop Bible study. As Jake grew in faith, he invited other skeptical friends, and that began a quiet small movement in the city.

Allen Hampton, a strong Christian, who worked in the firm where Jake was employed, saw the change in the young lawyer. He had followed the happenings in the city during the past year, and after connecting with Pastor Black, and seeing the sincerity of

Jarret, no publicity hound, Allen gave leadership to the Nehemiah side the growing coalition of Christians across the city.

Jarret and his friends are a long way from a formal Prayer Council for their city and yet, they are laying the foundation for a unified sustained prayer effort. It wasn't something they intended to do, they backed into it, but they are on the way to seeing their city changed, and they have learned, prayer is the first element in the transformation process.

STORY

It was the hedonistic hot spot of the city – and for that matter, known throughout the nation. A palatial mansion-like structure on a sprawling multi-acre spread, fenced and gated. In terms of elegance, it added to the upscale neighborhood in which it was located. Limousines with darkly tinted windows made their way frequently by the guardhouse and through the front gates. No one entered without a passcode, which meant they had an invitation.

Until a group of pastors and intercessors called attention to what they termed 'decadent and immoral, indecent and wicked' behaviors, no one knew that the unsigned palace-looking estate was anything more than another millionaires' playground near a famous world-class stretch of beaches. And the common sentiment was – it is a private matter, whatever is happening inside isn't our concern. More investigation by the group of concerned Christians revealed that renowned movie types and the wealthy frequented the place when they were in town. It was a hotspot for the cause of sexual liberation.

The local zoning authorities said there had been no complaints, and the owner was within his rights to hold as many private parties as he chose as often as he desired. It was a dead-end. The news media showed little appetite for exposing rich and powerful elites who either visited or resided in the area. Local politicians saw the concerns of the small group of Christians and pastors as exotic. What was more acceptable to them was the hedonistic paradise, contrasted with moralistic pastors.

There was nothing left to do, but pray! A group of pastors gathered at the gate of the palace. It was a small group, less than twenty. They were told to disperse, or the police would be called. They asked only for enough time to pray – and pray they did. Within three days, fire destroyed the facility completely.

7   This is actually a national average. Check the ratio in your city or county.

CHAPTER 9
It's Already Happening

Meet the Threads and Stands of our Story

Lyle – *Lyle is a former youth pastor whose business ventures and joy of daily sharing Christ became the great value of his life. He is a natural prayer mobilizer. He loves to start things and hand them off. He is natural people person and has the knack of coming alongside people and situations, speaking into their lives, expanding their vision, without making them insecure. He has no desire to control, but genuinely to empower others.*

Shelly – *A prayer organizer. She has been involved in community prayer efforts for years. In Lyle, she discovered an unselfish partner whose vision reached beyond prayer events, and who facilitated a community-wide connection between prayer leaders that has enabled each event leader to feel that they are a part of wider, ready-made team.*

Nancy – *Shelly's daughter who is deeply involved in the community's 'Prayer House' and the teen 'Cry the Night' prayer experience that takes place weekly and draws dozens, sometimes as many as a hundred to the 'Prayer House' parking lot for prayer and concerts. The event is baptized with prayer and witnessing opportunities.*

Thomas and Nell – A retired pastor and wife (Nell) who have become involved at 'Prayer House.' Thomas had mobilized intercessors across the region. He is trusted leader by other pastors. In addition, he is a great stabilizer for the intercessors across the city. They do an all-nighter once a month and maintain a prayer chain.

Jimmy – Leads a group of marketplace pray-ers affectionately called the '4-Fs'. It has touched more than two-hundred marketplace men from forty different churches and has become a connection point for Christian men in the city – safe and non-denominational. It is officially called 'E320'- 'one hour' in three twenty minute sessions: twenty minutes of fellowship, a twenty minute Bible Study, and twenty minutes of prayer (the 20-20-20 plan). The key is not letting prayer be squeezed out. 'E' for Exodus and Ephesians; and 3:20 for the verse. The first passage is a prohibition – 'No other gods." The second, a promise, 'Now to him who is able to do immeasurably more than all we ask or imagine ..."

Lyle is a prayer mobilizer. It is a term he had never heard, but when he did, he knew it was an apt descriptor of what he did. For a brief season, he was a youth pastor. But he found that his part-time tent-making to support his ministry became the main thing. Wherever he went, he found believers to pray with, and people who wanted to believe, but needed someone to kick-start the prayer process in their lives. "I'd get 'em talking to God, and I'd get 'em a Bible, and before you knew it, they were in church somewhere, loving God." Even in college, he gravitated to prayer gatherings. As the area representative for a sporting goods company, he had first worked with athletic directors of schools – that was by design, a good fit he thought for the youth ministry. Now he works the full range – schools, retail, trade shows and he has a regional team under him. Nevertheless, his passion has become prayer.

Natural and Relational

If it prays, Lyle is somewhere near. When Shelly, the National Day of Prayer (NDP) coordinator became ill, Lyle picked up the mantle and carried the ball for a few years. When Shelly was well again, he relinquished the reigns, "I missed doing it", Shelly recalled, "It had become so important to me." Suddenly, Lyle found himself serving as the area representative for the movement. Soon he was involved in NDP, the Global Day of Prayer (GDOP), See-you-at-the-Pole (SYATP), prayer for unreached peoples, and more. "If it prayed – I was there, if possible." He would find a new prayer cause, champion it, get it going, and then find someone to take it over. "It was a joy to show up and pray, and watch it all move forward," Lyle recalled.

Shelly remembered, "At times, I felt like I was all alone. As the NDP approached, I started looking for people to help me. This one was busy, that one had moved – every year I had to gear up again. When Lyle came along, he got so many prayer initiatives going, and also kept us connected, and suddenly none of us felt alone. Like a flock of geese, one took the point on this prayer initiative and the other on that one, all of us happily honking each other on. It was a relief to be a part of a team of prayer leaders."

"It seemed the natural thing to do," Lyle reflected "to help one another out. So those of us who believed that prayer was often the key to unity and certainly, the hope of the nation, would get together several times a year. I would have a barbecue at my house, and invite all these leaders of these prayer initiatives over. I certainly did not see myself as 'over them,' but we had a relationship. We loved the Lord, and we loved one another. We'd talk, and dream and pray! We had no intention of starting a 'PC²LN.' That was not our plan. We just knew that each time we gathered and prayed, something new seemed to be birthed."

Over the years, Lyle and Shelly had cultivated relationships with more than a dozen key prayer leaders and almost a hundred folks who would faithfully show up, pass out flyers, set-up and take-down. Their upside down humor and attempt to keep everyone humble was one of the reasons they called themselves, half-jokingly and half-seriously, the 'F-Troop!' Technically, Lyle says, "4-F: faithful, fruitful, fervent, forerunners." They had learned to insist that, before leading, one had to follow, and serve faithfully. "Our best leaders bubbled up from the bottom," he recalled. "They were not only faithful, but fruitful. They engaged others. They helped us enlarge the movement – and they did so with a servant heart." The next mark is passion. Shelly explained, "We want someone with a burning-heart. Organizers and leaders are not enough; the person has to be committed to prayer, and not prayer as an activity, but as a relationship with God." The last marker of the membership in the '4-F troop' is forerunner. Lyle explained, "We don't want to become stale and territorial, so we often urge new leaders to start something, but do so with the mindset of handing it off. That prevents a control mentality." Shelly smiled, "It doesn't always work! We have some leaders who have served certain prayer initiatives for more than a decade. They are a fixture. It is what they

> At the heart of every successful movement is a group of people who love one another.
> ➤ Joe Aldrich

do, and who they are – but they still represent the principle we are after: a servant heart, a non-contentious disposition."

Praying Teens

Now they have a little county 'prayer house' that is open to intercessors and to the public, seven days a week. It was donated to them rent-free. Young people fill it up two nights a week; one night for a Bible Study and the other for their weekly 'Cry the Night!' Youth pastors rotate in leading a Bible Study, but the real focus is on church kids bringing unchurched kids. And so is 'Cry the Night.' Lyle explained, "We are on a busy intersection, and we have a large parking lot, so we sometimes set up a stage and do live music and in-between songs, kids give their testimony, or do a short presentation, and we pray. We have teens that rove through the crowd gathered around the stage. Some kids stay in their parked cars, and the prayer team moves among those, as well. The prayer house is open for kids that want to go inside for prayer. We have popcorn and pop, sometimes hotdogs. Even when we don't have the concert, this has become a cool place to hang out. Kids bring their own entertainment – skateboards, music, games. It is a kind of managed chaos. And in the middle, we have seen some pretty amazing interventions by God."

Shelly's daughter, Nancy, is one of the leaders, "When the crowd leaves, usually it thins after midnight, the leaders gather and pray until the sun comes up. That's why we call it 'Cry the Night!' And we pray for the kids whom we have just witnessed to, who haven't made the commitment to God."

Connecting Intercessors
and Marketplace Prayer

Intercessors do an all-nighter at the prayer house, as well.

Thomas, a retired pastor and his wife Nell, coordinate that effort. "We're quite senior," Thomas said laughing. So when some of these intercessors wanted to stay all night, some in shifts, but a few for the full eight hours (10 PM until 6 AM), we had to find some young blood." That is when Nancy asked the youth to join the intercession. "We are beginning to see older and younger intercessors coming together in these sessions. You have a seventy-year old intercessor and a seventeen year old praying and crying together. You catch prayer, and it happens at the 'prayer house.'"

Lyle turned to Jimmy, who had been sitting quietly as the story of prayer in the city unwrapped, and urged him to tell his story. "Last year, we started a once a week marketplace prayer event. Well, actually, it was Lyle's idea. He kicked it off and I offered to help, but he quickly walked me through the '4-Fs.'" Everyone laughed. Jimmy began,

> The prayer house is relatively new, but so far, we estimate that we have touched well-over two-hundred marketplace men from about forty different churches. It is also becoming a contact point for Christian men in the city. It's safe. It's non-denominational. It's relational evangelism. Yet, it has its fervent moments. We call it 'E320.' I think some of them feel more comfortable in going to an 'E320' meeting than to a 'prayer' meeting. But it is a praying meeting – twenty minutes of fellowship, a twenty minute Bible Study, and twenty minutes of prayer. And we try to adhere to that 20-20-20 rule, and not allow prayer get squeezed out. We make it 'one hour' in three twenty minute sessions; get 'em in and out. If they want to stay and chat, we're here. But the meeting itself adheres to a disciplined sixty minutes. We start on time and end on time. And they appreciate that.

Why E320? Lyle noted, "We call it 'E' for Exodus and Ephesians, and 3:20 for the verses. The first passage is a prohibition – *'You shall have no other gods ... Or make for yourself an image ... of anything in heaven ... the earth ... You shall not bow down or worship them; for I, the Lord your God, am a jealous God, punishing the children for the sin of the parents ...'* No other gods! Business, pleasure, or whatever. It is our kids that get punished – by our sins. God is not a vengeful God, a debt collector that gets a generation behind. Our sins impact our children in negative ways. We say 'Embrace the discipline of faith with the destiny of your children in mind.' The second passage is a promise, *'Now to him who is able to do immeasurably more than all we ask or imagine, according to his power that is at work within us.'* Some dance between prohibition and promise. Discipline is essential to be a godly man, and promise is offered by God to help him reach his potential.

We have an E320 'guest day' four times a year, when these guys work hard to recruit others, and we begin a new series. Even men who are not believers attend – and they are saved at a Bible study and prayer meeting. We have 'bring your wife day.' And so now, there are three women's Bible study and prayer groups that meet at the prayer house. Twice a year, we do a 'bring your kids' day. And we pray with our kids. Here are men, some in business suits, sitting cross-legged on the carpet, praying with their kids, and then their kids praying for them. Doesn't get much better."

Jimmy explained, "We have found the prayer house to be a great meeting place. It is neutral. It does not belong to one church or denomination, and it is not anti-church or denomination – that is toxic. We had a bit of that going on, but we addressed it. So pastors feel safe. On and off, we have pastoral prayer events here as well."

PC²LN – Formal or Informal

Lyle, along with Shelly, Nancy, Thomas and Nell, Jimmy and a dozen others have already established the spirit of PC²LN. Do they formally organize? Only if they sense that it will help their local cause. Do they need a more formal structure, elections, etc.? Not necessarily. A formal political organization that diminished the relational ethos they currently would set the process back. How can PC²LN help them? It might be the reverse – how can they, using the network being created across the nation, help other cities? How can their story and model be an example to others? Of course, PC²LN can help them through new resource awareness, communication with other cities, transforming their local story into a national story, connecting them to a national movement, while at the same time; they retain autonomy with regard to their local initiatives.

> Where the dynamic of a PC²LN process is already at work, do you formally organize? Only if you sense that it will help your cause. You can still benefit from the national connections. ▬ ➡

All over the nation, there are local constructs of prayer leaders already in place. There is no need, if that is the case, to move through all the previous steps – unless fresh reorganization would be helpful.

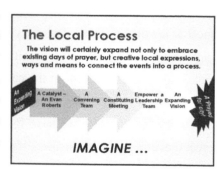

The Local Process

The vision will certainly expand not only to embrace existing days of prayer, but creative local expressions, ways and means to connect the events into a process.

An Expanding Vision — A Catalyst – An Evan Roberts — A Convening Team — A Constituting Meeting — Empower a Leadership Team — An Expanding Vision — A Prayer for a city!

IMAGINE ...

There are situations in which wineskins have quickly hardened. There are prayer leadership teams that have become unconsciously closed to newcomers. Some have developed a culture that permits one prayer style, but prohibits another. Some are the extensions of a particular denomination, and in all those cases, they are too narrow to forge a partnership that engages the larger Christian community. In such a case, some of the previous steps would be helpful.

What would be helpful to the movement would be for these local prayer and unity initiatives, orchestrated by the Holy Spirit, who is racing ahead of us, to be aligned nationally. In the early going, local leaders of initiatives and networks already underway might end up giving more than they receive. But in the end – a national, grass roots, bottom-up movement, that connects thousands of local prayer leadership teams across the country – that is a goal worth working towards together. What is desperately needed is a national construct of lay-prayer leaders, who serve various prayer causes, but share core prayer values that transcend any particular prayer effort.

And of course, there is a process of expanding what may already be happening in a local community beyond the current vision, and as we walk together, learning from one another and listening to the Holy Spirit, we will discover that our vision will grow and mature, our strategy will evolve, our tactics will become sharper and more effective. We will gain much by walking separately together.

STORY

In the town of Courier Ville, the president of the Chamber of Commerce is a believer. And he has worked hard to attract new business to the area, and more so, to attract godly businesses, morally clean businesses. When the negotiations broke down with a company who planned to build an assembly plant and employ more than three-hundred people, he almost cried. He made another effort to reach out to the company; they had three communities that had been targeted in their new plant location study. The one they had chosen was in Florida. He knew the Florida location well, and he also knew that Courier Ville was a quaint southern town, charming by his standards, full of decent, hard-working people, but it was no match by other criteria with the seaside metro Florida location. Local leaders had offered tax incentives. The labor pool was healthy. The potential salary scales proposed were competitive. But the deal was dead.

Sharing his disappointment with a small Bible Study group, they consoled him – and then challenged him. A friend asked, "Do you believe in the resurrection?" He was an orthodox believer, "Of course I do" he responded without seeing the immediate connection. "Let's pray for a resurrection!" A group of intercessors picked up the prayer theme. In less than sixty days, the owner of the company happened to be driving south to the new proposed plant location in Florida, when he stopped for gas in Courier Ville. At first, he was not even aware he was in the city where his company had considered locating. The study, with the Florida recommendation, had come to his desk a few weeks earlier and had barely mentioned the other potential sites. Something about Courier Ville attracted him. Rather than getting back on the freeway and heading south, he drove through the little town. Nestled at the edge of mountains, on a freeway, great transportation options, and conservative values – he rolled it all over in his head. He dialed the company that had done the research on new plant locations, and told them, "I am on my way to Florida to the suggested site of our new plant, and I don't mean to delay the process, but I am in a little town called Courier Ville. I wonder, could we explore yet another alternative, and do so quickly, without a great deal of delay?" Before he could ask how much the delay and the separate exploration would cost, his consultant explained, "Courier Ville is one of the options we looked at!" What followed was a quick explanation of why the Florida site was recommended, and the pros and cons of the Courier Ville location. Within a matter of weeks, the company reversed its decision and chose Courier Ville.

The President of the Chamber believes – God blessed the city with new jobs, because we prayed!

CHAPTER 10
So Much Rubble

Joe, Albert and Beth are all in different cities. But had they been in the same room and been able to talk about the 'Constituting Meeting' for their PC²LN in each of their communities, they would have laughed and cried together. Their stories, though diverse, would have been similar. They were simultaneously exhilarated and exhausted. Now, the really hard work would begin.

While Lyle did not intentionally follow the developed template, his model was not that far removed. He was the catalyst, although Shelly had been at the process and in a leadership role longer than him. And Thomas and his wife Nell had been around prayer groups in the city for decades. Still, it was Lyle who began to envision something beyond annual prayer events. And it was Lyle who became a convener of prayer leaders, along with intercessors. At times, he used the relational collateral of others – of Thomas with the intercessors, of Nancy with teens, of Jimmy with marketplace leaders. He stepped through the same processes informally. While there was no constituting meeting, had there been a formal process of selecting a slate of prayer leaders that were experientially vetted and were trusted by other prayer leaders, by intercessors, by pastors and marketplace Christians, there is little doubt that the team would have involved Lyle, Shelly and Nancy, Thomas and Nell, and Jimmy.

If a prayer leadership team already exists that is genuinely empowered, trusted and representative of a larger prayer process, not tied to one prayer organization or cause, one movement or style, one focus or emphasis, that team should be in a position to move the process forward. It should do so humbly, never trying to control, always to serve.

Whether the team emerges from a formal or informal process, the community will not be well served, and the prayer cause will remain narrow, until some team, empowered by the Holy Spirit,  and their relational collateral more than title or position, owns responsibility to serve the prayer process. Their first focus is always their own community; and then the nurture of similar movements in neighboring towns and cities, until a collage of mutual networks of prayer aimed at great awakening, have been formed.

The flash point of national spiritual renewal is local. Adam was placed in the *garden* with the *globe* in mind. The ultimate mission was unbounded, the potential for impact was unlimited – subdue and have dominion. But the specific stewardship challenge was bounded and attainable. The locus of control, the leverage point for impacting the earth, was to be found in Adam's capacity to both cultivate and tend, to *grow* and *guard* the garden. The first focus has to be on our own garden – wherever God has placed us. By the way, the term *'guard'* in Genesis has implications as a *prayer word.* It is the idea of *'watching.'* Later in Scripture, the watch and the watchman become synonyms for prayer and the intercessor. God wants us to guard our communities, and that starts with a prayer covering that blankets the city. Adam's sin was not what he did, but what he did not do – pray! And thereby, guard both himself and Eve through prayer. Our greatest failure is always in prayer.

Moving forward, what are our next steps?

STAGE ONE
Task One - What

The first assignment was to define major public prayer events to be mutually supported by the local prayer leadership team. Joe sent Megan and her teen group to the library with the charge, "Search through newspapers, local publications, the internet, for all the prayer events you can find in our local area. And do a survey of local churches." A good bit of that work had been done in the days leading up to the envisioning sessions.[8] They came up with a list of several national prayer initiatives that were observed in the community. And a good number that were unknown.

Task Two - Who

The next task was to discover 'who' led these initiatives; who coordinated these events. There were only a handful, and with the networks already in place, most of the leaders were known. Next, the leadership team needed to get these representatives of these nationally resourced prayer events/efforts to the table for a collaborative envisioning session. The half-day event would include time for each of them to tell what they did, when they did it, and how effective their prayer effort had been. The goal: Increase the effectiveness of all prayer events – an all-for-one effort. No longer should a slice of Christians support one day of prayer and others another, but there should be a more selfless approach. Without an attempt to control any specific prayer effort, the entire community prayer leadership team would own promotion of all prayer events.

Task Three - What's Missing

If there were significant national prayer initiatives for which there was no local representative and that prayer effort was considered essential to the overall prayer strategy in the community, the leadership team would connect with the national prayer organization and assist them in launching their local effort.

Task Four: When

The next step was to place on the calendar the existing prayer events, and then note other initiatives that might take place, those that were already resourced by national organizations, but currently leaderless.

The ultimate goal, they agreed, was a movement of prayer through the year where almost seamlessly, one prayer event flowed into another. And eventually, prayer events became the public measurement of the degree to which they had mobilized the churches and Christians in prayer; and further, where prayer events were driving the process of prayer, one that was constant and relentless, decorated by various public events, but taking place daily in different ways throughout the city.

STAGE TWO
Engaging the Movements

In addition to prayer events, each community is likely to have prayer movements and networks. These non-event relational movements are as significant as the prayer events, though often less noticeable.[9]

They too need to be convened. In some instances, this may be done in conjunction with the 'Stage One' gathering. Spend time allowing each to explain to the

Don't copy, collaborate; don't duplicate, cooperate; don't separate, synergize! ➡

others their efforts in the community, the scope of their network, their resources, and their vision.

Pray together – this is critical. Consider how each prayer ministry compliments the others, and discuss a means to develop a strategy for mutual support. Practice the principle – Don't copy, collaborate; don't duplicate, cooperate; don't separate, synergize! Consider the different contribution of these prayer movements in the city contrasted with prayer events. Find the common connection between them.

Now you have both prayer 'events' and a prayer 'movement' with leaders at the same table. You are making great progress! On to the next challenge.

STAGE THREE
Engaging the Congregations

Discovering prayer leaders of events and movements is less daunting than finding local congregations that are in every phone book. But convening the pastors is like herding cats – far more difficult. And finding the prayer leaders of those congregations, which ones have prayer leaders is climbing Mt. Everest. Begin by sending an invitation to the pastors, inviting them to bring their prayer leader. Do so with an inside/outside campaign. Have every member of the leadership team make contact with their pastor 'from the inside.' Have them inquire, if they do not know, 'Who is the prayer leader in our church?' Have them make a personal connection. Build a bridge, and extend a personal invitation to join the PC²LN.

The goal is to convene every pastor and/or prayer leader of every Christ-exalting, Bible reading congregation in the community. Give them a report of your efforts. Share the resources that are available. Envision them regarding a 'prayed-for' community – a 'Great Awakening!'

Develop a strategy to support congregations in their being houses of prayer for the community and the nations. Find your existing models. Champion them. Connect them to other pastors and congregations.

Focus areas:

1. At-home prayer – the restoration of the family altar;
2. Church-wide prayer meetings;
3. Identified, mobilized and directed intercessors;
4. Collaborative prayer evangelism efforts.

STAGE FOUR
Mobilizing Intercessors City-Wide

Identify intercessors across the city – first in connection with their home congregations. Then, geographically, in neighborhoods/zip-zones; and finally, by vocational tribe. Eventually, you will want to identify them in terms of their passion and intercessory focus.

In order to move from random intercession to informed intercession – do some primary research on the city. What is the strength of the church in the area? How many congregations are there in the defined area? What is the ratio of congregations to the population? (Ideal: 1-750; Significantly Under-churched: Less than 1 – 1500; Densely churched: More than 1 – 500. Average 1: 1000.)

How many people are in church in the defined area on any given Sunday? Percentage of the population in church on any given Sunday (National average – 17%).

A. It is estimated that some five percent of all believers have a specific call to intercession. With that as a standard, how many core intercessors should you be able to identify in your community, given the strength of the Christian community?

B. All believers are called to pray – and to pray for those in authority (I Tim. 2:2). Set a reasonable goal (recommendation – 10%) of the Sunday attendance, and begin to mobilize them in prayer.

C. Issue a city-wide call to all intercessors to gather to pray for their community.

D. Remember, prayer events test our capacity to mobilize. And the prayer events themselves often reveal training-teaching gaps. Without these events, we are guessing at our disciplined strength and the health of our practices.

E. Consider 3-4 community-wide prayer gatherings annually.

STAGE FIVE
Gathering Data

A. Map congregations involved in the prayer process. Map congregations not involved. Key these to their respective zip-zones.

B. Map the location of key intercessors.

C. Begin a basic spiritual mapping project.

STAGE SIX
Strategic Prayer Evangelism Deployment

I. Focus groups:
    a. Educators
    b. Government Workers
    c. Social Services/Family
    d. Medical
    e. Arts and Entertainment
    f. Media/Information
    g. Banking and Finance
    h. Service Sectors
    i. Trades
    j. Sales/Services
    k. Manufacturing/Industry
    l. Science/Technology

J. Who is the largest employer in your city? What are the moral implications of the work – is it something God can bless?

K. What drives the economy of your entire city?

L. What the character of your city? River, coastal, railroad, resort, interstate, border, retirement, bedroom, educational, medical, banking, blue-collar, manufacturing, welfare, ethnically distinct, historic, tourist? Is it growing or declining? Healthy or unhealthy? Is sin hidden or open? Are the controlling influencers, godly or ungodly?

> If a shop is locally owned and operated, then money spent there circulates up to eight times before it leaves the community.
>
> Ray Bakke,
> *The Urban Christian,* 104

M. Where does the light need to shine more brightly?

N. Who are the leading Christians in the above city-sectors?

O. Are there organized prayer efforts for or in any of the above sectors?

P. What about the groups without Christian insiders? Crime,

drug areas, gangs, prostitution, abortion clinics, human trafficking, addictions ... etc.

Q. Goal: One cause identified community prayer group for every 1000 residents of the community (With a church-cultural saturation ratio of one congregation per 1000 population, which equals one group per church). As a bare minimum, you must have at least one prayer group inside of or praying in behalf of each of the city-sectors.

STORY

Police and Pastors Fighting Crime

"We want a partnership with the religious community," declared Police Chief David Hixson. An outbreak of violence had catapulted the community to the top ten most violent cities in the US per capita. "We are trained to fight crime, but what we are dealing with here, this escalation of murder, is more than crime. It is symptom of something bigger, something we as police were not trained to deal with."

So, a publicly funded effort called Operation Good Shepherd was started by the police department that partners pastors and police officers. These pastors go through training and then have access to crime scenes to offer counseling to victims and witnesses. Almost forty pastors have now volunteered to be 'on call' as adjuncts to the police in tense situations.

The police chief noted, "Bullets won't stop people who mad – crazy mad. It is not something on the outside that stops them, but something on the inside, and that is what we are missing. I think

139

a stronger dose of Christianity in the city will help reduce crime."

Police Chaplain, Merl Keely noted, "In almost every case, there is an unhealthy family in the background – a missing father, a violent live-in boyfriend, drugs, an emotionally abusive climate. What we are seeing today is the result of the breakdown of the family. We are reaping the whirlwind of sin. These seeds were sown a long time ago."

Already, there are detractors to the effort citing church-state violations. A local economist noted, "With budget cutbacks, and private money, this may be the best recourse, faith volunteers".

---

8   Examples: The National Day of Prayer, the Global Day of Prayer; the Call-2Fall; Cry Out America; 30 Days of Prayer for the Muslim World; Seek God for the City; See You At the Pole; Prayer for the Peace of Jerusalem; Day of Prayer for the Persecuted Church, the Billion Souls Prayer Campaign, etc.

9   Moms-in-Prayer; Christian Educators Prayer Network; Adopt a School; Neighborhood Prayer; Aglow; Intercessors for America.

SECTION TWO
Wading through the Statistical and
Philosophical Bog!

CHAPTER 11
The Prayer Rope

"A three-fold cord," the Bible says "... is not quickly broken!" (Eccl. 4:12). Of course, this book is not about ropes, but about relationships. How do we forge a *relational construct* that can carry forward the weighty purposes of God and not easily break under the stress of the task or be easily severed? The goal is not the construct itself or the formation of a new organization. Quite simply, it is obedience to God. A task remains, the Great Commission, which we cannot accomplish given the current broken and divided conditions between Christians and congregations. Without stronger and broader relational connections between evangelical Christians in our cities than those that presently exist, we will fail in our mission. We all long to launch a rescue mission aimed at the lost, indeed, at the city itself

> How do we forge a *relational construct* that can carry forward the weighty purposes of God? ‒ ‒ ‒ ➤

– and we feel there is no time to waste, and yet, we lack the *relational construct* to move forward and make our efforts both systematic and comprehensive. We must build a rescue rope, one that we can share in our efforts to reach our communities.

For most of us – a rope is a rope! For those who depend on ropes – for climbing, for securing, for lifting, for binding this or that, a rope is not merely a rope! It is a scientific marvel requiring great care. A

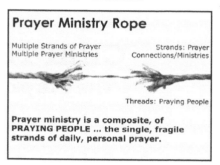

Prayer Ministry Rope

Multiple Strands of Prayer
Multiple Prayer Ministries

Strands: Prayer
Connections/Ministries

Threads: Praying People

Prayer ministry is a composite, of
PRAYING PEOPLE ... the single, fragile
strands of daily, personal prayer.

stressed rope can lose as much as 50% of its capacity, and stressed relationships also experience diminished capacities. Making sure a rope is dry, stored correctly, which means without knots and in its most natural coiled resting position – are all necessary factors. I am sure you are thinking – completely irrelevant to prayer ministry in the city! Not quite. Relationship strength is necessary to sustain a movement of prayer and transformation – and knotted, tangled relationships create stress that is counterproductive. Rope construction is almost as old as man. Ancient ropes were bundles of fibers or threads woven together; modern ropes may even use wires twisted together. Why not make a rope from one thick single strand of fiber? Great question – for us. While a single strand *should* have

A small group of people often hold it all together. When challenges come – they bind together and bear the load. They lead by example. They show up faithfully. And those people connecting together! Thus, corporate prayer! And 'prayer gatherings,' groups, etc. ▬ ▬ ▬ ▬ ▬ ➤

the same strength as a multi-stand rope the same size in diameter, it does not. There are several reasons why a rope is often a better solution than a thicker single strand of fiber.

The first is obvious. If one fiber fails in a multi-fiber, multi-strand rope, the rope itself, though damaged, remains intact. If the rope were made of a single, but even colossally large fiber, no matter how thick its diameter, were that single strand to be frayed or broken, the rope would fail catastrophically. And its mission would also fail. Quite surprisingly, scientific studies show that thin fibers usually have greater strength together than thick ones made from the same material. Glass fibers, for example, are stronger in tension when they are thin, because they are unlikely to contain what is termed, "a strength limiting defect". All of us have strength limiting factors! We need one another. We need one another precisely because of our unique differences both our strengths and our weaknesses. Drawn polymer fibers have higher mechanical properties than polymer products, but only when they have smaller diameters. Moreover, a multi-strand rope is more flexible than a single strand of the same diameter, easier to bend and work with.

If it is true, 'Without Him, we can do nothing!' And the means by which we invite Him into the work, declare dependence on Him – is prayer. You do not want a single-dimensional, fragile prayer existence! ➡ ➡ ➡

So we are stronger when we are together – God blesses unity. And together, we reduce our failure rate. And quite mysteriously, there is even greater flexibility with a multi-strand rope. And then there is the safety issue. Parachute lines and climbing ropes, where safety is the most important requirement, have an applied "safety factor". They are designed not only to be strong, but to survive five times the expected maximum load. When a rope is required to maintain the force of 200 pounds, it is designed to sustain a thousand pounds. Functionality is never targeted to meet the minimum threshold for performance, but to exceed that minimum multiple times! Certainly, the load of community transformation is not borne by us, but by God – and yet, the analogy is apropos. Relationships that lack depth, that are only minimally functional, that cannot stand the test of pressure will fail to sustain a significant community transformation effort.

In rope construction, the *fibers* are twisted together to form yarns; then the *yarns* are twisted together, but in the opposite direction of the *fibers* in order to create the *strands;* and then the *strands* are twisted in the opposite direction of the *yarns* to create the finished *rope.* This twisting or intertwining of each new element in the opposite direction, balances the rope! And that design is intended to prevent the components of the rope from 'unlaying' or unraveling when a load is suspended on it. Think about the implications for our unity – twisted together, in the opposite direction for balance, intertwined, strong enough to prevent unraveling under pressure. Coalitions across differences. Balance. Intertwined relationships and interests. Shared callings and commitments. Healthy tension. Profound unity.

> Relationships that lack depth, that are only minimally functional, that cannot stand the test of pressure will fail to sustain a significant community transformation effort. ➡

So powerful is the unity of fibers and interwoven strands in a simple new 3-strand, 1-inch diameter rope, it has a 9,000-pound capacity. Still, you would never attempt to test that maximum capacity! For safety sake, you limit the use of the rope to a fraction of its capacity. After any use, rope experts say that capacity is reduced. Environment affects it, and a rope can be shocked. That may happen in your prayer and city-impact effort – hostile spiritual environments, shocks as sin is uncovered and resistance is encountered from unlikely places. Knots and sharp bends of a rope can reduce the strength potential as much as 50%. Knots and sharp bends in our relational construct, along with different kinds of personal and spiritual stress will affect us, as well. Spiritual warfare, we will learn, is very real.

A few decades ago, the most common prayer coalition in local communities were among pastors. There were 'strands' of prayer *within* the congregations, but they were not usually connected across the community, uniting congregations. There were also strands of prayer in the community connected to various national prayer organizations and initiatives, but those efforts rarely intertwine – and sadly that remains true today. Efforts of community-wide, collaborative prayer are growing. Twenty years ago, when the 'single' strand of pastoral prayer coalitions formed, there was great hope that unified prayer would emerge across whole cities. But the links were severed or weakened with frequent pastoral moves. Congregational crises, rope stressors, emerged which demanded the immediate attention of a pastor to assure his continued role in a given church and the community. Sadly, such moments, at times, separated pastors from their peers. They were by necessity drawn back into an almost exclusive preoccupation with the congregational crisis. In far too many cases, the 'strands' were made of too few 'threads' – too few pastors involved in the city-wide process to bring change to the entire city. The average stay of a pastor in a local church is a bit less than five years. And new pastors do not always come with the same openness to prayer with other pastors across denominational lines as their predecessor. Even if that does occur, relationships require time to develop. As with ropes, single strand pastoral connections are not adequate.

The concept of PC²LN is that with multiple strands of prayer and prayer leaders bound together – many streams in confluence - the 'community prayer rope' has holding power. If the individual threads break or are severed, even if an entire strand breaks, the prayer rope holds. So, the goal is for strands, or streams, of prayer in the community – a fellowship of praying pastors, prayer leaders connected in prayer and prayer strategy, intercessors mobilized for prayer across marketplace prayer strands, youth prayer connections and more.

Through the wonder of computer simulation and modern technology, science has gone inside of multi-strand ropes. To the natural eye, a rope appears to be somewhat static, but under a microscope, when in use and under stress, the different strands in a rope appear dynamic. They appear to move as the stress of energy flows through them. The threads and strands appear to interact. Inside each strand, the individual threads appear to become dynamic, acting as if they were flowing rivers, conveying the energy of the rope, threads sharing stress within the rope, shifting the burden from one strand to another to absorb the weight and tension.

Many individuals, multiple strands – one rope! One purpose.

The idea behind PC²LN is the creation of multiple strands of single individuals (threads) bound and woven together, linked and unified, to sustain a movement of prayer, not only across the city or county, but across the nation. Not one thread – one person. Not one strand – one group, one sector, one stream, one movement. But many strands – dynamically moving and working together! Bearing the community to God in prayer. Maintaining the bridges of communication open. Holding things together when the storms come.

STORY

Bud and Amelia finally decided to make the move. The Midwest would be a more economical place to live. It was half-way between his kids and her kids. A small town would be a better place to raise the teens they shared. They would be less than an hour from a military base where medical care and other benefits of Bud's twenty-five years of service could be accessed.

The small quiet hamlet seemed in the middle of nowhere. It was the closest town to the farm Bud remembered spending time visiting each summer, the farm his grandfather had owned, and on which his father had grown up. There were no active family ties that encouraged them to move, just a sense of the need for change and the positive memories associated with a place. Both had previous marriages that still occasionally had livewire issues, and children with needs, though grown and married. Because of Bud's military service, in the eighteen years he and Amelia had been married, the longest period in which they had lived together had been nineteen months – except for the last three unbearable years.

A change would do them good. A smaller house. A less expensive lifestyle. They had not counted on times being so tough, and Bud's military retirement pay being so inadequate. The small hamlet into which they settled was a place of high stability. Everyone knew everyone. And everyone knew a new family had moved into the little house on Third Street. Seven churches were located on the streets of the little town, one only a block away from the home into which Bud and Amelia moved. But sadly, the couple was never invited to attend that church or any other. They knew of course that they could go! That they should go. But not one pastor made a call to welcome them or invite them. Neighbors waved, but no one came over. And so no one knew the secret emotional, relational pain of Amelia or the depression with which Bud struggled. Not until their relationship imploded and became the talk of the small town.

How do we balance personal privacy and the command to love our neighbors? How do we dig out of the deep cultural commitment to self-interest? How do churches see the city as a mission field, and accept a gracious responsibility for its neighbors? How do pastors serve not only their congregations, but pastor the community? How can we create ministries that are not mere harvesting nets for the church? Ministries that care, that don't coerce, and yet reach out to the hurting? How do we keep caring when people stop caring about themselves and others? "We can't save the world," we tell ourselves. "We can't make people receive our message of hope," we conclude. But are we doing all we can do?

After the tragedy that shocked the little town, Pastor Grayson, whose church was so near Bud and Amelia, wept before his congregation. He mapped out four blocks in every direction around the pretty little white church building that had set on the corner for eighty years. "This," he declared "is our mission field." Only three families that attended the church lived in the area. One other church was in the perimeter, and another on the edge. In the next few weeks, he knocked on every door in the four-block area. He didn't invite them to church or attempt directly to do evangelism. He simply introduced himself and the church as a neighbor. Where there was a warm response, he asked how the church might be a better neighbor. Bud and Amelia's story was still on everyone's mind. He made the fellowship hall of the church available to the neighborhood, not just the members. Suddenly, there were barbecues, yard sales, family gatherings – a buzz of activity that had never taken place before.

Other pastors in the city inquired, and eventually, five of them came together and concluded that each could share responsibility for the whole town of some 1000 people. There were 323 houses, 47 apartments, a nursing home with 67 residents, and three trailer parks with more than 75 living units. They divided the city into five grids, the city center and the four quadrants around it. Each had a population of approximately 200-300. Their churches ranged in active attendance from twenty-five to about a hundred. Each pastor committed that not less than once a year, they would find a way to get to each door. They approached the Mayor and asked him to declare a "Celebrate the Church Day!" He reluctantly refused. A number of business owners were equally reluctant to identify with the churches. On the weekend before the National Day of Prayer, the churches took out a full page ad in the local town paper announcing a unified prayer gathering and special day at each church the following Sunday. All during the week, every home in the city was visited.

Months before, they identified strong believers in each of their churches and got them into the same room, envisioning them regarding the little

151

town. They displayed a map of the city with the quadrants drawn, the location of the churches, and they asked each of them to identify the quadrant in which their homes were located. Then, they suggested that these people in each quadrant meet as Christians of influence. Each agreed to designate a peer lay-leader in each quadrant and continue to meet together, as Christians who cared about their little town.

During the week of the National Day of Prayer, these lay connections became critical. They led the charge for visiting friends in their quadrant. In the parks that Saturday, numerous gatherings took place. The Sunday following the National Day of Prayer, each church experienced a bump in attendance. But, the pastors knew the emphasis had to continue to be on their influence Monday forward.

CHAPTER 12
Values, Society, Culture

If ropes seemed an odd place to continue our discussion, then a discussion about values-society-culture may also seem a strange place to begin to launch a simple discussion about citywide prayer ministry, but let us be a bit philosophical for a moment.

- *Society* – A group of people living together forms and constitutes a "society". There are of course shades of variation within any given society due to economic, educational differences. The larger the group becomes, the more variations emerge.

- *Culture* – The customs, traditions, the ceremonies, the manners, the relating patterns and more. These distinctive ways mark and differentiate any given people [society] from another! The way they do weddings, and funerals; create lines and say "thank you!" Their food, language and music; the way they define family. The relating patterns that show deference and respect are *expressions of the values* underneath in which the society believes. Behavior is an expression of belief – the two are inseparable. The cultural *ethos* determines cultural *praxis* – practices. *Ethos* is a reference point for ethics, what a culture deems appropriate. And ethics derive from values.

- *Values* – Are moral and relational reference points for the people of the society, and they stand behind the culture, the cultural symbols, the behavior and relating patterns by which a people live. Values are what drive us. They inform our conscience. They are like inner lines by which we determine right and wrong. They are informed by some theological and philosophical system – atheistic, humanistic, socialistic, theological.

All peoples have "faith". These beliefs – moral or amoral, theistic or atheistic, belief in creation or belief in evolution, belief in the eternal or the existential – all beliefs are seen in the way people live together! Faith, whether traditional or contemporary, religious or secular, is never a private matter. The culture war that seeks to repress Christian expression, quiet public Christian prayer and eliminate Christian symbols, is a blatant war against faith which then allows the secular faith of humanism to be alone on the public social stage.

The collective beliefs (values) of the people (society) determine their customs and manners (culture), their traditions and practiced morals, the assumed behaviors the people practice with one another, thus, the culture they create. It involves holy days. Every culture worships in overt or subtle ways. Worship is an expression of values – it is an ideology, evidenced by our preoccupations,

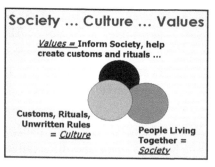

Society ... Culture ... Values

Values = Inform Society, help create customs and rituals ...

Customs, Rituals, Unwritten Rules = *Culture*

People Living Together = *Society*

the life-drivers considered 'worth' more than other things. In our society, we impose taxes for stadiums, not temples. Government subsidizes concert venues and the like, art museums, educational institutions all carefully designed to encourage anything but faith. Christianity as a social glue, a cultural center, a source of common values is gone. Independence and self-determination are virtually worshipped, as is freedom 'from' religion. Belief or disbelief determines shared behaviors. There is no in-between.

The _values_ inform society and help create customs and rituals. Those people living together form a _society_. And then customs, rituals, along with unwritten rules define the _culture_. When a dif-

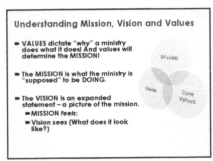

Understanding Mission, Vision and Values

- VALUES dictate "why" a ministry does what it does! And values will determine the MISSION!

- The MISSION is what the ministry is "supposed" to be DOING.

- The VISION is an expanded statement – a picture of the mission.
  - MISSION feels;
  - Vision sees (What does it look like?)

ferent 'value' reference point is established in society, it tends to gather supporters, creating a differentiated cluster of people who then move to challenge traditional customs and rituals. They may eventually displace the previously accepted value system, and if not, they typically resist them. They may even wage a culture war against the values as they manifest in different ways in society. And of course, this is exactly what we have seen in the US.

In simple terms, Judeo-Christian _values_ were those owned by most of the people who came to settle in America. The _society_ they created was informed by these Biblical values; and the _culture_ they celebrated, the holidays and the customs, were drawn from Biblical ideas and images. Their first public building was typically a church. Now, _Biblical values_ are consistently challenged and have been almost thoroughly displaced from mainstream society. In some cases, they have been declared illegal. A _'culture war'_ is being waged against prayer, the name of Jesus, public crosses and

Bible reading. This is not a superficial matter. It is the indication of a seismic moral values shift. A *new society* has emerged. For a season, the shifting legal standards seemed to aim at neutrality, supposedly taking a passive position toward 'Christian culture' in the context of the larger society. Now that is changing. The new values, liberal values, anti-biblical and anti-Christian values have become the core around which the new society has emerged – and the new majority have decided to live without Christian principles, more to the point, to wage war against them. This militant humanistic society has been dismantling the Biblical-Christian culture for nearly a century, and now the process is almost complete. Humanistic values are now at the heart of an amoral society that has created a godless, self-centered, hedonistic culture. The new anti-Christian values have become the norm for the new social core, which has now become dominate in the culture. And the seismic shift we are feeling is the center of culture shifting under our feet. This is not the only problem – the values of the now dominate, secular culture are also radically bending the shape of the church. Entire denominations have thrown overboard Biblical absolutes, such as, creationism, God's special claim to the earth. The virgin birth and the incarnation – and thus the other worldliness of Christ, and subsequently, the idea that he was sinless and that he arose from the dead. They have – abandoned 'the faith' without leaving the ship.

The fundamental key to the recovery of a Biblical *ethos* is found in prayer! Not prayer as prayer requests. Not prayer as acquisition. But prayer over open Bibles. Good prayer touches every aspect of our faith. There is an obvious connection between prayer and conversion, prayer and repentance, thus prayer and the recalibration of our orientation in life; between prayer and the Holy Spirit's Presence, prayer and regeneration, prayer and sanctification, prayer and our understanding of Scripture, prayer and spiritual formation, prayer and spiritual discipline, prayer and spiritual warfare, prayer and temptation, prayer and praise, prayer and petition, prayer and meditation, prayer and peace – and on and on. Virtually every aspect of our faith and walk is related to prayer. It is not only the 'saying' of prayers that is necessary, it is the cultivation of a culture of prayer – a culture of humility, one that aims at holiness, takes sin and the necessity of repentance seriously, honors the sovereignty of God and leans on His understanding, refuses the strength of the arm of flesh, champions unity, celebrates community, waits expectantly for God's glory, prays for fire from heaven. It is not the practice of ritual that is important, but the embrace of a deep personal habit of abiding in Him, of deep dependence on the Lord.

Ten Prayer Values
– what we believe, and how we behave:

- We value prayer; *therefore we will* encourage pastors and congregations to _make prayer the central element of all ministry, and we will integrate prayer into the fabric and rhythm of our vocational-daily lives._

- We are a praying people; _therefore we will nurture at-home daily prayer, and at-work regular prayer connections,_ providing resources, training and nudging new and old Christians to deepen their prayer lives.

- We believe that **we are a kingdom of priest** and that prayer and worship are our highest calling, and that as priests we are not only recipients of a blessing, but the conveyors of blessing; _therefore,_ in prayer, we will encourage Christians to pray for the favor and blessing of God, protective care, upon the pastors of the city, our churches, our places of employment, our neighborhoods, city and county as well as our nation. _We bless;_ we do not curse. We ask God, not for what we deserve, but for blessing – for grace and mercy!

- **We value holiness and righteousness,** and we recognize that our nation needs revival; *therefore we regularly and consistently cry out to God for a great awakening* for our nation.

- **We believe in the power of petition,** and that God answers prayer; *therefore we faithfully take the needs of the church, the city and the world before the throne of God and ask for grace!* We provide a means whereby requests for prayer are taken seriously, passed on to intercessors, specifically needs related to the moral and spiritual condition of the city.

- **We believe in the power of intercession;** *therefore, we identify, train, team and mobilize intercessors* across the city with a focus on community spiritual awakening and the various mission endeavors of the collaborative process. We will work to see embedded prayer triads and quads throughout the city.

- **We believe prayer is essential to the success of every endeavor,** and that without Him we can do nothing, and whatever we do in his behalf without dependence upon Him is less than it might have been, given dependence in prayer; *therefore, our rule is no one works, unless someone prays!*

- **We believe that the reception of the gospel unto salva-**

━ ━ ━ ▶ "Values" – as defined by use today does not constitute what we articulate as important, but what we demonstrate as important by behavior. Prayer may be esteemed as important, but it technically is not a "value" until it is held in such regard that it is practiced, so that it impacts behavior. Things articulated are not necessarily values. Things practiced are values.

tion is a spiritual issue; *therefore, we pray for the harvest,* that blind eyes will be open to the gospel, that closed hearts will be open to the truth of Christ – and that the gospel will go forth in power, out of prayer. Our goal is a systematic plan to make the city-county, a prayer-for place.

• **We believe that there is a definitive connection between prayer and the harvest;** *therefore, we insist that our prayers have a missional dimension,* that we must pray for lost loved ones, for the unreached in our city and the world.

• We believe, **"God governs the world by the prayers of His people";** *therefore, we pray for our city, state and national leaders.* We pray about world conditions and various global crises.

STORY

Darren is a young pastor. He came to the little town of Deerfield a year ago. And he has met with incredible success. The little church, averaging about fifty, exploded by a hundred new attenders. He quickly became the second largest church in the little town. It humbled him. The added members moved him to a deeper prayer life. As he surveyed the city, the spiritual condition of young people bothered him. Deerfield is a quiet little town and the county seat, with only about 15,000 people. Just off the main street is the Happy Hour Club, the hottest bar in the county. The parking lot is almost always full. And Darren knew, by his connections in the community, that the barkeep from time to time served underage kids.

The deputy sheriff attended his church, and he shared his concern with him. They suspected the bar for violating the age limit on alcohol but no action could be taken without proof. The kids did not want to self-report their drinking. Darren began to drive by the bar, and then he parked in the lot and prayed for those coming and going, looking for kids. Then he began to emerge from his car and prayer-walk the bar parking lot. That is when the bouncers met him outside and asked, "Are you coming in?" He told them no! "Who are you and what are you doing here?" "I am a pastor, and I am praying," he told them. They disappeared into the bar and emerged to warn him not to harass anyone. Later he would learn that the bar owner had told them, "Leave him alone. If he is only praying, not harassing anyone, that's harmless". But, prayer is never harmless. Darren became a regular at the Happy Hour Club – walking and praying, praying and walking.

Two tragic funerals captured the attention of the small town, and Darren was involved in both of them. The man who had built the structure and operated it as a bar for a number of years, had now leased it to the current bar owner. He sat in those funerals – both young people, both of whom had died far too young, both with profiles of lives far removed from God. It stirred the man. A month later, sitting across the street from the Happy Hour Club, the bar he had built and leased to someone else, drinking himself, he later said God spoke to him, saying, "This is not a good thing you have done." The moment sobered him. He called the bar owner, and informed him that he might not renew the lease. And then he called Pastor Darren. "Preacher, you don't know me. At least we have never met. But I heard you preach recently" and he mentioned the funerals.

"I have heard that you been hanging out in the parking lot of the Happy Hour Club – I built that bar, and now lease it to a friend." Darren listened quietly. "Preacher, the lease is coming up on that building. And I have been thinking about my own life and about those kids that died recently. If I gave you that building, what would you do with it?" Darren's heart leaped. Spontaneously, he declared, "I would create a community youth center." Within months, the Happy Hour Club became "Deerfield Connect!" – a Christian meeting place for teens.

CHAPTER 13
Fixing Us First

E zra, the key pastoral leader in the restoration of Jerusalem a generation after the devastation and conquest of Judah by Babylon, is found in the Biblical record engaged in personal prayer over the open scrolls in his charge. God changed him there and made him a catalyst for the restoration of the city. Around him, a small group formed that relocated from Babylon to Jerusalem, and arguably, out of their passion and example, with Ezra's prayer life driving the process, they launched a movement of spiritual renewal in the city. One person, in prayer, over an open Bible – this is where the change begins. This is what must inform and empower the process.

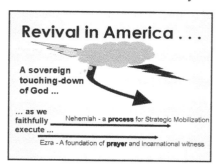

Nehemiah was civic leader on loan to Jerusalem from Persia, modern Iran. He had been a personal assistant to the king. He was a non-cleric. But he too recognized the importance of prayer. Under Nehemiah's leadership, the work of rebuilding the sections of the walls of the city was adopted by each family, who lived along each section. Each family rebuilt in their own neighborhood, what a powerful concept. They build separately, independently, and yet together, next to one another in a coordinated manner. There was a moment, when the work was almost halfway completed, when the walls had been joined together, but they were not entirely up, that the people despaired. "There is too much rubble," they complained. The task was overwhelming. They were tired. Under-resourced. Understaffed. Threatened in physical ways they did not anticipate. Moreover, they were ready to give up.

Each family rebuilt in their own neighborhood. ------▶

Amazingly, Nehemiah knew, the answer was not to double-down on the work, but to double-down on prayer. There was fierce and threatening resistance, death threats against the effort, emotionally debilitating distractions – and Nehemiah's response was more prayer. He partnered intercessors and workers. Half worked, and the other half watched, a metaphor for prayer. With the work needs assessment escalating, the labor requirements increasing, he does exactly the opposite of normal logic. He decreases labor and increases prayer. He moved to a twenty-four hour watch. He created a system and signal for rapid deployment of the support of one group for another. He knew working in isolation was a real and psychological concern, so he created a network of support. Every worker

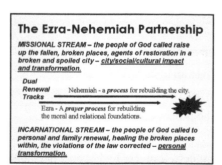

The Ezra-Nehemiah Partnership

MISSIONAL STREAM – the people of God called raise up the fallen, broken places, agents of restoration in a broken and spoiled city – city/social/cultural impact and transformation.

Dual Renewal Tracks — Nehemiah - a *process* for rebuilding the city.

Ezra - A *prayer process* for rebuilding the moral and relational foundations.

INCARNATIONAL STREAM – the people of God called to personal and family renewal, healing the broken places within, the violations of the law corrected – personal transformation.

had a watcher, a prayer partner. Everyone who felt distant and removed in their work had a means of connection and were assured that they were not alone. The result was that the work went forward. The doomsday prophecies against them, the threats by their opponents never materialized. When they won the prayer battle, they won the psychological war, and the finished their mission.

In your work toward city-impact, you will inevitably discover that you have underestimated the degree of rubble in the city – the levels of entrenched sin, the commitment to vice, the justification of immorality, the damage to children and to the family, the ideology of post-modernism. The rubble is great. Strength of the workers and tenacity will be an issue. And prayer is your only recourse.

You may find challenges to the balance between pragmatism and principle. As any city-impact, movement intensifies, and the numbers enlarge, this tension will manifest and could become a deal killing issue. You will want to make prayer central to all you do; you are fundamentally, beyond city-impact and serving the needs

The answer was not to double-down on the work, but to double-down on prayer. ▬ ▬ ▬ ➡

of the city, beyond repairing the walls of the city, at the roots of your evangelism and discipleship efforts, a prayer movement, a people of prayer. Any attempts to delegate prayer to a special group of intercessors so that an action team can accomplish the mission is doomed to fail. Prayer must be seen, not for what it does for the mission, but for what it does to and in us. It fundamentally changes the missionaries, the doers. The spirit of humility, grace in interaction, gentleness in navigating difficult decisions, and love one for another as well as the city, joy in the journey, peace in the storm – these are critical to the mission. Prayer is not for ancillary power; it is fundamental to our own Christlikeness. And without prayer, we fail.

There may be a tendency to assign prayer to the pastors and the spiritual folks, and make the task of reaching the city, the work of the Nehemiah's. "You folks go pray, and pray for us; we'll reach the city." Nehemiah had resources Ezra could not muster, as do lay-leaders. He had authority that was different and far more extensive than Ezra. But he knew the importance of prayer. In many places, a tension develops between the prayer people and the pragmatists. One group is about principle, the other about results. One group champions prayer, the other action. One group measures impact by quality of lives, the other by quantifiable cultural change. One group wants the church to grow, the other the city to change.

Business Leaders and Pastors – the Divide

This tension is at times found in the fault lines between business leaders, so critically important to this process, and pastors, who are equally critical. Laura Nash is Professor of business ethics at Harvard Business School, and Scotty McLennan is Dean of Religious Life at Stanford University. In their book, *Church on Sunday, Work on Monday,* Nash and McLennan, have done research focused on the divide between marketplace Christians and pastors. They state that Christian business leaders often feel "very close to pastors on issues of family, personal well-being, or community outreach ..." However, with regard to their role as business people; they feel ignored, even disdained. And they think that what they do is beyond the comprehension and experience of most clergy, often their own pastor. Indeed, Peter Wagner points out, that 99% of all clergy have no training with regard to relating to ministry in the workplace[10] and little context to understand. Bi-vocational pastors may be better prepared to assist here than seminary trained ministers whose only world is too often that of faith and the church.

The average pastor sees the vocation and workplace location of his people as irrelevant to the ministry of the church. He may claim bragging rights by having a 'doctor' in the congregation or some other respected profession, but he sees the work of the doctor or corporate president, even educators, as outside the function of the church. This rigid bifurcation of the sacred and secular is so debilitating. All of life is to glorify God. There is no such division between life with God and life in the world. We have failed as a church to help people connect their daily lives, as acts of worship unto God. We need a completely new effort to teach the sacredness of all life.

The sense that pastors do not understand business, do not understand the 'real' world, and live in a kind of bubble is not an isolated notion. Nash and McLennan point out the divergent views between clergy and church-going business people. The differences are stark in the areas of money, poverty and business attitudes. According to these two authors, clergy tends to see business people as centered on money or profit, as greedy and selfish, as focused on excessive salaries and consumption, their lifestyles and materialism. Underneath are the more sinister negative associations of idolatry, sin, materialism, false values, wrong priorities, selfishness, and injustice against the poor. These are at times the unspoken assumptions that not so silently bounce off the walls when the marketplace meets the altar.[11] They are not openly explored, but they shade meanings and alter the posture of each group in the course of decisions.

Nash and McLennan also note, according to their findings, that clergy felt simply "powerless to have a significant impact on business people ..." They also confessed that they felt "business people were simply too greedy or indifferent to care about real spiritual issues ..." If their conclusions are right, there is a great deal of trust that must develop between the Ezra and Nehemiah streams.[12] And even if their findings are correct in specific situations, generalizations will impede the process of understanding and partnership. One of the places this tension arises is along the fault lines of principle and the pragmatic. Pastors who claim the turf of prayer and business leaders who see themselves as innovative get-it-done leaders are likely to divide the work – you pray, pastor; we'll roll up our sleeves and get the job done. Any decision to leave the praying to the pastors and intercessors, and real impact to the Nehemiah leaders, is deadly to unity and spiritual health. Business leaders tend to feel more comfortable on the turf of pragmatic decision-making, and more confident of their commercial ability than they have confidence in pastors with whom they are called to partner. That often includes financial management and planning, human resources, decision-making, goal completion, not only with respect to efficiency but also with regard to effectiveness. In the church arena, they often feel compelled to suspend their sense of business acumen, and they quietly feel that the church is not always wisely managed. Pastors need their expertise, and they need the center of prayer and faith that pastors can provide. One thing will become clear, compellingly clear, there is no comparable enemy opposed to effective corporate management and success, as there is to the kingdom enterprise. And that battle is only won through prayer, the kind of prayer that cannot be delegated.

The harness that connects the Ezra-Nehemiah streams does not now exist. It is being fashioned. It must elevate the Nehemiah as a peer in the process. It must simultaneously increase respect for the Ezra stream. Pragmatism and access to resources cannot alone drive the process. It must be anchored to sound godly principles and Biblically centered. That is a key role for pastors who must learn to *co-lead* without attempting to dominate and control. Great respect must emerge from both streams, clergy and lay-leaders, one for the other. A city-construct of believers informally gathered, two-or-three in His name, is critical to the mission. These should be salted into every vocational location in the city and every neighborhood. A strategic plan should be developed for collaboration between these believers in the marketplace and their neighborhoods. In addition, a citywide or countywide strategic plan that forges new ways for the collaboration of churches for increased impact is necessary. Christians and congregations alone must give way to congregations and Christians in community. No congregation can accomplish the task alone. Nor can a group of determined, well-financed business leaders. The Nehemiah and Ezra streams must flow together. Any plan that leaves out the church will fail, and any plan that attempts this process out of the campus-based, Sunday morning church model now in existence will fail.

Faith in the Marketplace

The word *vocation* comes from the Latin word for *calling*. That is, God calls individuals to a vocation, a way of life, a profession; it's their life work. The Greeks and Romans pioneered *liberal* education. The term was applied from the Latin word for *freedom*. The goal was the development of the free citizen, freed because they had been taught and trained to use all their gifts and abilities, and were capable of being self-sustained. Free.

All over the nation, believers are seeing with fresh eyes the workplace and faith connection. It is gaining momentum. In 1990, there were only twenty-five formal workplace ministries. By the year 2002, there were 1200 organizations seeking to integrate faith and work. By 2005, that number had leapt again to 1400.[13] There are now at least 10,000 Bible and prayer groups in workplaces throughout America that meet regularly. That is only one for every 33 churches. Our goal, nation-wide, should be not less than a million, or about 318 per county; one per 300 or so residents. This connection between faith and the workplace has been addressed in books dating back to 1930's. But their number is increasingly almost exponentially. By the year 2000, some 350 titles had been published. Five years later, more than 2000 titles by Christians about faith in the workplace were in print.[14]

In Colonial days, the church was at the center of life. In recent times, in the age of Darwin, Freud, Dewey and post-modernism, the church has been increasingly marginalized. And faith itself, specifically, the Christian faith treated with contempt and distrust. Some allege that Christians are the most underrepresented group in the arena of public–policy discussion and debate in America today. Panel after panel has a special interest representative, people of color, gender identity and balance, advocates of this sector of culture and that. But not a Christian, a conservative Christian, a Bible believing Christian –as a Christian this may be due not only to resistance, but sadly to the complacent dispositions of Christians. The nation's minority and special interest groups, with their particular agendas, advance far more energy and seem to have more influence on public issues than do Christians. Art, literature, movies, music, and television can be anti-Christian without impunity. Politicians may articulate anti-Christian positions and are not challenged. The most despicable things are uttered about Christ, but not allowed against Mohammed, Buddha, or any other religion. They may be said of Christians, but not other groups. Rarely are

> **Marketplace Christians need to become more effective agents of salt and light!** ------➤

the people who so publicly denigrate Christianity, its personalities both historical and contemporary, its beliefs and practices, called into account in a measured, intellectually persuasive, and gently instructive way.[15]

Speaking with One Voice

Bob Briner in his book, *Roaring Lambs,* suggest that we need to have a strategy to retard the growth of evil in our community. That we should develop a policy and methods for speaking to people outside the four walls of the church. To accomplish this, our own sense of awareness of the community's disposition toward Christianity is an issue. For example, do you know the status of the image of Christianity and the church in your community? Among common folk? At the newspaper? Down at city hall? Among school board members? The zoning board? At the tax appraiser's office? In any given bank? At the Chamber of Commerce? Among the owners and managers of the city's malls and shopping centers? Among the wealthy, whose holdings entitle them to so much influence? Among business owners and corporations? In the social services sector? In the news and editorial rooms, the programming office of the local TV and radio stations?

When the average person in your town thinks of a Christian, who comes to his mind? A real Christian or a caricature? An authentic believer or the last public scandal involving a pastor or Christian leader? Is there a single *layperson* in your community who is known as an articulate advocate for a Christian point of view? He speaks not as a professional clergyman, but as a community leader? How does the church respond to media distortions, misconception, and misinformation about Christians and their motives?[16] Is there a plan? Is there a group of pastors capable of wordsmithing a reasoned and Biblical response? These are excellent questions. Typically the answer to all of them is – No! We do not have a unified strategy. We do not speak with one voice, especially as conservative Christians. We are unaware of the degree of support or adversity there is to Christianity in various sectors of the city. When community problems surface, we are too often a non-player or a reactionary non-contributor, because we do not have a plan to deal with, for example, teen pregnancy, underage drinking, the proliferation of bars and nightclubs, the practice of abortion, the introduction of occult practices, the drug problem, the human trafficking problem, poverty, homelessness, racism, family disintegration, on and on.

There may be noble models of Christianity in a community, but they are too often stealth. The community may see them merely as humanitarian, not as distinctively Christian. There is a growing trend to separate goodness and Christianity, and connect goodness with all humanity – a trend away from mankind as sinners. And so often Christians have the idea that they should not wear their faith on their sleeve. It is at one level a noble and humble notion, and at another, deadly to the cause. What we do must be done now 'in the name of Jesus,' and for the glory of God. Finally, in answer to Briner's question, rarely does the church have an articulate advocate who offers a Christian perspective in the face of media distortions and misconceptions.

We have an increasingly privatized faith, we are failing at witness. Behind the stained glass windows, our arguments may remain sound, but in public, we stumble. We have no united plan. As Elton Trueblood reminds us, "The test of the vitality of religion is to be seen in its effect on culture." Jack Graham, pastor of the prestigious Prestonwood Baptist Church in Dallas, TX, says, "Revival will come when we get the walls down between the church and the community." We should be reminded again that the Hebrew word for work is *avodah,* also translated *worship.* Work is sacred; it is an act of worship because our whole lives are to an act of worship unto God. Worship and its vertical God-centered tether find expression in our work. And the values of our work are informed by our worship. The dichotomy between Sunday and Monday must be healed. And the only way, given the current social and political constraints against the church has an organization may be the coordinated action of believer citizens, the Nehemiah's, who more boldly live out their faith in the marketplace.

Personal Vitality in Christ

Why is our impact on the culture so anemic? Greg Hawkins and Cally Parkinson in their extraordinary study identified church attenders on a spiritual continuum in four categories. First, there were those who were *exploring* Christ and his claims. Second were those who had made a faith decision, and were *growing* in Christ. Third, there were those who felt *close* to Christ. Fourth, those who were *Christ-centered*. They discovered the telling mark of the most devoted Christians, almost 80% of whom agree *very strongly* that they *love God more than anything,* is their characterization of the relationship, not as duty or faith, but as love. The study also pointed out the gap between lips and lives. A full third of those who so fervently profess that they 'love God' don't serve the church frequently.

One of the differentiating factors between those who are *exploring* Christ and those who are *growing* in Christ is their increased participation. Fifty percent of those who think that they are *growing* in Christ commit to a service function in the church at least once per month. Eighty-five percent of them attend church three out of four weekends. Forty-seven percent participate in a small group, and at least 50% of them serve in some capacity. Growth in Christ demands a contribution from us. Christianity does not allow us to be happily passive and inactive.

Approximately 10% of church attendees are *exploring* Christ. Some 38% are *growing* in Christ. Another 27% feel *close* to Christ. About one fourth, 25%, consider themselves *Christ-centered.* There are extraordinary differences in these groups related to personal spiritual growth. Fifty-eight percent of the *Christ-centered* group perceive themselves to be growing at a moderate-to-rapid pace in their Christian experience, nearly six-in-ten. These are highly charged individuals who are more deeply satisfied. In contrast, only eighteen percent of those who are *exploring* Christ, feel that they are *growing* at a moderate-to- rapid pace. That is a significant differ-

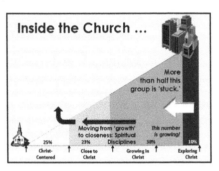

ence. The growing in Christ has 27% who classify their growth as moderate to rapid. Of those who are *close* to Christ, 47% classify their growth has moderate-to-rapid. The evidence seems compelling; growth in Christ is related to the perception of *closeness,* and beyond that, a life that is *centered* in Christ. This perception of closeness propels spiritual growth and development. Christianity is relational. And it is personal. It is not merely about principled living; it is about a vital connection to the living Christ.

According to Hawkins and Parkinson, some 26% of church members are stalled or dissatisfied with either the church or their own personal spiritual development. The segment in which stalled Christians show up in greater abundance than any other is in the *growing* in Christ group. Fifty-two percent of all stalled Christians are in this second segment. They have moved from *exploring,* and have made a decision to follow Christ, indeed, they are *growing* in Christ, but they do not yet feel *close* to Christ. The inability to

174

transition into a deeper relationship in which they feel *close* to Christ and then into a *Christ-centered* life, seems to be the source of their frustration and dissatisfaction.

Why have they stalled? Dominating the data is their lack of discipline in daily spiritual practices. Busyness crowds out prayer. Other activities take precedence. The lack of spiritual discipline applied daily, time with God, reading the Bible, pausing for reflection, is the dominating factor. It is more decisive than any lack in a church community. It is more decisive than ineffective church leadership. It is more of an issue than any personal emotional concerns. It is greater than any doubts they have about faith. It is more significant than any trauma they may be processing.

How do people get uninstalled? Again, dominating the data is this simple idea - they connect with God through daily spiritual practices. The management of their own personal daily time with God, the embrace of spiritual disciplines, was more of a factor in getting people unstuck than switching churches. Or increasing the frequency of regular church attendance. More effective than joining a small group. Or sharing their struggles with a friend and mentor. Or having a moving spiritual experience. Or being inspired. The answer is so simple that it is mystifying – daily prayer over an open Bible, learning to listen to God and feeling his love.

This one factor, the daily practice of prayer, separates those who feel *close* to Christ from *explorers* and those who are *growing* in Christ. The close to Christ group pray daily for guidance. Almost half confess their sins daily. Their frequency in daily engagement with God in prayer and Bible reading, in spiritual reflection, in solitude is more than twice that of the *growing* in Christ segment. It becomes clear that the personal time devoted to prayer and Scripture, is the most powerful catalyst for spiritual growth and satisfaction.

Moving from growth in Christ to rapid *growth,* and then to

feelings of *closeness* with God and deeper satisfaction – is not a feeling matter at all, but action issue. It demands obedience. When a believer feels *close* to Christ, there is also an increase in their love for others. And when individuals move from *exploring* Christ and *growing* in Christ to feeling *close* to Christ, their satisfaction with the church's role escalates to some 67%. Little may have changed in the church. But their relationship with the church and their perception of it, get transformed as they become *close* to Christ. Sadly, in many cases, we are asking the church to do for us what only a personal relationship with God in Christ can do.

Some 25%, one-in-four churchgoers, are in the *Christ-centered* segment. They excel all other groups – they serve the church more, serve those in need, evangelize more frequently, and tithe more consistently and at higher levels than any of the other three segments. Their sense of love for God and being loved by God is significantly higher than the close to Christ segment. They also feel

> **Best practice churches don't simply serve their community. They act as its shepherd.- - ►**

more equipped to share their faith. And they are more aware of their spiritual gifts.[17]

The more an individual progresses from feeling close to Christ to a Christ-centered life, the more concerned there is for the community and for friends and family around them who may not know Christ. In the beginning of their journey to spiritual development, the focus is on *reading* the Bible, *reflecting* on its meaning, personal purity and confession of sins, studying the Bible for *truth* and *direction* for their lives, and setting aside time to *listen* to God daily. As one moves from being merely *close* to Christ, to being *Christ-centered,* they report that God is *calling them* to be involved in the lives of the poor and suffering. They are more proactive in inviting non-Christians to participate in faith experiences and to know Christ. The more Christ-centered life they live, the more personal initiative for evangelism there is in their own lives. A higher level of personal faith satisfaction rises out of their own personal experience. They become less reliant upon the church and more reliant upon Christ. The move from being merely *close* to Christ, to being *Christ-centered* means daily reflection on Scripture and time in prayer. A growing trust in the authority of the Bible. A congruence between their own personal sense of self and their identity in Christ. The placing of Christ first in everything, knowing Christ, not only as Savior, but as Lord. Finally, the giving of their life away in service to other people for the cause of Christ.

According to Hawkins and Parkinson, "Best practice churches don't simply serve their community. They act as its shepherd, becoming deeply involved in community issues and frequently serving in influential positions with local civic organizations. They often partner with nonprofits and other churches to secure whatever resources are necessary to address the most pressing local concerns." In addition, in these churches, leaders model how to grow spiritually.

The makings of a disaster in a congregation are growing numbers of people in the exploring Christ group who do not make a decision to grow in Christ. And individuals who have made a decision to follow Christ, and sense some growth, but do not feel close to Christ. These are the people who stall in the spiritual life. They need a clear pathway for spiritual growth. They need to feel like they 'belong'. They need help understanding the Bible in depth. They need someone to challenge them. They need living models for growth.[18]

177

STORY

An evangelical church in New Delhi stands on a busy street, in the heart of one of the greatest mission fields on the face of the earth. Nevertheless, its doors are closed during the weekdays at which times the great crowds of lost people pass. In contrast, the Muslim mosques and Hindu temples are open. The church will open its doors Sunday, at 11 o'clock, and close them again for a week. It is functionally closed to the harvest, with dying people all around. Its location is prime real estate to win the lost; its strategy to use the resource of its location is non-existent. Sadly, it is not even aware of either its problem or potential.[19]

Jesus wept twice in the Gospels. First, at the death of his friend, Lazarus. Second, over the coming death of the city of Jerusalem. He loved Lazarus, and he loved Jerusalem. If you only see the city as a target for mission, you will fail. You need to love people. And you need to love your city. And that is proven by weeping over it. Without love, there is little chance of impact.[20] And without tears, there is little evidence of love.

10   Peter Wagner, *The Church in the Workplace* (Ventura, California: Gospel light, 2006), 94.

11   Ibid, 61.

12   Ibid, 95.

13   Ibid, 80.

14   Ibid.

15   Bob Briner, *Roaring Lambs* (Grand Rapids, Michigan: Zondervan, 1993), 64.

16   Ibid, 58.

17   Ibid, 87.

18   Ibid, 186.

19   Ray Bakke, *The Urban Christian* (Downers Grove, Illinois: Inter-Varsity Press, 1987), 46.

20   Ibid, 51.

CHAPTER 14
A National Profile

In our little book, we have considered a number of fictitious places, among them, Prayer County, named for the dream we have for all our cities and counties. Like your city, Prayer County is a long way from living up to its name. It is like Canaan, CT; St. Cloud, FL; Angels Landing in Zion National Park and Angel's Trail in Wayne County, Utah; and Zion, IL. Then there is Bountiful and Eden, Salem and Bethel. Like Prayerville, these cities do not live up to their name either.

Prayer County as a prototypical place is one of 3144 counties in the 50 States. It is the county seat. The USA population is 313,847,465 million and the average population per county is 99,824.[21] [We will use the rounded up figure for Prayer County of about 100,000 residents.] The *average* city in America has 8,967 residents [We will use the rounded up number of 9,000] and is one of some 35,000 cities, towns and hamlets in the nation, both incorporated and unincorporated. In each county, there are about eleven cities/towns/hamlets. [These are projected averages, intended as helpful benchmarks, as you consider your city/

county prayer council. Of course, some counties have hundreds of thousands of people and a handful are in the range of a million in population.] Metropolitan areas may choose to develop 'prayer councils' that reach across numerous counties creating a collage of interconnected prayer streams.

No statistics are readily available for the population average of county seats. We will consider our fictitious city called Prayerville, a community of 50,000 residents, well above the national municipal *average* of 8967, [9000 for our purposes]. In a typical county, almost 80% of the residents live in population clusters ranging in size. Just over 20% live in unincorporated areas or towns smaller than 2500. Every county will vary in terms of population patterns.[22] Overall, statistical studies reveal, nearly 80% of the people of the Western world live in cities. In the US, 212 media market centers reach 96% of the nation's population.[23]

> The Hebrew and Greek words for city are mentioned 1200 times in Scripture. And 119 different cities are mentioned by name. ➡

Twenty-three percent of the US population lives in ten mega cities. Forty-three percent have settled into the largest thirty mega centers. That is almost half the population of the US, concentrated in thirty population clusters that reach across multiple counties, sometimes state lines.

We will project 52 churches in Prayerville and 105 in the county, average.[24] On any given Sunday, about 17.7% of the population attend the nation's churches.[25] For many years, the Gallup Poll reported that 40% or more of Americans were in church every Sunday - but that figure was based on self-reporting by individuals polled. There was no cumulative hard data to substantiate that number until recently. The figure of 17.7% is extrapolated from hard data, based on real attendance counts.

How many people are in church in your county each Sunday – 17.7% or 40%? The data is confusing. As noted by Marler and Hadaway, "Ask most pastors what percentage of inactive members they have — they'll say anything from 40-60%." The broad definition of regular church attendance is someone who shows up at least three out of every eight Sundays, and only 23-25% of Americans fit this category. Olson notes that an additional million church attendees would increase the every Sunday percentage from 17.7% to only 18%. "You'd have to find 80 million more people ... to get to [Gallup's] 40%", a number that is now doubted. Still, the Gallup number, which consists of people self-reporting their church attendance has held steady for decades. Then, if you ask Americans to identify their religion, 75% self-report as Christian (The Pew Forum, has that number at 73%]. Fifteen percent do not claim a faith – and they are the most vocal group. Sixty-two percent claim to be members of a church.[26] Important to us is that the number who identify as Christians has fallen precipitously from 89% in 1990.[27] We are watching a culture rapidly disengage from their historic faith.

Therefore, the actual numbers, the head count, of people in the pews each Sunday is 17.7% (Olsen). The number of 'regular-irregulars' [every three out of eight weeks] is 23-25%. Gallup's number is 40%.[28] The number of cultural Christians is 75%. Approximately 68% of U.S. adults celebrate Easter as a religious holiday according to data from the Mission America Coalition. Ed Stetzer, missiologist and director of the Center for Missional Research at the North American Mission Board of the Southern Baptist Convention recently finished a study on alternative faith communities and found that a growing number of people are finding Christian discipleship and community in places other than their local churches. The study found that 24.5% of Americans now say their primary form of spiritual nourishment is meeting with a small group of 20 or fewer people every week. "About 6 million people meet weekly with a small group and never or rarely go to church," Stetzer says. "There is a significant movement happening." Thus, for every nine people in a church each Sunday, there is another somewhere in a non-traditional Christian worship, growth or prayer group.

For our purposes, we will retreat to numbers reflecting core, casual and cultural Christians. In one church strength assessment, one person in the pew (*core* strength) equals an additional *casual* attender. In addition, for each *core* (the 17.7%) and casual attender (Olsen, 25%; Gallup, 40%), there is yet another person who in some way identifies with the church (Pew, 73-75%, cultural Christians). To use

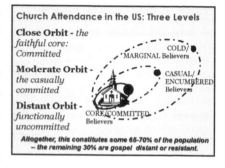

Church Attendance in the US: Three Levels

Close Orbit - *the faithful core:* Committed

Moderate Orbit - *the casually committed*

Distant Orbit - *functionally uncommitted*

COLD/ MARGINAL Believers

CASUAL/ ENCUMBERED Believers

CORE/COMMITTED Believers

Altogether, this constitutes some 65-70% of the population – the remaining 30% are gospel distant or resistant.

another set of terms, there are those in *'close'* orbit to the church, those in *'moderate'* orbit, and those in *'distant'* orbit. The individual in *distant orbit* is typically an Easter/Christmas/funeral/wedding attender. Their grandmother attended the church. A brother was married there. A family member was buried in the church cemetery. They went to Vacation Bible School at a church of the same denomination, but in another city. The *close orbit* constituency attends almost every Sunday; the *moderate orbit* constituency – attends irregularly; and with the *distant orbit* constituency, these three groups constitute the 60-70% of American's who indicate they are involved or connected into the life of some church.

Countywide, using our statistical model, based on Olsen's count, about 17,700 of the 100,000 population are in the pew each Sunday (core strength/close orbit) and that means a whopping

82,300 are NOT. In our model,[29] the number of core and casual attenders/close and moderate orbit is 35.4%. One statistic notes, to average 100, a congregation now needs about 200 attenders (the core and casually committed together). Therefore, we would conjecture, that 35,400 people in the county go to church, regularly to irregularly – and yet these are not the never-attenders or the seasonal attenders, the Easter and Christmas crowd. That number – core, casual, cultural/close, moderate/distant – is 70,800, a slightly more conservative number than the 75% who identify as Christian.

Here is the mission field. Out of 100,000 residents, optimistically, 35,400 are regular or irregular church attenders, leaving 64,600 countywide who are functionally unchurched. Olsen's number would be slightly higher – 75-77%. We are not considering here home-churches or house church-

> The way to reach the city is not through programs, but by being Biblical people.[32]
> ➡ Ray Bakke

es. That movement is growing significantly. Some estimate that it may comprise as many as 25% of all Christians. However, many of these families remain in some orbit around one or more churches as an occasional attendee; their children may attend a church-based school or participate in a church-based program. Still, 30-40% of the population in our model, 33.4%, are almost completely disconnected from any church. Some from any significant Christian influence. This detached group is the most critical harvest field in the nation.

All things being equal in Prayer County, as with your county, nearly 50% of that number would attend only eleven out of the 105 of the county's congregations. Most of the other churches in any county would be small, single-cell congregations. Nationally, the church attendance *mean* is 75, meaning half of all churches are smaller or larger than 75. About 90% of all churches are less than 350. Nationally, only ten percent, some 33,000 churches, 10.5 per county are larger than 350.[30] That is an average, but not a mean, of 170 per church.[31]

In our theoretical county with 105 churches, only ten-to-eleven (10.5%) would draw numbers of 350 or above. The remaining 94.5 would be less than 350. Half (52.5) would have fewer than 75 attendees each Sunday. Small does not mean unhealthy or ineffective. One study found that 98% of church satisfaction was found in measuring the number of intimate Christian friends within the congregation- relational health. More than the size or the quality of the church programs, even the level of preaching or the inspiration factor, the bottom line is found in the quality of the relational connections. Another factor is ministry opportunity. People who find avenues for service which are consistent with their gifts and passions, they are more fulfilled and motivated to grow in their relationship with the Lord.

━━ ━━ ━━ ━━ ━━ ━━ ━━ ━━ ━━ ━━ ━━ ━━ ━━ ━━ ━━ ━━ ━━ ━━ ━━ ━━

STORY

In 2005, The Journal for the Scientific Study of Religion published a study by sociologists C. Kirk Hadaway and Penny Long Marler — known for their scholarly research on the Church. Their report revealed that the actual number of people worshipping each week is similar to study conducted by Olson, who postulated that 17.7% of Americans were in the pews on any given Sunday. "We knew that over the past 30-40 years, denominations had increasingly reported a decline in their numbers," Marler says. Even with still-growing denominations, most mainline de-

nominations were reporting a net loss, and at the same time, the Gallup polls had remained stable. The data was inconsistent.

What was at play was "the halo effect" — the divide between what people tell pollsters and what their actions. Americans, it turns out, tend to over-report socially desirable behavior like voting and attending church and under-report socially undesirable behavior like drinking.[33]

Based on national averages, about 15-20% of the churches are vibrant. According to George Barna, only 10-15% of churches are effective in the area of evangelism.[34] That means some 16-21 congregations in Prayer County are healthy enough to influence the city and county. Others are stagnant or processing some crisis. On average, 20% will change pastors in a given year. In our model, Prayer County, that is about two per month out of 105 churches. Out of the 100,000 residents of Prayer County, about 34-35% attend church from weekly to semi-monthly (close and moderate orbit). Another 30-35% (distant orbit) would identify as Christians. To use another set of terms, the county has *committed* Christians, *casual* Christians and *cultural* Christians. Some 25-30%, the cultural Christians, are disengaged and typically disinterested. *Soft growth* is measured congregation-by-congregation in the movement of families from one church to another, usually in the *casually committed, moderate orbit* group, but that does little to change the overall impact of faith in the larger culture. What is needed is *hard-growth* measurements – the number of the uncommitted and the disinterested who become engaged in the faith; the transition of cultural Christians to committed status; and the intensification of the casually committed and distracted to more fervent faith practice. That is a task that the pastors of the county are realizing can only be accomplished in a collaborate effort.

There is another concern. Across the spectrum, the number of churches in America are not keeping pace with the population growth of 12.2%. Between 2000 and 2004, the net increase in churches, those opened less those that closed, in evangelical circles, was 5,452. Mainline and Catholic churches experienced a net loss of 2,200. Combined, the net increase of churches was 3,252. Olson says, approximately 3,000 churches closed every year in the last decade. While new churches were started, only 3,800 survived. The net increase in terms of new churches in this century is 800 each year. Consider this – from 2000 to 2004, to keep pace with population growth, a net increase of 13,024 churches was needed. When population growth is used as the benchmark, the Church incurred a deficit of almost 10,000 churches in that period. The U.S. Census predicts a population of 520 million in 2050. At the current growth trajectories, the church will increasingly lose ground. There is an alternative viewpoint. American's are leaving 'dead churches.' They are leaving liberal churches, and a realignment is taking place. And at the same time, the harvest is growing.

Prayerville does not have a Muslim mosque – not yet at least. Nevertheless, counties both to the south and north do have them (there are 2106 Muslim Mosques in the US, as of 2012; .66 per county – two mosques for every three counties). If Prayer County were typical, 827 of the 2.6 million Muslims in the US would reside in their county.[35] In addition, there would be about the same number of Buddhist, perhaps more.[36] And about the same number of Hindus, maybe more.[37]

Prayerville is just an average place to live. Last year there were 3,298 arrests countywide.[38] The violent crimes in the county numbered 465, the property crimes were 3,517. Five people were murdered.[39] Currently, 743 residents are away either in federal, state prison, or a city/county jail. An additional 2483, thus 3226 altogether, are on parole or being monitored for illegal activity, 2.9% of the population.[40] Prayerville is not a 'dry' place. While there are only about 20 bars, taverns, nightspots throughout the county, there are over 308 places to obtain alcoholic beverages.[41] [Again, our purpose here is to set forth benchmarks for your own city-county profile.]

STORY

One pastor visiting with a bar owner discovered that he had a regular customer who was too easily inebriated, and in that condition, he was bad for business. Bravo, most would say. The pastor, however, saw an opportunity for uncommon ministry. He offered to sit at the back of the bar in the evenings and entertain the rowdy patron and any others that the manager might refer to him. Here is what you can say, "There is a caring team willing to listen to you." The 'care and listening team' even had logos made for their jackets. The action of the pastor and his care team was disconcerting to many in the church. However, at the end of the year, more baptisms had come from that effort than traditional evangelistic outreach.[42]

Prayer County, as does the typical county, has 11 communities, incorporated and unincorporated.[43] About 80,000 of the residents live in those communities; the remainder live in the unincorporated county area. The number of families in the county[44] is 24,662 (with 65.1% owning their own home), the average number in each family, 3.14. Married couples number 17,974; the never married, 23,614; the divorced, 7,551; the widowed 4,561. This is average.

Last year (2007), 1,358 babies were born. Sadly, nearly 40% of them were without a dad either present or immediately anticipated in the life of the child. Every day at the local hospital or birth center, almost 4 children are added to Prayer County (3.7 a day; 26 a week; 113 month). In addition, every day, two more fresh graves can be found in county cemeteries, 15 a week and 64 a month (768 annually). Fifty-nine weddings take place monthly (two a day; 13 a week; 702 annually). Sadly, 360 marriages were also terminated annually, 30 a month, almost one a day. Though Prayer County does not have an abortion facility, estimates are that the number of abortions per residents are about 411 annually, a bit more than one a day, about eight weekly.[45] All of these significant events beg for ministry.

Across the county, there are four school districts, and forty-two schools (an average). Thirty-one of those are public schools. The county has two charter schools and nine private schools (religious and non-sectarian), and that is aside from the two Catholic schools. Some 15,670 kids go to school in Prayer County – and as is typical, the school day does not have a prayer! About 617 are in the charter schools.[46] About twice that many attend private schools (1,643) and almost 500 are home-schooled (479). Catholic school enrollment is 708. Approximately 1024 teachers serve these students in the public system. If national church attendance averages hold true, that means that only about 174 of these teachers give themselves persistently, weekly, to the spiritual nurture of their own souls. Some 23 teachers serve the charter schools, and 145 private schools. Catholic teachers number 47.[47][48] Like the rest of the country, Prayer County is struggling with a high school dropout rate of about nine percent.

Prayer County, like other average counties, is divided into

ten geographic zip zones.[49] The average population in each zone ranges from 7,500 to 10,000 (nation-wide, the number is 7,474 with difference accounting for those who have no physical mail delivery apart from a PO Box. With a zip-zone designation, Prayer County can be analyzed – where are the churches, the schools, crime, the densest population, the bars, drug activity, teen/youth hangouts?

[All the above is to establish NORMS, based on national data, pushed into our mythical community, Prayerville, whose name is more about our dreams and hopes for our communities, than its current condition.]

Beginning Your Data Collection
Phase I: The Basics
The Harvest Field

1. Demographic data on the city/county or definitive geographic area.
2. Crime (types, particular challenges to a healthy safe community).
3. Major community challenges.
4. Nature of your community (health center, education, commerce, recreation, tourist, banking center, technology or science; on the freeway, back-roads).
5. What is its history?

The Harvest Force

1. Demographic data on the churches.
2. State of the congregations (are they growing? New church plants? The conditions: unity/division; Nature and type of the larger churches. How does the church influence the city? Is it still predominately Christian, or multi-ethnic? What is the state of the pastors? Stable, long-term, united,

bi-vocational?

3. How is the church perceived in the city?

4. Is there an interface between the police force and the pastors? The judiciary and the pastoral community?

5. What are the bright spots, the promise, and the hope?

6. What are the great challenges?

7. Where are the fathers? How many gangs are active in the county?

8. Has there been a significant revival?

9. Who are the power brokers of the city/county? Are they godly?

10. What is the nature of the primary money stream into and out of the county?

11. Are there racial tensions?

12. Are their agencies, with a Christian worldview, ministering to community pain? The homeless, marriages, teens, gangs, the incarcerated and their families, hunger, prostitution, abused children and youth.

13. Is there any mechanism for collaborative action?

14. Is there a forum for dialogue between churches and helping agencies?

15. Is there a grand evangelism plan, a multi-year plan, for reaching every home with the gospel?

Phase II and III research will be covered later in this publication. Research investigates and confirms; it informs and inflames the process. Bad data can send you in the wrong direction and waste much valuable time.

There are numerous cultural indicators of social decline in the history of civilizations. Here are a few:

- The society no longer worships or publicly acknowledges God.

- Political correctness reigns. Pluralism emerges first as the preferred faith posture, but that quickly devolves into some form of totalitarian paganism.

> Our purpose here is to establish norms – for your county or city, to assist you in establishing your own norms. ━ ━ ➤

- There is a low view of life – abortion, suicide, euthanasia give birth to a culture of death.

- Hedonism, pleasure, base and immoral entertainment become acceptable. Rome at the height of its power developed an insatiable appetite for debauchery and immorality. Perverted entertainment was carried to the streets and polluted the common language. Open homosexuality was practiced and encouraged. And in Rome's case, it crumbled.

- Violent crime becomes common.

- Economic despotism. The rich tend to become increasingly powerful and then directly or indirectly begin to oppress the poor. The middle class disappears.

- The Government becomes ineffective and insolvent. The French Revolution occurred against the backdrop of a bankrupt government.

- The Government contributes to social, moral anarchy. They live off the corruption. Today, government use of lottery funds, a tax on the poor is an indication of its broken moral compass.

- Related to this, a government that lives off society's moral decay is another sign of the end of a civilization.

- The loss of moral objectivity – in government and judicial decisions. Judges that reign as kings and make up the law, reversing the Founder's Maxim – *Lex Rex*: the Law is King. We were an experiment in government – no king, no emperor, the people would rule by ruling themselves. Here, the law would be informed by moral law, no one would be above the law. Now, Judges act as kings and make up new laws or extend rights based on dubious legal grounds. Their decisions are forced on the people in the form of law, but it is more of a form of legal tyranny. Anarchy cannot long be restrained in such a climate.

History has a long line of past civilizations that witnessed these cultural indicators of moral demise, but failed to act. Thanks to modern methods of education, history is no longer taught in our schools. The NEA president has declared, "The day of basic skills is over . . . we will be the conveyor of national values." No longer is it the goal of Washington for the schools to teach the 3-R's, it is the goal of public educators to transform the culture. This was at the heart of Dewey's philosophy. It has taken 80 years for it to infect the mainstream and become dominate.

Who will become the voice crying in the wilderness? Will it be you?

STORY

In Portland Oregon, as research was completed on that city, one area revealed an African–American church for every 177 African–Americans. Exceeding all standards, that neighborhood was saturated with churches, pastors, Christians and abundant witness. However, the same area had the highest crime rate in the city. Murders had been committed on church steps. Seemingly, the gospel had penetrated the area, but community transformation was minimal.[50] Saturation church planting alone and church-to-population ratios do not always indicate spiritual health and vitality.

Across the nation, in one section of Miami

noted for its crime, there were thirteen churches. However, only two had any activity from Monday through Saturday. And only one of those had a human present in their facility during the week. The church was an absentee neighbor, a non-contributor to the neighborhood. Drug dealers confided that the dark alcoves of the unused church facilities, the parking lots, were some of the choicest 'dealing' turf available to them.

21 Population data reflects the number of males: 151,781,326 (49.2% of pop.); females: 156,964,212 (50.8% of pop.). Ethnically: White - 223,553,265 (72.4% of pop.); Black - 38,929,319 (12.6% of pop.); Asian: 14,674,252 (4.8% of pop.); American Indian and Alaska Native - 2,369,431 (0.8% of pop.); Hispanic/Latino [can also be white/black]: 50,477,594 (16.3% of pop.); Native Hawaiian and Other Pacific Islander - 1,225,195 (0.4% of pop.). The median age is 37.1 (2012). This extrapolates to a population profile in the mythical 'Prayer County' as: White, 72,000; Black, 12,000; Asian, 4,800; Native Indian, 800; Hispanic/Latino, 16,300.

22 According to the US Census data from 2000, 79.2% of the population lived in urban areas, population clusters of 2500 or more people; and 20.7% live in rural unincorporated areas or small towns and hamlets of less than 2500. The break down is as follows: 153 Urbanized Areas over 200,000 population, a total of 166,215,889, representing 58.274% of the US population; 310 Urbanized Areas 50,000 - 199,999 population, a total of 310 29,584,626, 10.372% of the population. 1838 Urban Clusters 5,000 - 49,999 population, a total of 25,438,275, 8.918% of the population; 1328 Urban Clusters of 2,500 - 4,999 population, a total of 4,717,270, representing 1.654% of the population. Source: http://www.fhwa.dot.gov/planning/census_issues/archives/metropolitan_planning/cps2k.cfm. Accessed December 16, 2013.

23 Waymire, Intro – 6.

24 It is estimated that there are 330,000 churches nation-wide [Source: Rebecca Barnes and Lindy Lowry, *7 Startling Facts: An Up Close Look at Church Attendance in America*, http://www.churchleaders.com/pastors/pastor-articles/139575-7-startling-facts-an-up-close-look-at-church-attendance-in-america.html? Accessed December 16, 2013.] The exact number is not known. Church closure rates have escalated in recent decades. Further, it is estimated that some 80-85% of these churches are in maintenance mode and not considered, in terms of community impact, life-giving churches. If you divide the number of churches, by the number of counties – the average is 105, our example. If, however, you divide the population by the number of churches, you come to a ratio of one church to 937 people. For our purposes, we are using the benchmark of one church per thousand population. Ask the question - is your county above or below the national average?

25 Ibid. This is a study conducted on the basis of actual attendance data by Olsen. Other studies show slight variations. For our purposes we will use 17%.

26 Finke, Roger; Rodney Stark (2005). *The Churching of America, 1776-2005.* Rutgers University Press. 22–23. ISBN 0-8135-3553-0. online at Google Books.

27 *American Religious Identification Survey.* CUNY Graduate Center. 2001. Retrieved 2007-06-17.

28 For many years, Gallup reported that 40% or more of the population attended church each Sunday: "No matter how we ask the question to peo-

ple, we get roughly 40% of Americans who present themselves as regular church attendees." Of course, from actual attendance studies, as contrasted with self-reports of Christians, we know that number is around 17%. But that is not the whole story, "Although about 40% of Americans are regular church attendees, it doesn't necessarily mean 40% are in church on any given Sunday". There is a growing trend toward worshipping in non-traditional ways, such as small groups. There are informal churches that meet in gyms, storefronts, social halls or even homes. Non-denominational independent churches, if considered together, now constitute the third largest segment of congregations in the US, behind only Catholic and Southern Baptist movements. In another study, Marler and Hadaway discovered that while the majority of people they interviewed do not belong to a local church, they still identify with their church roots. "Never mind the fact that they attend church less than 12 times a year," Marler observes. "We estimate that 78 million Protestants are in that place." [Source: Rebecca Barnes and Lindy Lowry, *7 Startling Facts: An Up Close Look at Church Attendance in America*, http://www.churchleaders.com/pastors/pastor-articles/139575-7-startling-facts-an-up-close-look-at-church-attendance-in-america.html? Accessed December 16, 2013.]

29 One church growth model suggests, for every regular attender you have an irregular attender; and for every regular and irregular attender, you have a 'prospect.' For our discussion, we will use this 1:1:2 model. Using Olsen's number, we would say, for every approximate two in the pew (17.7 %), we have another one (23-25%) who is irregular. Our model is a bit more generous and falls between Olsen (23-25%) and Gallup (40%). Another church growth model uses the categories – those in close orbit (every Sunday), moderate orbit (irregular), and distant orbit (Easter and Christmas, or less).

30 Another striking trend has surfaced, the smallest (attendance 1–49) and largest churches (2,000-plus) grew. The small single-cell churches grew 16.4% in a recent study; the largest grew 21.5%, both above the national population growth of 12.2%. However, mid-sized churches (100–299), declined one percent. According to some studies, the average Protestant church in America is 124. Olson believes people see larger churches as an upgrade. Growth of the larger churches has come from people leaving mid-sized congregations for larger churches.

31 Some sources project a national average per congregation of 184.

32 Bakke, 62.

33 Rebecca Barnes and Lindy Lowry, 7 Startling Facts: An Up Close Look at Church Attendance in America, http://www.churchleaders.com/pastors/pastor-articles/139575-7-startling-facts-an-up-close-look-at-church-attendance-in-america.html? Accessed December 16, 2013.

34 Waymire, Intro – 1. Quoting George Barna, *What Effective Churches Have Discovered.*

35 Muslim claims of US population in the range of 6 – 10 million are exaggerated; however, the number of Muslims in the past decade, since 9-11, has doubled.

36 Estimates for the number of USA Buddhist range from 2.4 – 4 million.

195

37 From 1,700 people in 1900, the Hindu population in America grew to approximately 387,000 by 1980 and 1.1 million in 1997. As of 2008, the estimated U.S. population of Hindus of Indian origin is approximately 2.29 million (mainly of Indian and Indo-Caribbean descent). Today's analysis on the US Hindu population. Estimates are that there may also be as many as 1 million practicing American Hindus, not of Indian origin, in the U.S. http://www.hafsite.org/resources/hinduism_101/hinduism_demographics

38 Total nation-wide arrests (2005): 10.369 million. The number in state, federal, and local prisons was (2005) 2,186,230. Thus about 695 from the county.

39 National statistics for annual murders (2005) is 14,860; violent crimes per 100,000 people (2004) was 465.5; and property crimes per 100,000 people (2004): 3,517.1. Homicides per 100,000 people (2004): 5.5.

40 The US has the highest documented incarceration rate in the world; in 2009 it was 743 adults incarcerated per 100,000 population. According to the U.S. Bureau of Justice Statistics (BJS), 2,266,800 adults were incarcerated in U.S. federal and state prisons, and county jails at year-end 2011 – about 0.7% of adults in the U.S. resident population. Additionally, 4,814,200 adults at year-end 2011 were on probation or on parole. In total, 6,977,700 adults were under correctional supervision (probation, parole, jail, or prison) in 2011 – about 2.9% of adults in the U.S. resident population. In addition, there were 70,792 juveniles in juvenile detention in 2010. In 2008 approximately one in every 31 adults (7.3 million) in the United States was behind bars or being monitored (probation and parole). In 2008, the breakdown for adults under correctional control was as follows: one out of 18 men, one in 89 women, one in 11 African-Americans (9.2%), one in 27 Latinos (3.7%), and one in 45 Caucasians (2.2%). The prison population has quadrupled since 1980, even though crime is down, and that due partially as a result of mandatory sentencing that came about during the "war on drugs."

41 The US bar and nightclub industry's drinking establishments primarily engaged in the retail sale of alcoholic drinks number around 65,000, according to Dun & Bradstreet, which generated approximately $20 billion in combined annual sales revenue, with the average establishment accounting for about $200,000. Taverns were the largest sector within industry, with 19,660 drinking places. Combined, they shared more than 32% of the market. Bars and lounges represented 19.8% edging out drinking places share of about 19.5% of the market. Cocktail lounges held 11.5% and night clubs had 8.6%. Per the U.S. Census Bureau's Statistics of U.S. Businesses, there were about 351,912 people employed within the industry with nearly $4.1 billion in annual payroll in 2005. Last year's total Restaurant and Bar Industry Sales accounted for $632 billion with 970,000 locations and are projected to be the same or increase 1% in 2013. Sales of spirits, wine and beer increased 4.9% to reach $93.7 billion in 2011. Of the Top 100 survey participants, 42.8% identified their venues as nightclubs; 70.6% of them described their hotspots as dance clubs. Of those identifying their venue as bars, 31.7% are sports bars and 29.3% are traditional bar/taverns. DJs and

live entertainment are featured by 88.3% and 73.6% of total respondents, respectively. Nearly 80% offer a dance floor, 70.1% provide VIP areas and 65% offer bottle service.

42 Ray Bakke, 117.

43 There are an estimated 35,000 cities, towns and hamlets in the US. Many metropolitan area are a collage of smaller communities, each with their own governance.

44 According to census data, the number of USA families is 77,538,296; the average family size, 3.14; with 65.1% of population owning their own home. Married couples numbered 56,510,377; the never married, 74,243,000; the divorced, 23,742,000; the widowed, 14,341,000. Read more: An Overview of the U.S. Population — Infoplease.com http://www.infoplease.com/ipa/A0004925.html#ixzz2cK1C9HNI

45 The number of births (2007): 4,269,000 (14.16 per 1,000 pop.) Deaths (2007): 2,416,000 (8.27 per 1,000 pop.). Marriages (2008): 2,208,000 (7.3 per 1,000 pop.). Divorces (2008): 3.6 per 1,000 pop. Infant mortality rate (2007): 6.37 per 1,000 live births. Legal abortions (2002): 1,293,000. Life expectancy (2007): Total U.S., both sexes, 78; total men, 75.15; total women, 80.97; white men, 75.3; white women, 80.5; black men, 69.0; black women, 76.1 Read more: Vital Statistics | Infoplease.com http://www.infoplease.com/ipa/A0004929.html#ixzz2cK1WmeZ3

46 The largest network of charter schools in the nation is Islamic.

47 Side bar note, the average district public school per pupil expenditure is $12,744 (Digest 2010, Table 190) compared to Charter School per pupil costs of $8,001 (The Center for Education Reform, Annual Survey of America's Charter Schools, 2010, page 15).

48 Total number of public school districts: 13,809 (Digest of Education Statistics: 2010, Table 91). K-12 schools: 132,656 (Digest 2010, Chapter 1, Table 5); Elementary: 88,982; Secondary: 27,575; Combined: 14,837; Other: 1,262

(Digest 2010, Chapter 1, Table 5). The total number of public schools, 98,706; Elementary: 67,148; Secondary: 24,348; Combined: 5,632; Other: 1,587 (Digest 2010, Table 97). The total number of charter schools: 5,714 (Center for Education Reform, National Charter School & Enrollment Statistics, November 2011). The total number of private schools: 28,220; Elementary: 16,370; Secondary: 3,040; Combined: 8,810 (Digest 2010, Table 63). Catholic Schools 7,400; Elementary: 5,960; Secondary: 1,080; Combined: 370 (Digest 2010, Table 63).

Total K-12 enrollment: 55,235,000 (Digest 2010, Table 2); Elementary: 38,860,000; Secondary: 16,375,000 (Digest 2010, Table 2). The total Public School enrollment: 49,266,000; Elementary: 34,286,000; Secondary: 14,980,000

(Digest 2010, Table 39). Total Charter School enrollment: 1,941,831 (The Center for Education Reform, National Charter School & Enrollment Statistics, November 2011). Total Private School enrollment: 5,165,280; Elementary: 2,462,980; Secondary: 850,750; Combined: 1,851,550 (Digest 2010, Table 63). Home School enrollment: 1,508,000 (estimate) or 2.9%

LAUNCHING COMMUNITY PRAYER MOVEMENTS

(estimate) of America's school population (Digest 2010, Table 40). Catholic School enrollment: 2,224,470; Elementary: 1,457,960; Secondary: 620,840; Combined: 145,680 (Digest 2010, Table 63). On-line enrollment: approx. 250,000 (iNACOL Key Stats).

The number of teachers: 3,219,458; Elementary: 1,758,169; Secondary: 1,234,197; Unclassified: 227,092 (Digest 2010, Table 69). Charter School teachers: 72,000 (Digest 2010, Table 105). Private School Teachers: 456,270; Elementary: 207,230; Secondary: 69,240; Combined: 179,800 (Digest 2010, Table 62). Catholic School teachers: 146,630; Elementary: 94,800; Secondary: 42,400; Combined: 9,430 (Digest 2010, Table 62).

49 One of the easiest ways to manage the outreach to a city, more consistent and less subject to change than a voter district, is by zip-code. There are 41,801 zip codes in the USA. That is deceiving, in this sense, 29,812 (71.3%) are general zip codes; another 9,363 (22.4%) are PO boxes – that is 93.7% of all zip codes. Military codes number 535 (1.3%). Unique business codes account for 2,091 (5%). *Focus on the 'general zip zones.'* Some counties may face a moderate challenge using this system since 9,897 zip codes cross county lines (23.7%). However, that differentiation is overcome by computer sorting. Eliminating all but general zip codes, with 3144 counties, all things being equal, each county would have some 9.48 zip codes. Based on population, that number is 12.

50 Waymire, 1-6.

SECTION THREE
Research Suggestions

CHAPTER 15
Phases of Development

PHASE I
AWARENESS – The Catalyst

The process always begins with a catalyst! It is an 'Ezra' praying over an open scroll (the Bible). A 'Nehemiah' moved by the report about the condition of his hometown Jerusalem. A Mordecai who bravely confronted the queen, Esther, and moved her toward action that saved the Jewish people. It is a Moses before a burning bush and Elijah on Mt. Carmel. It is Martin Luther nailing debate issues to a church door sparking the Reformation. It is Livingston heading for Africa. It is William Seymour renting a broken down abandoned church building that had fallen into disrespect and disrepair to begin a prayer meeting on Azusa Street. It is Jonathan Edwards ascending the pulpit with a heavy heart to confront complacency in his church. It is Jeremiah Lanphier persisting in prayer in Fulton Street for more than thirty minutes before others showed up, sparking a revival throughout the city of New York and the third great awakening. Every city and movement needs a catalyst. But a catalyst does not work in a vacuum. His effective work is in the shadow of God's work, though rarely discerned at the pre-awakening stage.

One of the first key elements, and a critical factor for motivation, is awareness that God is up to something! Pastors (Ezra) and community lay leaders (Nehemiah) must be linked to intercessors, and all become aware of the desires for the community that are on the heart of God. As they begin to share glimpses of hope together, they become strangely aware that they are seeing components of the same vision. God is calling the church of the area to a joint mission, out of a new sense of shared

Holiness and social impact are seen in a seamless way.
------►

community, in and through the power of the Spirit. Holiness and social impact are seen in a seamless way, and the evidence of a culture not seeded with the influence of holiness, with the salt and light of Christian influence, is dismally apparent. A simultaneous dissatisfaction with the status quo meets spiritual empowerment. Fresh hope blossoms. Signs of awakening appear. Unity intensifies. Mission becomes clear – "It can be done", folks whisper to one another, "But not in isolation from one another". A hunger for a divine visitation increases along with a willingness to walk and work together. The greater the humility, the greater the anointing.

'Can do' optimism is not enough. There must also emerge a deep sense of contrition – specifically, repentance. The change agent, the church itself must first be changed. Any sense that we can change the city without undergoing deep transformation ourselves is an indication that while we may be disillusioned, we are not disenchanted! And without breaking the cultural spell and stepping outside the paradigm in which we have been trapped for at least five decades, we will not see either the solutions necessary for lasting change. A growing and deep sense of contrition must grip the church resulting a movement of repentance for our lack of cultural and social impact. New levels of 'holiness' and holy living must rise out of deep levels of repentance, and that must be tethered to God's love. Truth cannot be allowed to eclipse love, and love must not be allowed to mute truth. A cultural devolution, a radical version of immorality resulting in a moral freefall has happened on our watch, and only a sovereign visitation of God can arrest that trend. There has to be acceptance of some sense of responsibility for the conditions of culture by the church and its leadership. And that is a good place to begin the process of repentance and change.

God is calling the church to a new level of relating and living, a new paradigm for missional impact and harvest, but we will only advance "on our knees!" And we will do so, not as we rush the city, but as we rush the cross. The constant change mantra must always focus on us, our need for Christlikeness, before it focuses on either the church corporately or the city.

> 'Can do' optimism is not enough. The change agent, the church itself must first be changed. ➡

Action Steps

1. As a catalyst, make a short list of people whom you sense, after prayer, might be open to beginning the process of city impact, out of prayer.
2. Meet with them. Share your heart.
3. Make a long list. Start gathering the names of prayer leaders – start meeting with them. Let a relationship be foundational; not mission. Joe Aldrich would say, "At the heart of every effective organization is a group of people

who love one another". City reaching *praxis* will be more effective if it is released out of a healthy *ethos*. The relational environment is as important as the mission, "My how those Christians love one another." A competitive church is not a good witness to a watching world.

4. Consider vision-prayer gatherings, groups of people, who gather to pray for the city; pray to be a better witness to the city; pray for unity among pastors and humility in Christians.

5. Share the vision with small and large groups.

6. Make a list of significant pastors and community leaders, intercessors, and make contact with them, sharing your heart. After some season, your passion will begin to open doors for you and your character and message will affirm you.

7. Consider a Solemn Assembly of intercessors, pastors and leaders, to lay a foundation of repentance.

Creating a Circle of Concern

It is becoming increasingly clear that touching a whole city in a redemptive way that results in widespread conversions, revival in the church and cultural impact will require a healthy church in unity. This is not an optional factor, but one that is essential. Great care must be taken to attempt to link arms with as broad a cross-section of the Body of Christ as possible on the foundation of core theology.[51] Identifying the major streams of the church open to unity and collaboration – Evangelical, Liturgical, Pentecostal, Messianic - and both their clergy and lay leaders is vital. The broader the coalition at the start of the process, the better chances of wide-spread support. The readiest connections are often across the evangelical-Pentecostal divide. If the early relational work is sacrificed for the speed of the process and groups are left out, the need for reconciliation with them does not go away

– it presents itself later as a greater problem.

Those who will be part of the solution must be part of the initial formation of the initiative. Where divisions have been identified, great effort must be made to reconcile the individuals or groups, particularly along racial lines. Decisions regarding collaboration and participation should be made relationally rather than institutionally.

1. The major streams of the church are identified.
2. The key leaders of each stream are identified.
3. The need for reconciliation between specific leaders and/ or streams is identified.
4. Action plans for reconciliation are established.
5. It is understood that reconciliation is not an event, but an on-going process. Make earnest efforts, document them, and revisit the process until trust levels deepen, understanding grows across differences; appreciation exists in the face of contrasting approaches, and you have created a culture of affirmation and collaborative mission.

Prayerful Dependence on God

The last instruction of Christ, was to send his followers to a *prayer meeting*. The constituting assembly of the church was a *prayer meeting*. Prayer is critical to both initiate and sustain effective community transformation. Community transformation comes from the collective impact of the work of the Spirit on the community's congregations, and that comes from significant numbers growing and being impacted through daily time with God. Personal prayer and corporate prayer are inseparable twins that invite community transformation resulting from the supernatural work of God, a work he has determined to do through spiritual and functional partnership. God's presence in the church gathered leads to a diffusion of the Spirit through the church scattered, and that releases spiritual power into the city.

The work of God in a city begins in prayer. Out of persistent prayer, a vision for the city emerges. It is prayer that awakens in all a clear sense of God's love for the city which manifests, grows and is nurtured through continued extended times of prayer and worship, not only by the pastoral community, but also by networked intercessors. The exponential explosion of this movement of prayer is when Christians begin to connect in prayer triads/quads thoughout their professional tribal work settings during the week.

Make no mistake. The city reacher who does not spend personal time in prayer, waiting on the Lord for clarity of vision and specific next steps will fail. Spending time in prayer, putting oneself in a position to hear from God, is a primary key for each person with a heart for the city.

At the very beginning of the process, the movement is likely to experience a fork in the road called *prayer*. Some will want to delegate prayer to the intercessors – that will be a great mistake. Some will suggest that prayer is good – who wants to be against prayer? But they will argue, 'doing' is as or more important than prayer and doing should not be held hostage to prayer, "Let's take the city!" – that will also be a great mistake. Others will suggest that you 'pray as you go,' making prayer a casual and corollary element in the process, not primary and standalone in value. Still others, the purist, may insist that you pray and do nothing, that you wait for 'a sovereign touching down' of God. Avoid these extremes. Most of all, remember that only a leadership team and community that understands that 'without God they

> **The city reacher who does not spend personal time in prayer, waiting on the Lord for clarity of vision and specific next steps, will fail.** ➤

can do nothing!' will grow to be both dependent on God and one another. Prayer focused on the Supremacy of Christ and personal transformation weeds out the *Rambo's* who can be devastating to the unity of the group and the character of the mission.

One of the roles of the apostolic was to answer the question that arose from the people in response to the coming of the Spirit in Acts 2. They asked, "What does this mean?" A leadership team consistently articulates 'meaning' in the context of change. Revival can become an end in itself, fixated on experientialism, and subjectively personalized in a manner that misdirects its energy, causing it to fail to engage the culture in change. The role of leadership is to help steward the move of the Spirit. Peter gave 'action steps' – "Repent and be baptized, every one of you, in the name of Jesus Christ for the forgiveness of your sins. And you will receive the gift of the Holy Spirit" (Acts 2:38). Renunciation of the old. Recalibration of values. Redirection. Baptism – death of the old and resurrection into the new; the public announcement of identity with Christ; of the need for cleansing; of the recognition of sin and the need for forgiveness through Christ; subsequently, a life lived in and by the enabling Holy Spirit. These are action steps for the individuals who wanted to join what God was doing in Acts 2.

Peter and John were sent to Samaria and Barnabas to Antioch to assist in clarifying the role of believers in response to the work of the Spirit in those given geographic context. This is the most important component of 'vision casting' – What is God doing now? What is God's desire for our community? What would he have us to do? The primary catalyst for city-transformation is a prayer-birthed, God-given vision.

Nothing is more important than the understanding that this is God's mission – *Missio Dei*. You are not asking *Him to join you*, or to bless what you are doing. You are joining Him in mission. And that demands *a culture* of prayer. And a culture of prayer will keep character and holiness at the heart of what you are doing, and it will nurture humility which will foster unity. And unity will create a synergy of your efforts with a special anointing from God (Psalm 133).

I have watched the prayer movement as it unwrapped locally, morph into the city-reaching movement until city-reaching swallowed prayer and made it a mere servant of that process. And then the city-reaching movement, in some areas, transitioned to community development – that is where the money is! And that is where we feel most fulfilled pragmatically. Yet, if we build all the houses needed for the poor and provide food for the hungry – and those are things we should do – but to do so without significant numbers of people in the city repenting, and finding a new center for their lives in Christ, we will have failed in our mission.

Never leave prayer! And never disconnect prayer from the Great Commission, done in the spirit of the Great Commandment. And never believe that Great Commandment work alone is enough. The music begs for the words.

Action Steps

1. To lead a prayer movement, you must be a person of prayer – and you must pray now more than ever. Deepen your own personal commitment to prayer.

2. Surround yourself with a small group of trusted intercessors with whom you can regularly prayer and share your heart, as well as the development of the process in the city.

3. As the Lord leads, begin to meet with a small group of pastors, community leaders who are Christians, and intercessors – at least once a month for prayer.

4. Keep the main thing, the main thing – dependence on God. Prayer.

5. Don't draw lines, draw circles. The most eager, but undisciplined enthusiast, might be changed into a significant catalyst, a team-player extraordinaire, but someone has to help with that transformation. Draw circles. Work with 'potential' city transformers.

6. Keep your balance. Maintain missional poise and personal grace.

7. Stay on track – prayer, care, share.

PHASE II
Engaging the Pastors as Intercessors

The city-impact movement is impossible without pastors as leaders in the process, and simultaneously, it will fail with pastors alone leading the process. A number of things must change – pastors must see their prayer roles as primary; they must see Sunday Morning Campus ministry, not as their main function, but as a worshipful gathering to glorify God, the overflow of which supports the lay missionary force of the Church. They must see laymen, not as mere members of their congregations, but as their critical missionary force to an unreached city – and they must work to transform members into ministers, and accept them as ministry peers. They must emerge from the silo of the one congregation that works alone and connect with other pastors. They must transform ministry models from independent work for a single congregation to models designed to team with other ministries to serve the city open to the gospel. They must share their resources, human and material, with other congregations, indeed, with other movements beyond their own denominational stream.

Most evangelical pastors see themselves first as 'preachers' – it is the task they most look forward to. Their weekday role is as the CEO of a non-profit organization, the church. And around that role, pastors tend to create supporting ministry that reflects their own gifts and callings. For example, they may offer personal, family counseling, establish a counseling center. Run a Christian School. Work with a youth program, build a gym to offer a youth basketball league. Sponsor an adoption agency. But rarely, does a pastor see his central role as *prayer.* And by this, I mean prayer that is devotional, connected to Christ, that value's time with God, but then specifically opens to the ministry of *watching* which focuses both on the *harvest force* (the church) and the *harvest field* (the city). Like a shepherd called to watch *the flock and beyond them the field* in which they feed and rest, this is the call of a pastor. This is the meaning of the term – *pastor.* His public work on Sunday may not be either the primary or most important narrative of his ministry. Sunday, at-church functions, have far too limited impact on the city. And sadly, on members. But in his prayerful watching, as a shepherd, of both *the harvest force* and *field,* he is awakened to the dangers facing the congregation and the community. In prayerful listening, the Spirit whispers things to him he could not otherwise know. Suddenly, we feel an increased sense of urgency. The burden felt is the burden of the Lord for the church and the city. The greatest call of a pastor is to prayer! To *'watch'* the flock and field is a metaphor for intercession.

Ministry can be so seductive. And the church is so easily substituted for Christ. So many pastors have fallen into the deception that their love expressed in *service for* Christ equates to a love relationship *with Christ.* Preaching, rather than prayer, becomes the means by which the pastor senses the Spirit in his own life, blind to the fact that he is high-jacking the anointing on the scripture and spiritual gifts for personal fulfillment.

Many pastors are wounded today, in hiding, at least psychologically, and in relational isolation. Many have been wounded by an increasingly embattled congregation. Division is far too common. Church splits. Lawsuits. Controlling boards – all work to wear down a pastor, not to mention the very personal spiritual enemy he faces. The average pastor is at a church for less than five years. A significant number would leave the ministry if another occupation were available, and that number is often higher among spouses. Marital failure rates rank among the highest among professionals. The professional fallout rate that may be the highest of any grouping – only one of 100 who begin in pastoral ministry are in ministry at their age of retirement.

No city impact can be considered without addressing the health and vitality of the leaders of the *Harvest Force*. Where can they go for help? For counseling? Are there effective pastoral prayer groups in the city? Is there a climate in churches that encourages ministerial affirmation? Is there a means for remedial assistance? On-going continuing education? If we field a team that is playing so hurt, and so taped up, that they are minimally effective, we will not fulfill our mission.

Any assumption that we are 'ready to receive vision for the city' may be blind to the present condition of clergy. They are weary and often without a vision for their own congregations.[52] Most have never considered what it means to *pastor the city* together. To speak of a vision for city-transformation and impact is intimidating. Education for a new paradigm of relating, a new paradigm of mission in and to the city is critical.

Personal/Pastoral Steps

1. Complete a personal inventory of spiritual vitality completed. (See LifeWay's Spiritual Growth Assessment: www.lifeway.com/lwc/files/lwcF_PDF_DSC_Spiritual_ Growth_Assessment.pdf Worksheet).

2. Start the habit of daily personal prayer or strengthen the practice.

3. Join a prayer triad/quad; start one.

4. Get in a small prayer group.
5. Spend time specifically praying for the city.
6. Identify catalytic leaders – both Ezra's and Nehemiah's.
7. Identify other intercessors or intercessory networks.

PHASE III
Creating the Vision Community

The vision community is a diverse group of participants – Ezra (pastors) and Nehemiah (lay leaders/marketplace) types along with intercessors - who become a committed and trusting community in order to shepherd the transformation process. The vision community guides participating congregations and Christians in discerning God's vision for the city out of which emerges vision-guided, strategic decisions that lead to the broad commitment to and achievement of that vision.

> Soon after the completion of Disney World, someone said, 'Isn't it too bad that Walt Disney did not live to see this!' Mike Vance, creative director of Disney Studios, replied, 'he did see it – that's why it's here.' ▬ ➡

The vision for community transformation should be clearly stated, in concrete and compellingly ways, and comprehensively so, and it will vary for each community, at times, from communities within the larger community. It is the shared core vision that results in shared direction guiding the efforts to reach the city. The church of the city, both the Ezra and Nehemiah streams, with intercessors, agree not only that change is necessary, but they also agree about the shape and direction to take.

The Vision Team

1. The vision team baptizes itself in the practice of prayer.
2. A critical connection is established between the vision team and the intercessory prayer community.
3. Personal intercessors for the vision team and process are recruited.
4. Communication intercessory networks are established and verified.
5. Intercession is focused upon identification and empowerment of spiritual leaders.
6. A vision and strategic process emerge out of prayer in the light of clear and compelling research.

Owning the Vision

It is one thing for a small core group to forge out a vision statement for transformation and own it. It is another to communicate that vision, moving it from private to public space. This demands a comprehensive, intentional, process. The vision must be clear and compelling, and it must be owned by a significant group of churches and Christians. Vision unifies, a perforated vision – *di-vision* – results in fractures, lost energy, competitive actions, division. The intent of the vision process is to generate a high level of understanding and commitment to what is believed to be God's vision for community transformation by the broadest cross-section of the Church possible.

You moving toward the realization of God's vision through carefully chosen specific steps, coordinated, high-leverage initiatives. Implementation flows directly from the distinct and clear vision. Shared information and common goals enable effective use of resources and collaboration hastening community impact. Increased momentum and collaboration accelerate transformation. It is important to measure and monitor effectiveness by results and not merely by activity.

The Vision Community Action Steps

1. Here again, prayer must be at the foreground. The evidence, the facts and data, can be some mesmerizing, that prayer is pushed back out of curiosity. Prayer must be the central activity of leadership.

2. Intercessory networks now begin to unite for citywide prayer gatherings.

3. Local congregations increase participation in prayer activity.

4. Pastoral prayer cells increase in number.

5. A rhythm of prayer among leaders is begun (weekly cells, monthly city-community gatherings, quarterly all pastoral prayer, an annual day of prayer or extended prayer event).

6. The burden of the Lord for the city will become the catalyzing and compelling motivation. Vision will be clarified. Boldness will emerge.

7. Vision will find itself expressed in the language of prayer.

STORY

The Heights is a section of Houston with a population of 100,000. Churches and ministries began spiritual mapping research on the area. They discovered a collage of diverse cultures and ethnic groups, and began to learn about their relating patterns. They looked for the causes of crimes. They studied the ways joblessness was affecting the area. They determined the number of single-parent families and speculated about the implications. The more they learned, the clearer the mission became. Fifty-two churches developed a cooperative program. They teach leader-

ship skills. To help kids find jobs, they maintain a job bank. They offer a range of activities – sports teams, drama, inner-city camps. They have afterschool care programs. The mayor and other city officials now believe that the primary cause for positive change in the Heights was the work of these local churches and para-church groups who demonstrated the loving care of God for all. The impact could also be measured in increased high school completion rates, improved education and a lower crime.[53]

PHASE IV
Unity- Sustaining the momentum

Authentic community is essential to sustain momentum. The church will not regain its credibility in the world until there is a confluence of its various streams, a celebration of its differences. Anti-denominationalism is non-productive, often toxic. As has been often observed, the non-denominational movement morphs into a denomination-like movement.

What we need to do is more clearly see our differences as "tribal" and legitimate, but illegitimate if they are meant to define the whole of the Christian community. We long to "bring the full force and flavor of our diversity" into the streets of the city, retaining our "tribal distinctive" while at the same time manifesting our oneness as "the nation of God's peoples in the earth".

We inherited a post-reformation system defined more by an emphasis upon our diversity than by our core theology. In a world that was almost exclusively Christian, we came to define ourselves by comparison and contrast with one another – and that condition is now accepted, sadly, as the norm. Folks from different denominations spoke of being from 'different faiths' – so significant were the differences suggested to be. There may be a great theological divide between the ecclesiology of a congregational church and an episcopal form of government, between Calvinists and Armenians – but they are not different faiths. We have failed, until recently, to "discern" how counterproductive such an adversarial relational system among Christians can be.

There are three dimensions of order rising from the Scripture, most clearly seen in the foundational writings of the Old Testament. They are the spheres of *sovereign, moral* and *relational* order. Each is tied generally to one of the three principal offices of the OT – patriarch-judge-king, prophet and priest. From these come the three great social institutions – the state/government, the church and the family.

> **Information is a message that reduces uncertainty.**
>
> Claude Shannon,
> ▬ ▬ ▬ ➤ *Bell Labs*

The great push in the last 400 years, among Protestants, has resulted in a preference for the theological-moral-truth dimension of order (prophet), over the relational dimension of order (priest). We have, in our attempt to correct the church theologically, damaged the church relationally. While the priesthood of all believers was core to the reformation, prayer was pushed to the background as different splinter groups put forward their own ecclesiology and theological inclinations. Theology could be debated; prayer was not so susceptible to arguments. Brotherhood was not defined vertically, in prayer alignment, but horizontally, by theological agreements forged. We are still in need of reformation. We may be as straight as an arrow, morally, and we may cross all our theological 't's – but we are disordered relationally, by our division.

It is not that we should no longer emphasize doctrine or

"core-theology" or even renounce our "tribal distinctive" – it is rather that we need to begin to equally emphasize the missing dimension of "relational order". Truth need not eclipse love.

Action Steps

1. Identify personal factors and behaviors contributing to disunity.
2. Identify corporate factors preventing unity between major streams of the church.
3. Identify potential vision partners.
4. Invite key partners to join partnering relationships.
5. Outline personal objectives and specific actions to strengthen and develop relationships – across denominational divides, racial and ethnic divides, different sides of the city, any stream where a chasm exist.
6. Outline initial personal objectives and actions to reconcile poor relationships.

PHASE V
Research: Increasing understanding

In the beginning, much of the data cited will be anecdotal. It will be incidental and far too narrow. High profile issues will drive awareness and heighten concern. Catalyzing reactions may occur to community events or news, but the unity that forms around such data and events tends to be reactionary and short-lived. It is not without value, it often provides on-ramps into your coalition. It may give leaders an opportunity to speak into the moral-social intersection. In the end, you need better data, holistic data, and that demands quality research.

So often the tendency is to react to some social-cultural issue. We then deal with symptoms, rather than the systemic concerns. In order to be relevant, and a positive force for community change, we need information that, in the past, we have considered irrelevant. This information is on both the community (Harvest Field) and the church (Harvest Force). In addition, diagnostic data that assesses the conditions of darkness, the negative spiritual forces (Spiritual Mapping) behind this current reality is important. The Church must see the city as it is and not as it appears. These data, with prayer, directs the process. We are 'informed' by both hard evidence of needed changes – 'we have seen the broken walls; we have surveyed the damage', and by the Spirit's direction. This is the means by which we discover God's agenda, and move to leverage resources that will result in impact.

At every strategic planning and goal-setting session, decisions must be informed by reality as opposed to vague supposition. Information gathering is critical to effective and strategic city impact.

Harvest Force (Noted earlier)

1. A directory of congregations, denominations and para-church ministries is created.
2. Church-based and community para-church ministry resources are cataloged.
3. Description of Church and city current reality is completed.
4. Geographic limits are identified – Is our focus this city? The county? What area are we focused on?
5. Zip Zones are identified.

Harvest Field

1. Information about current reality is disseminated to leaders and intercessors.
2. Citywide briefings take place in zip-zones, in different towns/cities, in various sectors of the society (among pro-

218

fessional tribes).

3. Prayer gatherings intercede for the major issues facing the city.

4. Leaders now gather to seek God for His priorities and direction.

5. All levels of prayer are increasing.

6. Vision out of concrete data is becoming more compelling.

PHASE VI
Vision to Strategy: Envisioning – The Completed Task

So many of our congregations are without a clear and compelling mission.[54] George Barna writes, "But when we asked these pastors, 'Can you articulate God's vision for the ministry of your church?' we found that roughly 90% of them could articulate a basic definition of ministry. But only two percent could articulate a vision for their church."[55] The result is wonderful activities 'for us' that fail to touch the lost and invite them into the kingdom of God. The church becomes a silo isolated from any community impact other than its incidental impact.

Thus, aligning the Church's activities with the activity of God to "rebuild the walls of the city" must become an increasingly clear vision and mission and its possibility believed to be concrete. This demands continuous interactive vision casting, formally and informally, until shared vision emerge, along with shared values and common goals. This happens intra-congregationally, as well as between congregations. Common language emerges enabling a deeper understanding and commitment to vision, principles, and processes.

A critical question: "What is God doing in our community?" and "What is His desire? How can we join His work?" The answer to these questions enables each individual to adjust their behavior in order to align their activity with the activity of God. The commitment to alignment is at the heart of the city reaching effort. Personal vision must move beyond the vague sense that God is up to something unique to a more concrete reality that perceives the framework in which God works and what he appears to be doing and getting ready to do. At that point, vision empowers.

Awakening occurs when many leaders grasp the fact that God is at work and commit to join him in that task – together. The idea is not to create a vision and sell it to a larger group, but to allow multiple visionaries access to the canvass. Thus, genuinely 'shared' vision emerges when the vision of many individuals is integrated into a larger and more compelling vision, and affirmed by the whole. Urgency intensifies as the larger group sees both the problems and the possibilities, and agree that the mission cannot be accomplished if they remain in isolation.

Vision materials are distributed throughout the Christian leadership community, to both pastors and lay leaders, along with intercessors.

Empowering leaders and articulating strategy

Empowerment requires a growing circle of core committed leaders and the removal of the barriers that prevent them from serving together effectively. These leaders then move to develop the structures and strategy to accomplish God's vision, one owned by a larger community. Strategy rises out of prayerful planning that has identified God in action in the community, and calls are made, with structures, that allow unity and collaboration to join God in that activity.

A growing inner desire among many to witness a divine visitation resulting in the transformation of the city is necessary.

Measurements and Action Steps

1. Personal calling to action verified, "God is calling me to join this effort ..."
2. Pastoral networks and key leaders identified, "I can work with you; we can work together ..."
3. Relational pathway to key leaders identified, "I know him. I will get to him, and connect the two of you ..."

New relational structures must emerge, new spheres of leadership that do not exist now, to steward a fresh move of God. This is only possible through trusted and credible servant leaders. Such trusted leaders invite the whole Church to mobilize to reach a whole city. Some such leaders are self-evident while others emerge in the process. The cultivation of relationships between these leaders is a key priority.

Next Steps

1. Initial envisioning team formed
2. Envisioning team sponsors initial level of research.
3. A clear plan for reconciliation between key leaders and groups is created by the envisioning team.
4. A clear plan for ongoing interactive vision casting is completed by the envisioning team.
5. A clear plan for mobilizing pastoral prayers groups is completed.

Learning - Increasing Vision Capacity

The average church member sees their role as 'being good' and 'going to church' faithfully. They typically do not have a sense of personal mission. They do not always connect the dots of the crumbling culture and their inactivity and silence. Without condemnation, they have to be awakened – and that is the function of vision.

The mission is daunting. It is overwhelming. It is complex. It requires a new relational construct of the church, and changing paradigms, an evolving structure, new ways of relating and who new measurable, long-term strategy.

This also calls for a new level of learning by the average church member. We must teach missions, train laymen as missionaries, mobilize the church across the city/county, without demanding their disassociation with either the congregation that they call a church-home or the denominational family in which they have found a sense of belonging.

Markers of Progress:

1. Three crucial components of strategy should now be in place:
    a. A growing unified prayer effort.
    b. A growing pool of reliable data and information that clarifies vision and informs strategy.
    c. A formative leadership team.
    d. These three critical prongs of strategy – prayer, dependence on God; informed vision, a clear and compelling sense of mission in the face of hard data; leadership, an action team with a strategic process and linear tactical steps.

2. You move from vision to strategy, then to tactics, all informed and energized by prayer; and then the process is revisited.

3. The vision grows, is clarified; the strategy is adjusted; the tactical steps are realigned. Prayer deepens.

4. The belief is in place – as we seek God for direction and solutions to the needs of the peoples of the city, He is willing to unveil His plans and purposes. Doing God's will in God's way will produce God-sized results.

5. Decisions are made in the context of prayer, "It seemed

good to the Holy Ghost and to us!"

6. General intercession evolves to strategic intercession for leaders and the planning process.

7. A process for conveying research and analysis to intercessory networks is created. Communication links between leaders and intercessors verified.

8. Pastoral prayer cells prayerfully prepare their hearts to receive God's direction through their leaders.

Implementation Markers

1. As the process moves forward, expect to see Level One warfare – distraction. Strategic intercession increases in importance since the spiritual battle will likely intensify more than before.

2. The Church must be prayerfully alert to the potential spiritual counter-attack, but not obsessed with it. Discerning, but not debilitated. Aware, but not focused on it.

3. Prayer must not be diminished, but increased, and yet, not prayer for the sake of prayer, nor prayer obsessed on the darkness.

4. Now we move beyond preparation to implementing its plan for community impact.

5. The spiritual health of the pastoral community is increasing, and the prayer life of the pastors, and people are deepening.

6. Strategic intercessors are now adopting high priority needs in the city and building teams.

7. Prayer is mobilized in local congregations as they seek the highest leverage ministries to utilize.

8. The number of intercessors is increasing as intercessors mentor others.

9. There are increased numbers of answers to prayer.

10. Citywide and city-sector prayer celebration gatherings

are conducted. Prayer walks take place. Prayer missions. Faith and expectation are growing.

Serving

The *Great Commandment* calls for a loving and caring Church that demonstrates God's love in practical ways. The *Great Commission* calls for a Church that articulates a message of hope and salvation through Christ. The *Great Commitment* calls for a church that is praying for its community and leaders that 'peace' might prevail, and that men might be saved. The three go together. *Prayer* fuels the need to *care*. And, increasing the church's credibility through acts of kindness and compassion open doors for the gospel to be *shared*. It increases the capability of the church to gather the harvest and expand the kingdom.

STORY

In an area just southeast of San Francisco, forty evangelical churches began a monthly meeting to consider the unique needs of their community. It was estimated that only four percent of the residents of their community attended any church. They prayed for cultural bridges. For God to open doors to the diverse ethnic pockets in a community known for its diversity. One-hundred and thirty-six languages were spoken in their public schools. After some time, they felt it was important to move from merely praying about community needs to taking action about community needs. They knew that one congregation working alone would not create the wave of change necessary, so they joined forces. They asked for and received an audience with the may-

or and local officials. And they inquired, "What's the best way to serve the city?" They discovered it was through non-profits. So they formed a compassion network pool. They combined their resources and funded an office in the city's Family Resource Center where twenty-five other private, governmental agencies had offices. Each church contributed a monthly donation. They hired a full-time administrator and engaged five interns to assist. The administrator and interns then worked to connect church congregations willing to meet the needs of people within the community. Each week, the churches received emails with volunteer opportunities. Many were filled within hours of the postings. The Compassion Network received the local government's Nonprofit of the Year Award.[56]

On-Going Research

Your process moves constantly from vision to strategic process, and unwraps in various tactics. The fatal flaw, which you will not notice initially, and many may never perceive, is to omit *strategic process*. The church has been uncommonly lazy. It looks for the quickest, simplest way. It avoids the discipline and embrace of the tedious. Moving from vision – more correctly, from a small picture vision – to a tactical endeavor is deadly to the larger process. It may bring temporary relief, a victory on some front, it may seem to turn the battle, but it will not win the war.

Healthy process moves from an ever clearer *vision*, informed by research, to *strategy*, and then strategy is unwrapped *tactically*. If you move directly from vision to tactics, it is, to use an analogy, like pushing over one domino. Strategy lines up the dominos so they fall in serial (tactics) fashion. Vision is the *big picture.* Strategy is the *big picture plan.* Tactics are the small pieces, the one-by-one deployment. Vision sees. Strategy plans – and plans big. Tactics act. Without tactical deployment, there can be no feet on the ground, no action, no impact. Yet, without an overarching strategy, energy and resources are wasted on non-collaborative action. Research must constantly inform the vision and advise the strategic process. The *energy* of this cycle is deployed tactically – there will always be the fervor, once people catch vision, to *do something quickly.* But quick fixes fall short of the goal. One shot 'save the city' crusades win superficial victories. The end result is, *we tried,* and we don't have the strength to try again.

Research informs the process – it clarifies vision, it confirms anecdotal hunches, it corroborates spiritual impressions. Vision is then translated into a multi-year process (strategy) with ordered steps (tactics), timelines, benchmarks and outcome measurements. All along the way, you are re-visioning, re-strategizing, and calibrating your tactics.

There are some who will only be concerned about their piece, their domino, the tactical component in which they are involved. They will overvalue its role, see it as critical, place that tactic in the position of the strategic, "If you will only do this – this one thing will change the city. Can't you see that?" There may be value to helping them see the larger vision, the big picture plan, and yet, that may be a waste of energy. Their fixation on the thing God has called them to is a valuable part of the process. Use their passion for the piece about which they are concerned. Not everyone needs to think strategically – but architects are critical.

Don't skip the strategic. And research is a critical part of an informed vision and strategic plan. The research team will translate anecdotal evidence into verifiable data. Reliable data makes your claims credible both in the Christian community and outside. The research team you employ needs this first-step, short-term goal in mind – a compelling snapshot that profiles both the city/county (harvest field) and also the church (harvest force). This will serve to mobilize your movement. It should, in relatively clear fashion, point to the unfinished task, the unreached harvest field, and the harvest force to be mobilized.

This means an assessment not only of the conditions of the culture, but current measurable presence and influence of the church as felt in and by the city. One of the key elements is the discernable relevance, and therefore, 'presence' of the church in every sector of the social sphere, the marketplace. Of course, in the current political environment, not only is the 'church' kept atarm's length, but its influence, its presence in symbols and cere-monies is disallowed. And increasingly, Christians are barred. Our most underutilized asset is the invisibly present church throughout culture, through the influ-ence of believers. Howev-er, these must be practic-ing believers, not passive believers.

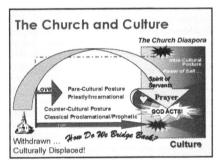

There are three per-vasive measures – prayer, care, and share.

- SHARE - Can Christians *share* faith openly? Are their Christians present, in any and all sectors of the culture, who could share? Who do share? Is there a systematic plan to reach the entire community with the gospel, to make it easy for people to believe? Is there an apologetic team? A proclamation team? A reconciliation task-force that aims at keeping peace?

- CARE - If the Christian message is suppressed so that it cannot be openly proclaimed everywhere? Is it then evident in silent, but powerful incarnational ways? Is it seen and felt in *caring* ways? Do the Christians in any given place intentionally live and relate in ways that honor Christ and reflect their faith values? Is there an organized means by which the church of the community, responds to the needs of the community?

- PRAYER - Finally, is there any on-going, intentional prayer *in* this place? *For* this area and its people? And that question should be asked of any place in the city, of every professional/vocational sector, in every neighborhood and zip zone. Are intercessors mobilized across the city? Are there intercessory leaders? Teams? Have vocational sectors been adopted for prayer? Are embedded prayer teams functioning in critical relational circles?

A mission *field* can be defined as any place – a building, a neighborhood, a company, a group, a social sector – any place or people, where Christ is not known or celebrated, not acknowledged as Lord; where Christian principles, openly or passively, have little or no influence. Thus the 'presence' of Christians – by prayer, care, and sharing of the love of God are essential.

The key question is the following? "What is the measurable impact of the church, and by extension, Christians, on the city/county? What is the effect of their faith?" The inverse question is also important. "What difference would it make, it there were no Christian values in our city? No Christians with influence? How would that change the quality of life, the conditions of suffering and pain, the hurts and hopes? And what difference do Christian values, applied directly or indirectly, have on the social systems and

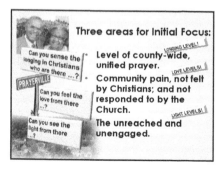

Three areas for Initial Focus:
- Level of county-wide, unified prayer.
- Community pain, not felt by Christians; and not responded to by the Church.
- The unreached and unengaged.

228

structures of the city/county?"

Such measurements do not come easily. However, measuring influence and progress is helpful; as is concrete data that informs the "What more must be done?" process.

The FIRST QUESTION – Where are we?

What is the current overarching status of the harvest field (city/county) and the harvest force (church)?

The SECOND QUESTION – Where are we going?

This is the primary goal setting stage that focuses both on the conditions of the people, places (city neighborhoods, etc.), and their problems.

The first questions gathers in "what has already been done!" The second question asks, "What is yet to be done?"

The THIRD QUESTION – How will we get there?

This is a critical strategic question. If you only respond to problems in a piecemeal manner, your effort will fail. A long-term, multi-tactic solution is needed. You need a map for the multi-year journey ahead. This is not merely a random list, but a sequential, strategically ordered list of steps toward city impact. Identify the problem. Propose a solution, often layered, with multiple steps perhaps over multiple years. Assess resources, human and otherwise. Cast vision. Align. Engage. Measure. Reassess. Baptize everything in prayer. Stay humble. Guard the unity of the team.

STORY

New Covenant Church in Clyde, North Carolina, joined with thirty other churches to address the community's homelessness problem. They started a homeless shelter. They supported it completely with cooperative, collaborative funds and staffed it with volunteers. Tasting success, they turned to the public schools. Public school budgets were tight. They pitched in to clean up school properties before the academic year began. Sixty-eight churches have now joined to adopt all the schools in the county. A formal agreement has been forged between churches and schools, the first of its kind in North Carolina. The churches have also partnered on other initiatives – mission trips, joint Vacation Bible School endeavors and more.[57]

Building the Research Team

Look for three different types of involvement by the research volunteers.

1. Strategic Thinkers - members who have a clear understanding not only of research processes, but out of a strategic framework. They must understand the vision of city-impact and the significance of the research.

2. Technicians – team members who are information managers, proficient with databases, spreadsheets, and mapping software. They may have assistants

The words civil and civilized are derived from the Latin civis, meaning one who lives in the city. City folks were considered cultured, in contrast to country folk. From the Latin word urbs, we have Urbane. From the Greek polis, city, we have the word politics.

helping, but they need to be responsible for managing the information electronically.

3. Assistants – the largest group. These are the data gatherers, the wonderful people who make trips, assess, see things first-hand, bring back reports, sometimes consisting of hard-core data and at other times, impressions. This is the largest contingent of the group.

A typical team may expand and contract, depending on the stage of information gathering. The typical size is seven to twelve individuals.

Quantitative methods of research focused on statistics. This is easy to gather. It can be found online, in libraries – and is a matter of numbers. On the other hand, *qualitative* research is more subjective, it is gathered by interviewing and observation. It connects the dots, often intuitively, but never leaves the *quantitative* research out of the equation. *Quantitative* research tells us how many churches there are and whether or not they are growing – the facts. *Qualitative* research probes deeper, telling us why they are growing or why growth in one group is not taking place.

Harvest Field Data (Going Deeper)

The listings of data below may need to be gathered, not only at the macro level, but at micro levels, as well.

1. Metroplex (Metropolitan Statistical Area/MSA) -- For example, the Census Bureau's geographic definition for the area. Charlotte, by some measures, is an eleven county area, spread over parts of two states with a population in excess of 2 million. Macro level research forms a baseline for comparison and evaluation of the smaller geographic units.

2. Move from the LARGER to the SMALLER. MSA data is gathered, then each county is broken out; then each city/

231

town; then zip-zones.

3. Census tract/block group, community districts or zip code – It may seem like overkill to extrapolate this data, but this is where the tactical implication must take place, and that cannot be effective, unless it is linked to the larger MSA picture. The Census Bureau typically has the general data for this micro breakout, and other sources include county and city planning commissions. Census Bureau information is available down to the block level.

4. Work with categories most commonly known and recognized by the general public.

5. Begin with the larger geographic focus, and move, incrementally, smaller.

Basic Demographics – (for the whole and the parts)

Total population calculations include both numbers and percentages of the whole.

Total Population – number.

1. Gender (male/female);

2. Age group (builders, boomers, busters, millennials and children);

3. Ethnic groups (first, second, third generation where possible);

4. Socio-economic – income;

5. Employment, etc., (number and percent).

6. Civil status -- married, single, single parent, divorced, widowed, etc.

7. Religious preference;

8. Households by type -- single, married, single parent, etc.;

9. Other pertinent demographic figures the research team feels is important.

NOTE: You need a cartographer who can help display

these figures for the appropriate geographic levels, in layers if possible. A map room is important, a kind of 'situation room' for the city/county effort. Both Harvest Force and Harvest Field data is best displayed using tables, graphs and maps augmented by descriptive narrative interpretation.

Because ethnicity is such an explosive and deeply held mark of identity, the raw data may be inadequate. You may need, in addition to ethnic composition and distribution for both the whole and the parts, a sense of ethnic history of the city/county. It is important that such data have the fingerprints of all the groups, particularly historical perspectives.

Growth Rates:

1. Population growth rate over the last decade.
2. Projections for the next decade.
3. Familiarity with the AGR – Annual Growth Rate and AAGR – Average Annual Growth Rate). That gives you a baseline. Four factors determine population growth for a given geographical area - births (B), deaths (D), immigration rate (I), and emigration rate (E). Thus, the growth rate of population = (B-D)+(I-E). In other words, the population growth of a period can be calculated in two parts, natural growth of population (B-D) and mechanical growth of population (I-E), in which mechanical growth of population is mainly affected by social factors, e.g. advanced economies may grow faster while backward economies grow slowly or even experience negative growth. (Growth can be both positive or negative i.e. growth can increase or decrease.) The CIA World Factbook gives the world annual birthrate, mortality rate, and growth rate as 1.89%, 0.79%, and 1.096% respectively. The USA population in 2010 was 310,384,000 up in twenty years from 253,339,000, a 22.5% increase.

At Risk Groups

1. Number of homeless individuals, families, children.
2. Number of gangs, number of kids in gangs.
3. Children from low income families
4. Senior beyond 75 living alone.
5. AIDS carriers, victims.
6. Children in the welfare system.
7. Teens in the welfare system.
8. Teens in juvenile lock-ups.
9. Others.

Social and Societal Concerns

With a focus on these area, though not exclusively, start the process of attempting to both discern and factually substantiate, the major moral, social and spiritual concerns of the city:

1. Mayor's Office – the degree to which the faith community has access and influence.
2. The interface between clergy and Law Enforcement; the court system and the faith community.
3. Social Services – who are key Christians in this sector?
4. Education – who are key administrators and teachers who are Christians?
5. Heath Care Services – sensitivity to faith concerns, doctors and nurses, medical supervisors and staff who are believers.
6. Other.

HARVEST FIELD ANALYSIS

1. What is the geographic area(s) of largest population concentration?
2. Where does the whole or part differ (higher or lower)

from national averages in each demographic category?

3. What geographic areas are the various ethnic, racial, linguistic, religious and social-cultural concentrated within?

4. In narrative fashion describe what has been learned about each high risk group and each societal concern.

5. What other harvest field realities stand out as particularly noteworthy?

Harvest Force
Harvest Force Data

Create a list of Protestant Christian churches. You will want, for spiritual mapping purposes, and for a comprehensive picture of the community, a list of other 'faith' movements – Islamic Mosques, Hindu temples, Buddhists shrines, satanic churches, new age churches, Mormon churches, Jehovah Witnesses, Jewish synagogues, Catholic and Eastern Orthodox gathering sites. In addition, you want a listing of para-church ministries. Create one comprehensive list.

If your community is host to denominational oversight offices or para-church ministry headquarters, note those. Also, be aware of ministerial associations, fellowships, networks or coalitions of pastors and/or churches. Include Christian education institutions. List and code these in categories.

Once you know the character and breadth of the Harvest Force, enlist key players who might make it easier to gather data. Generally, good data will be more difficult to obtain on the Harvest Force than from the Harvest Field.

1. Solicit assistance from denominational offices. Ask them to have their pastors and churches compete a Church Survey Form.

2. Mail the form to all churches. You will have to use multiple avenues to get this data out, and recollect it.

3. Enlist a group of volunteers to call pastors and churches, telling them about the process you are launching and asking for their help.

4. This will probably require multiple contacts either by both mail and telephone. If you have churches you believe to be critical, target those for in person visits to obtain the information.

5. In all cases, enter the data into the database.

6. Your goal should be participation by at least 60% of the congregations for the whole target area (city/county). Now, you are ready to begin analysis.

Harvest Force Analysis

1. How many churches are there in the county? Various cities/communities? Rural areas? Eventually, you want to know how many there are in each zip-zone.

2. You want a list by type – Baptist, Methodist, Presbyterian, Episcopalian, etc.

3. What is the aggregate *membership* size (both number & percent) of all Christian congregations combined? Compare that to the population.

4. What percentage and number of the churches are participating actively in the process? The goal – 20% of the churches! At least five percent of the total population. This is a starting point baseline.

5. What is the *aggregate average worship attendance* (number & percent) in the congregations surveyed? Is there comparative data, for example, from denominational statistics, re, Baptist in the area (Association Office), Regional Administrative Offices of any given denomination from which you can extract data for comparative purposes.

6. What is the Annual Growth Rate (AGR) for the congregations, in terms of attendance and membership, for each

of the last five years?

7. What is the AGR for church planting for each of the last five years? How many new church plants have popped up in the last five years? What is their survival rate?

8. What is your church closure rate? Number closed or merged in the last five years, track by year if possible.

9. Determine and classify the number of *growing churches* (they have a 5-10% increase, or more, over their baseline five years previously Color them green)? Plateaued churches (plus or minus three percent over the past five years. Color them brown)? Declining churches (More than five percent less in attendance; 10% -3 AAGR over the past five years. Color them yellow; more than 10%, code orange; more than 25%, code red; more than 50%, code blue)? Do this anonymously, detach church names from the released data. For strategic reasons, you may want to be able to differentiate the churches. How can you assist declining churches?

10. What is the *seating capacity of all the congregations*? Compare that to the population.

11. What is the *seating capacity based on the number of worship services* conducted? At what percentage do you run out of seating space were the whole community to come to church? Differentiate the seating capacity for growing, plateaued and declining churches?

12. Given the growth trends, what will the size of the Church be in 3 years, 5 years, 10 years based on the current growth rate?

13. Which denominations or types of churches are growing most/least and by what percent? What demographic of the population? What age groups?

14. Within which geographic regions of the city/county is the Church growing most/least?

Harvest Field and Force Overlay Analysis

1. What percentage of the population is churched?

2. What is the church to population ratio? (X number of churches per 1000 people; or, one church for every x number of people). In parts of the SE USA, the ratio is as low as 300:1. Optimally, it should never be greater than 1000:1. Which areas have the highest/lowest ratio?

3. How does the growth of the Church compare to past population growth and future projections? At what point in the history of the county/city did the church grow the fastest?

4. What is the church to population ratio for each major ethnic group?

5. What are the percentages represented in the church for each age group?

6. If the population is growing in the city/county, is the church keeping up with the population growth? If the population is in decline, how has that affected church attendance? What is the comparative ratio? Overall, is the church, in comparison to relative population trends, growing or declining?

7. How are the congregations distributed geographically? By county/city/zip zones – and the comparative population ratios.

8. Where is the Church most/least present in each level of geography? Ethnicity?

9. Are their geographic or demographic areas from which the Church is entirely absent? Who lives in those areas? Are there apparent reasons for the absence of a church?

10. Based on community population projections, what portion of the community will be churched if the following becomes a reality?

   a. The church grows at same rate for the next five years as it did in the past five years?

   b. The church stops losing members and maintains its

size – to what extent will it lose ground based simply on population growth?

   c. The church experiences a growth rate of three percent, 5 percent, ten percent. (Seven percent AGR is all that is needed to double in a decade).

11. Identify the top ten high risk groups and/or societal problems and the degree to which the Church is aware of and engaging those groups and issues (be specific).

12. Prepare maps for the following (minimum)

   a. Population distribution.

   b. Ethnic distribution.

   c. Church to population ratio for major ethnic groups.

   d. Church to population ratio for each level of geographic division.

   e. Church locations at various geographic levels (color code churches by major ethnic groups)

   f. Basic demographics (see Basic Demographics from harvest Field section)

   g. Churches coded by size and location (+1000, +750, + 500, + 200, + 100, - 99, - 50)

51 Consider the Lusanne Covenant or an adaption of it to create a construct of mission out of core theology. See Appendix.

52 According to George Barna, 61% of pastors admit that they "have few close friends." One in six feel under-appreciated. At any given time, 20% are dealing with a very difficult family situation. Ninety-eight percent describe themselves as an "effective Bible teacher". This is the high-water mark of ministry – ascending the public pulpit on Sunday. About 90% feel that they are an "effective leader" and are "driven by a clear sense of vision." Eighty percent see themselves as an "effective disciple maker." Another favorable perception for 70%, is that they are "deeply involved in the community". https://www.barna.org/leadership-articles/150-pastors-feel-confi-dent-in-ministry-but-many-struggle-in-their-interaction-with-others (June 10, 2006).

53 Waymire, 5: 3-4.

54 Lyle Schaller categorize pastors in four type categories. 1. Those who could not 'pay the rent.' They were always behind in delivering what was due. They were handicapped in some way. Their churches rarely grew beyond 100. 2. Pastors who paid the rent on time. They did what was expected of them but lacked vision for anything beyond the norm. 3. Goal-oriented pastors. 4. Pastors who moved past the numbers, goals, and were driven by a vision and had the capacity to share that vision. http://thomrainer.com/2012/08/27/four_categories_of_pastors/

55 Quoted by Aubrey Malphurs, "Developing a Vision: What kind of church would we like to be?" Building Church Leaders, Practical Training from Leadership Journal. See: http://www.buildingchurchleaders.com/articles/2005/042705.html

56 Greg Hawkins and Cally Parkinson, *Move: One 1000 Churches Reveal about Spiritual Growth* (2011), 242-243.

57 Ibid, 243.

CHAPTER 16
Starting the Spiritual Mapping Project

Project Overview
Step One: The Team

To complete a spiritual mapping project, you need a team of about a dozen individuals. In addition, you need to plan for a project that could take years – two-to-three years easily. The size of the city and the length of its history will determine the scope of the project. Doing spiritual mapping is somewhat like ancestry research. Some aspects are laborious – pouring through mountains of dusty historical materials, tracking to some site and looking for a clue that you don't fully understand. Then, there are those discovery moments that bring excitement. Everything you do will need to be bathed in prayer. You need spiritual insights and revelation, more than data, as you move forward.

Step Two: Constant Prayer

Before every battle, David inquired of the Lord (I Sam. 23:2, 4 and 30:8; II Sam. 5:19, 23).

First, pray. Then pray again. Pray often. Pray over data and for the interpretation of the data. Pray for one another. Pray for direction, protection and a sense of God's presence as you proceed with the project.

Step Three: Assign Projects

Find those individuals with time to go to the library and pour through old newspapers and records. Others, you will want to send to the records hall to examine old land records. Who first staked out the area? What amount of land did they own? Who did they acquire it from? Someone needs to visit the historical society. Another person might be especially adept at internet research. All along the journey, you want to share both discoveries and missing pieces. You need a chronicler, someone who has the charge of all the data. If someone drops out, you want to make sure you have his or her work saved. You are putting together a puzzle – a picture of the spiritual history and present condition of your city.

Hours will be spent in research – research you will want to save. Some you will not recognize as important until later. Everyone may be assigned reading in some area. Interviews should involve at least two people – we all tend to hear differently. In some cases, you may want to record an interview. Field exploration can be done by in individual – better two than one. However, field treks, those times when you go to pray, to discern, to consider or confirm data, should, when possible, involve the whole team.

Step Four: Discern Gifts

You will need to discover the gifts and talents of the team, their interests and passion. Some will be graced with sharper discernment than others. They will, more quickly than others, see the value of some insight or some historical data. Others should be equally valued, since they have the patience to pour through old newspapers or begin the process of recording current events. Those 'people oriented folks' are the ones you want to assign to the interview process. They are capable, not only of grasping quantitative data, but discerning the implications of qualitative data, and exploring its implications. When possible, have them operated as a team. The qualitative, discerning interviewing, who travels with a quiet, conscientious, detail hound.

Step Five: Engage Living Historians

There will often be people in the community who are walking repositories of community information. These "old-timers" are living treasures. You may only have one opportunity to hear their story. Take good notes. Record the interview if possible. Remember, they may not be a person of faith. Take that into consideration. Still yet, you will rarely find someone who will give you such direct data. You will find additional clues you need inside their story. Be patient. Do not force a narrow interview, "We are only interested in the spiritual history of the city!" Such a limited view will probably miss significant slices of data. Let them tell their story naturally, and as you listen, listen to the Spirit. At the same time, don't be afraid to press for specific information, "So your great, great-grandfather gave the logs to build the first church? And it was at the corner of Maguire and Main? And both the Methodist and the Baptist used the building – the same structure? For how many years? And what event triggered the separation of the churches?" Keep clarifying. Be polite.

Step Six: Go Stealth

As you explore the current condition of the city, and even its past, at times you will need your own clandestine operators, individuals who venture into places that Christians usually avoid. There may be streets in your city that 'decent' folks avoid – but someone may need to go there. Salt and light are needed in such areas. You may need to venture into bars – and have a cola, sit in the corner booth and read the spiritual environment. You may have teams that make a mission trip into clubs and theaters. The goal is not increased exposure to the darkness or heightened vulnerability. This should not be the main focus of the mapping project, but awareness, as opposed to utter blindness regarding the community's spiritual condition, and first-hand impressions are important.

In some cases, Christians have ventured into abortion clinics 'for advice.' They have sat down with Satanists. They have invited punk rockers for a chat – and listened. They have researched alternative faith avenues. They have sat in on high school, and college classes where Christianity was regularly trashed and the language, even of the teachers, was vulgar and explicit – and these spiritual mappers silently listened. They were there not to counter. Not to argue, but simply to gauge the spiritual atmosphere. They have even walked their upscale mall, with spiritual eyes, and found things they had completely missed on previous visits.

Step Seven: Be Cautious. Stay Focused. Respect Boundaries

As you explore, God will set boundaries. In addition, it might be necessary for the team to set boundaries. At times, the Lord may say to someone, *"Don't explore this any further"*. That may be a word for that person or the team. That is to be discerned. At other times, the team may need to say to an individual - "Leave that alone!" Awareness of the darkness is one thing. We are not to be ignorant of the enemy or his devices. Nor are we to become students of the darkness. The best counterfeit detectives are effective, not because they have studied the phony, but because they know the authentic so well.

Spiritual mapping must not become a descent into the darkness, a preoccupation with the bizarre or an invitation into the decadent. The darkness is alluring. It is enticing. It is an illusion. Sin or evil never represent itself as what it really is. Remember, Moses sent only the mature for the intelligence reconnaissance mission. Do not allow a well-meaning new believer to be a part of the team when they are neither mature enough to discern their own heart or adequately grounded in Scripture to resist the tug of some underworld spirit. A convert from deep sin or some cult may feel that spiritual mapping is a way for them to redeem some missed opportunity. At times for specialized purposes, you may find their insights very helpful. But don't put them in harms' way or on the front lines.

When the Lord draws a line in the process of your research, respect his boundary. Blessings stop when we violate boundaries. To obey is always better than sacrifice or the completion of some mission (I Samuel 15:22).

Expect Push-back

Any member of the spiritual mapping team may get special attention from the Evil One. While he is not omniscient, he is no dummy, and he has observers that want to stop our surveillance activities at the very beginning of our project. When an individual on the team seems to be experiencing an unusual confluence of negative happenings, consider the possibility of spiritual warfare. Moreover, when several individuals, simultaneously, are caught up in what normally might be explicable, but now a convergence of simultaneous distractions – perhaps more than distractions.

Stop – pray!

When cars break down on the way to an assignment, you are at one level of interference, one that might be explained away. When they break down in harm's way, without a reasonable excuse – you are at a different level. And when someone out investigating and exploring has a life endangering moment, that is yet another level – whether it is a near accident, a mishap that could have been fatal, a falling object that just missed them, an inexplicable and unprovoked altercation or confrontation with someone who was angry for seemingly no cause. Prayer is the ultimate and immediate response.

Cover One Another

If an individual on the team is a consistent target – get them a prayer covering, assign a partner, and if the uncanny continues, consider reassigning them to another task. Take such matters seriously. Pray about timing. Ask God for clarification. You should neither be baited by the resistance, nor intimidated by some Sanballat and Tobiah (Neh. 2:19; 4:3; 6:17, 19). Remember, Nehemiah refused to allow the enemy to stop him or alter his agenda. He rarely responded to them. He stayed on-task. The bottom line is that team members needs to be grounded and mature persons, who know their spiritual authority and position in Jesus Christ. The work you are doing almost certainly assures very real encounters with the darkness. Your team will need to resist the enemy and stand your ground without allowing the warfare to become the main thing.

Mature team members know to say calmly, *"I will say of the Lord, He is my refuge and my fortress: my God; in Him will I trust" (Psalm 91:2).* You will need to take the Evil One seriously, while refusing to be overawed by the Dark Lord or his princes. Luther reportedly awoke one night to find Lucifer standing at the foot of his bed. Legend indicates that the old reformer said, "O, it is only you!" And he went back to sleep. *"Submit yourselves therefore to God. Resist the devil, and he will flee from you" (James 4:7).*

Step Eight: Leadership Adjustment

The Spiritual Mapping Project leader needs to know their own gifts – and use the gifts of others efficiently. Discover your best interviewer. And the best chronicler of data, etc. Find out who loves to pour through mountains of historical materials. Make assignments consistent with gifts and passions. The leader, whatever their gifts and preferences in terms of data, interpretation, research and assessment, they *must* function both as a team member and as the leader. They cannot get lost in the details. Someone has to direct the project.

The team itself should be comprised of godly believers who work out of their calling and gifts. Mutual submission should be the relationship culture in which you work, *"Submitting yourselves one to another in the fear of God" (Ephesians 5:21).* No one should be working for the "Best Spiritual Mapper Award!" Paul would urge, *"Let nothing be done through strife or vain-glory; but in lowliness of mind let each esteem others better than themselves. Look not every man on his own things, but every man also on the things of others" (Philippians 2:3-4).*

The Ultimate Goal – The Harvest

Keep the ultimate goal in mind – a harvest of souls. A community-wide revival. A cultural awakening in the region. Spiritual Mapping is not the goal. Do not stop seeing lost people. Do not go on mapping expeditions, pass people in pain and not even see them. Cultivate a spirit of compassion. Working with hard data, and frequently encountering the darkness, you can become hardened, unconsciously. Keep wet eyes and a tender heart. Even in the course of research, the spirit in which we pursue truth must be love.

As you begin your spiritual mapping journey, you need the ongoing input of pastors and spiritual leaders. Without some tethering, the team can lose its way. The spies were given specific perimeters in terms of data to be collected. And they were to give a report when they returned. Any spiritual mapping team needs a group of pastors/elders or leaders with whom they have access and a regular opportunity to interact. *"Without wise leadership, a nation is in trouble, but with good counselors there is safety"* *(Proverbs 11:14).* And also, *"Every purpose is established by counsel, and with good advice make war" (Proverbs 20:18).* And then, *"For by wise counsel, thou shalt make thy war, and in a multitude of counselors there is safety" (Proverbs 24:6).*

Remember, you are making trips behind enemy lines for which you need prayer covering.

Beginning The Work

There is a tendency to make the work of spiritual mapping a bit exotic and even secretive. Neither the work itself nor the discoveries should be 'secret.' It is, however, important to be discreet – about incursions, treks, even interviews. Wisdom is needed to appropriately steward insights given by the Spirit, and those may need to season before they are openly shared. Further, you are mapping areas where there are actual and measurable strongholds. You will discover boundaries, the lines at which you can almost sense the heaviness lift or feel it descend. At such points, you are moving under a net or a snare, the web of a giant man-eating spider who wraps up its victims, binds them with cords that seem too fragile to secure any living thing, and devours them. Men and women move under its shadow without realizing the danger. Such discoveries are not always meant for public discussion. They are matters committed to the heart for prayer. In no way, does any spiritual mapping team desire for its data to be construed by the folks on the street, either those who are the exploited or those who do the exploiting, as adversarial. Cheap talk that fails to see the vilest place as potentially sacred, that treats a street or a group of people as a target or a mere outreach experience, is destined to fail – and maybe backfire with serious repercussions. The work of reconnaissance is a special function of warfare and should be maintained as a private matter.

Mapping Details

Do not ignore the obvious geographic features. Are you a valley town? A prairie? A floodplain? On the delta? Bordering a lake? On the seacoast? The plains? A mountain hamlet? Does a river run through your city, or border it? Is it adjacent to a water reservoir? A national forest? Look at aerial photos (You can usually find these on-line, i.e. – Google Maps.) Do you sit on an ancient highway or trade route? Were you an early railroad center? Does a mountain or ridge divide your city? Or serve as a boundary to it? Are there some folks who live 'on the other side of the mountain?' Are you at the end or mouth of a valley? What is the climate of your city? Dry or wet? Is rain seasonal? Are you in a hot or cold place? Two seasons or four? What are the implications of the obvious? Salinas is over the hill from Monterey – two different climates. A few miles apart, and a world away. Salinas is the setting of John Steinbeck's, *Grapes of Wrath*. And Monterey is home to Pebble Beach, playground of the elite and famous. One is agricultural, bucolic, and countrified; the other sophisticated, cultured, and suave. One is the Joad family, the other Clint Eastwood and Doris Day. Only minutes apart.

After you have looked at the physical features – altitude, rims and rivers, natural terrain, consider the unseen. Fault lines – the potential for earthquakes. Tornado or hurricane frequency. Mineral deposits. Health advantages and risks. Water quality and abundance, including the source. Wildlife (plenty or scarce) and the natural creatures and their eco-balance, the deadly and dangerous with whom you share the land. Why do people live here?

After you have considered features, a practical way to map present *activities* is to find a map of the focus area. Place on it colored and/or numbered pins or marks. Each pin/mark is keyed to a name and address. In a file is the data behind each pin/mark. In one system, this is their coding key:

RED - Cult and Occult Churches

#1 RED –   Church of Divine Light
             115 Maple Street
Formerly: Community Chapel
Character: New Age
             Shares it facility with a Wiccan Group

#2 RED -   Church of the Divine Master
             1234 NW 18th Avenue
Formerly: Warehouse building
Character: Wiccan

#3 RED -   Unification Church of the South
             9876 Sacred Circle Parkway
Character: Unitarian

YELLOW - (Pornography)

#1 YELLOW   Uptown Video Center

	1010 Slacker Lane
Note:	Been in business for five years.
	First of several similar stores in same five-block area
	Allegedly rents to kids

#2 YELLOW	XXX Books
	127 Cool Valley Road
Note:	Adjacent to the motel, rooms by the hour!
	Checking on ownership link.

#3 YELLOW	Gas & Go – Fast Food
	1596 Harness Lake Road
Note:	Large display of pornographic magazines
	Open display
	XXX Rental Rack
	May also sell underage cigarettes and alcohol

Additional materials can be added to each file over time, and appropriate amendments made.

You may want to differentiate between 'establishments', 'incidences' and significant 'events.' For example, the active presence of prostitutes on a given street corner is an 'incidence.' The use of a given hotel by prostitutes is identified as an 'establishment.' The murder of a prostitute is an 'event,' as are other murder locations, robberies, kidnappings, etc. Do the same for gangs: gang 'presence,' gang 'territories,' gang 'events.' Drug 'activity,' and drug 'territory,' and drug 'events.' Your team alone can determine how detailed you will be with your research. Here are some notes and categories you might want to consider.

MAP ONE - CAMPS

There are, of course, many layers to spiritual mapping. On one map, you might place "camps" - designed to show the location of physical establishments that have a definitive 'spiritual' character. Here the research team will detail a number of things about each establishment – the name, their nature, their size, and any alliances. Seven categories are in this focus area:

CATEGORY #1

Theologically Non-Orthodox, Cult and Occult Churches (Red Pin/Markers)

These 'churches' are not orthodox in faith. That is, the core of their theology is either missing a critical component (trinity, deity of Christ, resurrection, inspiration of Scripture, fall/sinful nature of man, need for redemption) or is held as higher truth than the Bible - Jehovah's Witness Kingdom Halls, Mormon Temples, Bahia, Unity Churches, Unitarian churches, Christian Science, as well as the more exotic, New Age Centers, Wiccan Groups, Satanist Associations, Mystic Centers, Pagan Groups, etc. The goal is not adversarial. "We wrestle not against flesh and blood ..." The goal is to discern locations where cult groups have built their nest and to discern why – if there is a why? Look for patterns. Trace trends. Moreover, from that, search for clues as to why folks are falling into such heart and mind deceptions.

CATEGORY #2

Cult and Occult Establishments (Orange Pin)

These are not churches, per se, but businesses that are involved in some way in cult or occult practices. These are places that perform metaphysical healings, Reiki teaching, reincarnation and past life therapy, astrology readings, chakra and energy works, I Chang. Some of

STARTING THE SPIRITUAL MAPPING PROJECT

these places masquerade as something else. A group of researchers in Miami found comic book and baseball card shops full of cult and occult materials. In addition to baseball cards, they also sell magic cards, the 'Dungeons & Dragons' game. The large chain toy stores, even those in the malls, sell these materials shamelessly.

The 'trump factor' in the arena of the occult does not appear to be devotion to an ideology, but the greater commitment to the money generated. In Miami, research revealed some 120 cult and occult churches, but some 350 businesses that dealt in cultic and occult goods.

CATEGORY #3

Pornography (Green Pin)
This includes the obvious, the 'XXX' bookstore or lounge with nude dancers, as well as the gas station or corner market that distributes pornographic magazines. Large chain bookstores also carry a great deal of pornography, as do airports, some lingerie stores, and neighborhood video stores.

Verification requires a visit – or at least call. Phone connections are not always reliable. If they perceive disdain or a 'parental tone' chances are, you will not get the truth. In some places where you find adult magazines, you may also discover 'an adult room' or adult videos for viewing or rent. These back-room dimensions are not commonly known except by word of mouth. You have to inquire, and you may have to buy a magazine or rent a video to gain access. Do not falsely accuse. Verify the information.

CATEGORY #4

Freemasonry [Including Easter Star] (Brown Pin)
These include temples and shrines, as well as Lodges. This is an ancient mystery religion veiled in secrecy, and

presented as a fraternity. In some communities, it is the meeting place of the power brokers of the city. Freemasonry is often in the foundation of important buildings in the city. Secret rites and rituals that affirm its hold or influence over city fathers and institutions are conducted. In its values, the sacred book is one of choice – the Bible, the Koran, the Torah, etc. The book itself is only a symbol since it is always subordinated to the new light of Freemasonry.

CATEGORY #5

Abortuaries *(Purple Pin)*

Covert reconnaissance will be necessary. While there is the obvious "Crisis Pregnancy Center" that usually performs terminations, there are additional clinics that are not so obvious. There are some HMO clinics that perform abortions, especially the smaller ones. In ascertaining the reality of the less obvious, you must once again be wise. In Miami, two women went to a suspected location. They would go to the receptionist's window and ask, as if nervous or embarrassed, if they did pregnancy terminations (preferred language over the term abortion). The receptionist would usually give a straightforward answer. If the answer were in the affirmative, an immediate invitation was offered to come in for counseling. At points, the team did so – to gain additional information or confirmation of the services offered. At times, the institution would offer a referral, noting other places that did discreet abortions. The ladies would thank them for the information.

CATEGORY #6

Homosexual Establishments (Yellow Pins)

In this category, the Miami team pinned only places that were owned or operated by the homosexual community. These 'gay pride' businesses either promoted or supported the lifestyle.

This list included Gay/Lesbian churches as well as businesses. The dominate Homosexual church in America is the Metropolitan Community Church (MCC). You will also find churches of a wide variety that advertise Gay-Lesbian-Transgender friendly.

The South beach area is awash with homosexual businesses, bars, etc.

CATEGORY #7

Prostitution (Blue Pins)

Here, the obvious street corners where prostitution is regularly practiced are pinned. In some places, lingerie shops are fronts for prostitution rings or an "escort" service.

Here is one experience of the Miami team. Each week, an ad was discovered in a newspaper that typically circulated in the more seamy sections of the city. It was a solicitation for 'models' for an escort service. A researcher called the number in reference to the ad. A woman answered, confirming that they were still looking for "girls". The researcher kept listening, and amazingly, the representative for the agency became very transparent, saying the agency was looking for 'models' – that the agency was into "slapping", "bondage", and "domination". The representative then asked the researcher if she had 'experience' in these areas. "In that split second," the godly intercessor recalled", my mind went blank." Then the Holy Spirit whispered, "Tell her you have had no experience with slapping, but you have had plenty of experiences with bondage and domination." (Obviously, of another nature. Life without Christ is a life of bondage and domination.) Satisfied, the interviewer agreed to mail the application. With the return address, the pin went onto the map and with that, another small glimpse into the depth of community depravity.

This will require multiple maps – layered maps. In addition, with this data, a picture of the city will begin to emerge. In prayer, the Lord will impress a focus on this area or that. This 'global' view will change the perspective of the mission. Instead of reacting to small bits and pieces of the problem, a more holistic strategy can now emerge.

In Miami, they continually reminded themselves that each pin on the map represented people – people who needed God, with whom an encounter with God could affect the quality of life in the city. The first response, therefore, is prayer – for people to know Christ. *"Ask of Me, and I shall give you the heathen for your inheritance" (Psalms 2:8).*

Second, they reminded themselves that each pin was the location of a doorway into the darkness, one where Satan had been empowered to operate. The team went to various locations to pray as directed by the Lord, often with incredible results. Sometimes, they would anoint the ground or building with oil. At other places, they planted a Bible. They prayed for the release of the grace of God into the area, believing that grace teaches godliness. *"The grace of God that brings salvation hath appeared to all men, teaching us ..."* Grace is a teacher! They would appropriate the work of the redemptive blood of Jesus *(Ephesians 1:7)*, to draw individuals close to God – those *"who sometimes were far off are made near by the blood of Christ" (Ephesians 2:13).* By invoking the blood of Jesus, the focus is to *"purge your conscience from dead works to serve the living God?" (Ephesians 9:14).*

Being on location usually results in heightened discernment. And that empowers more precise praying, more aligned praying, more effective prayer in and with the Spirit. The impact is greater and the results of prayer more evident.

MAP TWO – PUBLIC PLACES

The 'public places' map will have city parks, public attractions, public schools, colleges and universities, government centers and courthouses, as well as areas of transportation (airports, train and bus stations, cab centers, boat marinas, etc.). They may also note the 'gates' of the city, primary routes leading into or out of the city/county. These are not necessarily areas of darkness, but they are entry and exit points. Moreover, they are places where spiritual authority should be exercised, where Christian presence and influence is desired, and accountability is important.

MAP THREE - HISTORICAL

The third map is the historic map. It denotes, as the name implies, significant historic locations – the first courthouse, the first settlers, the first church, early historical occurrences and influences. What is the nature of the history – peaceful or violent, godly or godless? Was there, in the history of the city, some noble act or on the contrary, some egregious happening, that marred the community history? Was there some act of unrighteousness or injustice? A shocking homicide or trauma to the area? This data can usually be found in at the library, historical society or the newspaper office.

In Miami, they conducted a study of the county's history from the middle 1500's. They noted war sites, massacre locations, Indian burial mounds, race riots and the location of the original houses of prostitution. They also tracked major traumas to the people and the land. For example – meteorological, major hurricanes; financial, the collapse of Eastern Airlines; social, the Cuban immigration; social, a particularly bizarre murder.

Pay attention to architecture – is it unusual? What about statues, sculptures, paintings, other public works of art? Are there both public and private works of art – on or in front of buildings? Is their nature obvious, significant, and telling in some way?

MAP FOUR – THE CHURCH MAP

The fourth map might be the Church map. Team members should visit the churches, pray for them, and note the church on the map according to denominational or theological affiliation and their major *ethnos* group.

The group will readily see where churches are located and where they are not prospering, and that data should be correlated to a potential impact on neighborhoods, because of presence or absence of life-giving congregations.

As you create your map, you may want to distinguish between the types of churches -

- Churches (Generally)
- Evangelical/Pentecostal Churches (Special Note)
- Mega Churches – 1000 or more (Special Note)
- Ministry Outreach Centers
- Para-Church Offices/Centers/Denominational Centers/ Ministry Administration

ADDITIONAL MAPS

In addition to these maps, spiritual mappers might want to consider the following as well (Or make sure they are covered. Some are referenced above, but deserve special note):

- Murder Sites (Referenced in Map 3)
- Strongholds/High Poverty Areas
- High Crime Areas
- Robberies
- Gang Territories
- Drug Activities/Known Drug Sites

- Significant Monuments (Reference in Map 3)
- Historical Sites – Negative Implications (Map 3)
- Elementary/Middle/High Schools – Differentiate between public and private (Map 2)
- University/College Campuses/Vocational Schools (Map 2)
- Check-Cashing Locations/Exploitation of the Poor
- Bars – Level 1: Old fashioned bar; Level 2: Bar with Food; Level 3: Upscale Bar (i.e. Applebees, restaurant - family like atmosphere with bar).
- Liquor Stores
- Abandoned Buildings
- Industrial/Manufacturing Centers/Primary Community Employers (Is the activity godly? Are the owners/leaders godly? Is the work environment godly? Do Christians work there? What influence are they allowed to have?
- Spiritual mappers should also note the location of points of light, places of hope!
- Historic Places – Positive Implications (Whether they are Marked or Not) – Map 3.
- Government Offices – Local, County, State – Map 2.
- Police and Fire Stations
- Courthouses – Map 2.
- Malls/Shopping Areas (Types of Stores/Presence or Absence of Christian Witness).

Just a quick tip - do not put too many categories on one map! If the map gets too crowded, you will lose focus and miss any strategies the mapping is revealing. Pin only locations that have been verified. In addition, the verification should be sufficiently adequate to assure, with a certain level of reliability, that the location is being appropriately characterized. You want to produce a work of excellence, one in which leaders can have confidence.

Resources that can be used are:

- Yellow Pages - Look under Churches, Religious Organizations, Religious Goods, Metaphysicians, Clubs, Nightclubs, Bookstores, Video Stores, News Dealers, Clinics (Abortion), Psychics, Palmists. Remember to verify by making a phone call or visit. Some may have closed or moved.

- City Newspapers – Do not miss small neighborhood papers. Specialty newspapers published by such groups as New Age movements, the GLBT community, occult networks, and specialty publications for 'singles, swingers, swappers'. [Caution: Be aware of the darkness, but do not study it.] Newspaper archives – can be invaluable (Search a hundred years ago and see how faith and the Church was treated, etc.).

- Bulletin Boards – Health food stores. New Age bookstores. College campus bulletin boards.

- Libraries and historical societies. History books. Museums. Historic sites and markers.

- City Halls or Chambers of Commerce - Many have "New Resident" packets with a wealth of information. You will also find out what the city is officially promoting, how it advertises itself.

- Land Records – Who were the earliest settlers? Who granted the land rights? Who owns/owned certain property? Look for unusual borders/boundaries.

- Reconnaissance - Drive the city. Do it section by section. Notice the barriers, the ways freeways chop up the city. You are better to do this in pairs or triplets, for confirmation and protection. Remember the enemy knows you are invading his territory.

The Los Angeles Police Department has a refrigerated morgue where hundreds of young bodies are stored and stacked on shelves with a tag on their toe that reads, "Unidentified". They are kept for three months, and then cremated. Most are never claimed.[58] The number of runaway or throwaway kids is epidemic. Hollywood alone may be home to more than 20,000 of them. Each night, thousands are on the street.[59] There are 150,000 known gang members in Los Angeles alone. Nine out of ten have had a brush with the law by the age of eighteen. By the age of twenty, 60% are dead or in prison.[60] Such facts are rarely published. What pain exists in your city that is hidden? Who are your throwaways?

The group will need to secure a PO Box. You may want to use a fictitious name or only an initial and a name. This address will be used for literature or subscriptions.

There were times that the Miami team would go directly into some obliviously non-Christian setting. For example, in their area, the homosexual community has established its own Chamber of Commerce and hold meetings monthly to promote gay-owned business and businesses. Two team members became regulars at the meeting. They would quietly sit and listen. They were never asked to express their sexual preference. At each meeting, announcements, for example, regarding the opening of new 'bed and breakfast' locations that were gay fronts were made public. Homosexual clubs that were active were announced. Other pro-gay initiatives were unveiled.

Team members went to the Satanic and New Age bookstores. There they would take note not only of books and materials available, but also of the bulletin board, loaded with flyers and notices about speakers, musicians or conferences that were planned and being promoted. In some cases, they found when and where 'coven' meetings were being held, new groups being formed, what psychic fairs or events were coming to town, etc.

The late Dianne Buker, the lead researcher for the Miami Spiritual Mapping Project noted, "The Father asked me once, 'if you knew for sure that a thief was coming to your home on a particular day, at a particular time, would you leave the house unattended?' I, of course responded, 'No Sir, I would not.' He then said, 'Whenever you know a thief (an assignment from the kingdom of darkness) is coming into your county, you (someone in the army of the Lord) should be there.'" When the Nation of Islam comes to town. Or a decidedly obvious antichristian singing group or comedian (Example: the Grateful Dead). Or there is a New Age or Psychic Fair – should intercessors be there? The intercessors do not have to attend the event, pay the admission, immerse themselves in the darkness, but they do need to take a position in intercession in reference to the event and its potentially damaging impact on the community. Damage that is often invisible immediately afterwards. The spiritual damage manifests later in attitudes and actions, life decisions and direction.

Intercessors should be neither intimidated by the darkness nor enchanted by it. The focus is on the Lord, in reference to the needs of those who are agents of the darkness – and the souls they will influence. And on the community and the need to draw the line for righteousness and that can happen only by Divine intervention. *"As the bird by wandering, as the swallow by flying, so the curse causeless shall not come" (Proverbs 26:2).* Stay connected to the team. Do not allow isolation. Corporate prayer times should be agreed upon then kept. Never forsake personal time in your prayer closet.

The Cost of Spiritual Mapping

This project will demand a fair amount of finances. The preliminary expenses will include the purchase of maps, clear contact paper to cover them, creating layered looks, foam boards to mount them, straight pins with colored paper flags and file folders for the actual data. You may want to laminate the maps. In use, they endure a substantial amount of "wear and tear". Mounting them on foam boards make the data most visible and secure, even if a bit awkward. Straight-pins can be used to hold small labels enabling the ability to distinguish quickly the various items or categories.

However, the cost of not doing spiritual mapping work means we are working and living in battle zones as if it were peacetime. We are blind and oblivious to the nature of the harvest field, the tactics of the Evil One, the degree to which evil and resistance to the gospel is entrenched in the city – relational networks of influential citizens who are committed to promoting their religion free brand of community life. We do not know the depth and breadth of the 'web of iniquity' that is over the city. We sow our seed – without studying the terrain or the condition of the soil. We cast our nets without an awareness of what might be lurking under the surface of the water. We choose ignorance.

Note: This chapter appears here by permission. It is the third of four chapters on Spiritual Mapping that appear in the Praying Church Handbook, Volume IV, scheduled for release in the fall, 2014.

I am deeply indebted to Mission Miami for sharing so many insights from their journey. Further, I am indebted to the late Dianne Buker, spiritual mapper extraordinaire, for releasing this data from her work in the city and permission to use it.

---

58   Joy Dawson, Intercession – *Thrilling and Fulfilling* (Seattle, WA: YWAM; 1997), 67.
59   Ibid, 65.
60   Ibid, 70.

SECTION FOUR
Organizational Templates

All of these organizational templates
are available for download
at www.pc2ln.org.

— *Examples* —

Note: These are only intended to be models. The
movement is not so much organizational, as it is
organic. It is dynamic and relational, and yet, even
organizations have structure.
Hope this helps you start your journey!

Community Prayer Connect Teams

An idea whose time has come ...

The Prayer Connect Community Leadership Network (PC²LN) is intended to be a grass-roots group of community prayer leaders. The concept is to connect and envision, to mobilize local prayer leaders who are often divided denominationally and even by prayer-emphasis, though neither in heart or central purpose.

Denominations and national prayer organizations issue prayer challenges, release programs, and different emphases, many of which are wonderfully resourced, but typically adopted only in the context of a given stream. These noble efforts are embraced in pockets that are too sparsely concentrated, and mobilize too few people to have the kind of impact needed to spark awakening in the land.

Many local prayer leaders are advocates for one particular prayer ministry. They lead a one-cause prayer effort or an annual prayer event. Another emphasis may mobilize a wholly different sector of churches in the community. A greater level collaboration and unity is needed at the grassroots level to create a seamless community-by-community saturated prayer effort.

A bottom-up movement is needed. One that honors national prayer organizations and denominational loyalties, but for the sake of the kingdom, and in response to the present generational need of the nation, collaborates locally to blanket the community with prayer aimed at a Great Awakening. The resources clearly exist, but the relational infrastructure at the grassroot level necessary to mobilize across denominational lines and also synergize, locally, the various prayer initiatives, does not now exist.

The Prayer Connect Community Leadership Network could be that vehicle. The idea is an effort that is envisioned and resourced 'nationally', but owned and driven 'locally'. Vision and resources are often national, but the flash

The culture of the movement would be geometric, not hierarchical. ➧

point of revival and the place of tactical adaptation are local. As a network, the culture of the movement would be geometric, not hierarchical. The national construct would facilitate the flow of information, innovation, across community and state boundaries.

PURPOSE: Prayer Connect Community Leadership Networks will form to create a seamless prayer process owned and directed by the prayer leaders in every community in North America in consultation with lead pastors.

MISSION: The mission of the Prayer Connect Community Team movement is to synergize and facilitate community prayer efforts in collaboration with national/state/regional prayer organizations and other PC²LNs, to improve the spiritual and moral condition of both churches and cities through a unified, strategic and seamless prayer process aimed at edifying the saints and evangelizing cities.

VISION: Imagine a prayed-for city - systematic prayer walks, strategic prayer mapping and tactical prayer deployment. Imagine city/county leaders prayed for, and every school adopted for prayer. Imagine stronger churches praying for smaller churches; suburban-inner city prayer partnerships. Imagine identified, trained and teamed, directed and debriefed intercessors. Imagine prayer focused on both pain and promise. Imagine systematically identified praying Christians in every neighborhood. Imagine prayer efforts that engaged all the churches and organizations, instead of a hit-and-miss hodge-podge of poorly led and supported prayer efforts. Imagine seamless, year-round, 24-7 prayer process and strategy to mobilize prayer for the whole community.

GOALS: The seven goals of a Prayer Connect Community Leadership Network are as follows –

1. To pray – and nurture community prayer leaders, pastors and congregations as houses of prayer.
2. To coordinate a collaborative year-round prayer process.
3. To ensure that the city is a prayed-for community, including city leaders.
4. To press prayer into every vocational and tribal sector of the community.
5. To encourage the proliferation of community prayer groups.
6. To identify intercessors in the community who can be mobilized for prayer efforts aimed at a Great Awakening.
7. To consider strategies to insure that every home, every family, is a prayed-for family.

Prayer Connect Community Teams are intended to raise the level of community prayer by connecting, envisioning, resourcing and empowering local prayer leaders through unity and collaboration that expands the local prayer movement. The effort is facilitated nationally but owned and driven locally. Currently, excellent prayer resources exist, but tend to be adopted only in the context of a given stream. Though noble, these efforts affect sparsely concentrated pockets and mobilize too few people to spark widespread awakening. Local prayer leaders are often advocates for a one-cause prayer initiative; further, whole community sectors remain unengaged by national prayer efforts. Greater collaboration and unity at the community level could create seamless community-based, saturated prayer efforts aimed at a Great Awakening. The national resources clearly exist, but a community relational infrastructure does not; the components are present, but national vision and trans-local support are necessary. The movement would be geometric, not hierarchical. The national construct would facilitate the flow of information, innovation and offer implementation options. Local prayer leaders would continue their allegiance to various national prayer initiatives but do so in the fellowship of a larger community-wide prayer construct.

Who Serves on the Prayer Connect Community Leadership Network?

The Prayer Connect Community Leadership Network should be constituted by representatives of recognized national, state or regional prayer initiatives (National Day of Prayer representative, Global Day of Prayer, Moms in Prayer, Meet Me at the Pole, Intercessors for America, Awakening America Alliance) and by the prayer leaders of local congregations. At-large members should be considered as well, especially, those with a reputation for prayer and intercession. In addition, a pastor advisory team of at least three pastors is recommended.

In this sense, the PC²LN is self-constituting.

Constituting Questions:

1. Do we have a significant number of the representatives of national prayer organizations active in our community at the table?
2. Do we have denominational diversity at the table?
3. Do we have geographic diversity at the table (someone from every town/community at the county level, every community/city sector at the municipal level)?
4. Is the PC²LN consistent with the ethnic profile of our community?
5. Do we have men and women? Young and Old? Advocates for youth and children's prayer?
6. Do we have pastors and laypersons? Both the Ezra (church/pastors) and Nehemiah (marketplace/vocational tribes) streams?
7. Do we have veteran intercessors?

When Does The PC²LN Meet?

The Prayer Network should meet, not less than quarterly. Prayer calendar activities should be projected at least a year in advance.

In addition to regular quarterly meetings, the Prayer Network may develop 'action teams' working on specific prayer initiatives in intervening weeks and months. In some cases, these 'action teams' already exist. They are the leadership teams of existing prayer efforts who would benefit from a larger and broader coalition to assist their further efforts. The goal of the PC²LN is not to direct, but to encourage, aid and create a forum for collaboration for these efforts. In other areas, new action teams will develop new initiatives.

What Does The PC²LN Specifically Do?

It networks and collaborates. It creatively knits resources together for the benefit of the community. It mutually empowers. Using national prayer events and resources, the PC²LN commits to support various prayer events. The PC²LN is a representative organization. For example, the National Day of Prayer representative is appointed by that organization, as are leaders of other prayer ministries. Local church prayer leaders are appointed by the congregation.

The PC²LN is a network of duly appointed prayer leaders. All of whom would continue in their role, but now in the context of and with the collaboration of the entire community prayer network. For example, the local Prayer Network may now consider how, for example, one prayer event might be positioned to support a subsequent community-based prayer effort. The role of the Prayer Network is to synergize and unify current prayer efforts, drawing from the resources and expertise of national organizations and leaders.

Of course, not all prayer organizations are 'event' driven. Some are ongoing and relational. Others are cause or issue driven. The Prayer Network becomes the place in which events are used to catalyze on-going relational and purpose driven prayer groups, and the various prayer groups, along with collaborating congregations, become the pools from which people are drawn to support community-wide prayer events.

These events are flashpoints. The goal, in reality, is in the ability to nurture at-home, daily, to-be-like-Jesus transformational prayer, until the entire community feels the impact of the incarnational presence of Christ.

What Could Be Done?

1. Out of these networks could emerge a core of leaders whose trans-organizational unity (Psalm 133, John 17) is adequate to sustain a move of God in a given community.

2. Out of these networks could emerge a strategic process, and not merely tactical events – to measure the light density in every corner of the city/county.

3. Out of these networks we could strategically deploy intercessors.

4. With these networks, we could connect, through police/ sheriff chaplaincy officers, and offer the gift of prayer in troubled areas, high crimes areas, to people in pain, need, etc.

5. With these prayer networks, we could solicit prayer covering for the Adopt-a-Badge programs.

6. With these networks, we could mobilize prayer for every school in the community. Adopt a school.

7. With these networks, we could mobilize prayer, neighborhood by neighborhood.

8. With these networks, we could move toward 24-7 prayer in every community throughout the nation.

9. With these networks, we could give prayer support to struggling churches, church plants, inner city churches, lonely pastors, their wives and more.

10. With these networks, we could penetrate the cultural-vocational tribes that make up a community (Government [Judicial, Representative, Executive], Education, Social Services, Media, Arts and Entertainment, Commerce, Finance and Banking, Manufacturing, Tourism and Travel, Medical, etc.) By mobilizing and teaming intercessors, we could gain access to spiritual information, from their seasons as watchmen on the wall.

11. With the prayer networks, any emergency in the county could be covered immediately in prayer, with intercessors deployed.

12. With these prayer networks, we could develop strategic plans to prayer walk the entire county, regularly; to deploy prayer mission teams to pray at places of pain and

promise, light and darkness.

13. By linking prayer and compassion-based ministries, we could not only serve the needy with commodities, but with the gift of prayer.

14. By linking prayer and evangelism, we can pray for doors to be open into which the gospel is shared.

15. And more ...

Long Term Prayer Connect Network Benefits
Examples of Joint Endeavors

A RELATIONAL CONSTRUCT TO MOVE LOCAL PRAYER FORWARD

1. What we are after is a 'relational construct' of prayer stewardship at the county/city/community level. Connections that would last until Jesus comes. We want to resource and empower PC²LNs, connecting them with national prayer organizations, encouraging their development of a seamless prayer process for their entire city, a 24-7 prayer effort.

QUARTERLY COMMUNITY PRAYER LEADERS NETWORK GATHERINGS

2. In each community, the ideal is every prayer organizational representative at the same table, along with local church prayer leaders. This group, in some communities, could be quite large. We would suggest that they gather in the same room at least four times (quarterly) a year, planning and praying for their community. In addition, these gatherings would

provide a venue for learning about their joint resources and vision, as well as the needs of the community.

SERVANT LEADER TEAM

3. A smaller sub-set of that council would form a servant-leader team that would meet not less than monthly. They would provide humble, but executive leadership for a long-term prayer strategy, focused on their community and aimed at Great Awakening Transformation leverage points.

AN INTERCESSORS NETWORK

4. We want to encourage them to identify and find movement and venues to gather intercessors across the whole community/city/county. We want to identify intercessors, team them, mobilize them, deploy and debrief them. We would encourage a systematic adoption process – every geographic region of the city prayed for; every one of the eight or more sectors (so-called seven mountains), with identified and imbedded or adoptive intercessors; places of pain and darkness, adopted by intercessors.

CITY-SECTOR NETWORKS

5. Further, we want to encourage the mobilization and gathering of intercessors and Bible-reading Christians in every one of these sectors – to know one another, to adopt their sector as a mission field, to commit to be salt and light in

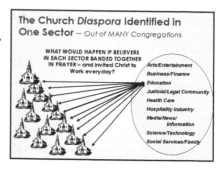

The Church *Diaspora* Identified in One Sector – *Out of MANY Congregations*

WHAT WOULD HAPPEN IF BELIEVERS IN EACH SECTOR BANDED TOGETHER IN PRAYER – and invited Christ to Work everyday?

Arts/Entertainment
Business/Finance
Education
Judicial/Legal Community
Health Care
Hospitality Industry
Media/News/Information
Science/Technology
Social Services/Family

that sector, to develop a plan to make that sector a prayed over sector. These, unlike the Sunday congregational gatherings led by 'Ezra's' (pastors), connect not once a week, but almost every day, Monday through Friday. This is where the light meets the darkness, the salt preserves and catalyzes. This is the Nehemiah stream, that construct of church, that we have not mobilized, and yet the one most promising if we desire to reach our culture. It is the church in a different construct, two or three gathered in his name. It crosses denominational lines. It defers to pastors, and yet it must be by and large, lay led. It is the organized church (Sunday), realigned and freshly constituted, reaching into areas the organized church cannot reach, in ways no program can touch. It goes where clergy garbs are no longer permitted. Where formal prayer is considered out-of-place. It is neither facility based nor program driven. Still, this is the church, scattered and sown. This is Nehemiah's stream, touching the broken places in the city, rebuilding, and digging through the rubble.

> Remember, salt works only if there is contact. Even if the church is doing a good job in the light area, it often suffers in the salt area. Salt has to meet decay, and by its power, quietly prevent it.
>
> ➡ Bob Waymire

STORY

Five Christian families in the same neighborhood became concerned about how to serve and more effectively witness. They made the decision to host a monthly informal dinner. All five shared in the cooking and rotated the dinner among their homes. They determined to do this for one year. They sent invitations throughout the neighborhood. Each evening was to be an open forum, neighbors sharing their concerns for the neighborhood – believers and unbelievers. In each meeting, two or three members of the Christian families briefly prayed for the needs that had been aired. The short-term partnerships proved to have long-term neighborhood implications.[61]

PC²LN Catalyst

General Role Description

The Catalyst is the John Knoxer of the PC²LN in any given community.

The Identity

In some ways, it would probably be ideal for the Catalyst to be a well-known pastor or prayer leader, the established leader of a para-church organization or a godly lay-business leader with name recognition and community credibility. However, that is not how God always works.

In some cases, the Catalyst may be an intercessor who deeply senses the need for Christian unity and collaborative prayer, who carries a burden to see their community bathed in prayer.

They may not be well known and may need the relational collateral of another person to convene an envisioning session. What they do have is a fire in their belly, a longing for widespread, seamless prayer in the community.

The Simplified Message to Community Prayer Leaders and Pastors

"What we are attempting to do individually, we can do more effectively together. Prayer and unity are partners. Some things may separate us as believers, but in the very least, we can pray together! *God promises a blessing when his people pray together* (Psalm 133). *And Jesus wanted us to be one – it was the centerpiece of his last prayer* (John 17). We have numerous prayer efforts already going in our community. How can we link these? How can we support one another in a unified prayer effort?"

Registering the Effort

Once an individual decides to move forward as a catalyst, they need to contact the PC²LN coordinating office via the website, by phone or email.

1. Determine whether or not an effort has already been launched in the community. If so, work cooperatively.
2. Register their name – as a catalyst.
3. Provide contact information.
4. Provide any credentials, connections – do you work with a national prayer organization (Helpful, but not necessary)? Are you a prayer leader for a local congregation?
5. Join vision calls, subscribe to the PC²LN ebulletin. Get connected.

Sharing the Vision

The Catalyst then engages other significant prayer leaders and pastors with the idea of the creating of a PC²LN. Hearing about this network, this person immediately senses its strategic relevance to the geographic city/county.

In some cases, an informal construct of prayer leaders may already exist, but no opportunity has been available for connecting the local team with a national network.

Using support materials, provided by the National Facilitator, the catalyst persistently shares the vision, beating the drum for the formation of a PC²LN. This vision sharing may be one-on-one. Or with small groups. The catalyst pursues potential conveners, men and women of prayer, along with him/herself, who have the relational collateral needed to call a larger envisioning meeting, and subsequently, a constituting meeting to launch the PC²LN.

The Catalyst

1. Shares the vision for a PC²LN.
2. Persists in connecting people of prayer and pastors.
3. Finds a team of three-to-five conveners, who will, together, call for envisioning meetings to consider the formation of a PC²LN.
4. Sees the project through to the constituting meeting.
5. Yields to the Holy Spirit and the will of the larger group when they are gathered and does not presume a leadership role. Retains a servant-heart. Refuses to manipulate the process.
6. Engages others with passion and yet with tenderness – let's God guide and direct the process. Exhibits patience, waiting for God's timing. May live through the death and rebirth of the vision – but is relentless in believing that the community will benefit from a PC²LN.

PC²LN Convening Team

General Role Description

The Convening Team is a group of leaders, drawn together with or by the Catalyst, the John Knoxer, who carried a vision to them for the creation of a PC²LN in their community.

The Identity

The Convening Team consists of a group of three-to-five Christian leaders who have a concern for prayer in their community. Together, they have the credibility and relational collateral to convene one or more envisioning sessions.

This Convening Team may consist of prayer leaders, pastors or other. They should represent some level of diversity. Ideally, they are ethnically diverse and from different streams of the Christian community. The prayer effort you want to mobilize should be broad enough for all Bible reading believers in the community and the churches they attend. It should embrace a variety of prayer styles and expressions, prayer focus areas and interests.

The Simplified Message to Community Prayer Leaders and Pastors

"What we are attempting to do individually, we can do more effectively together. Prayer and unity are partners. Some things may separate us as believers, but we can pray together! *God promises a blessing when his people pray together* (Psalm 133). *Jesus wanted us to be one – it was the centerpiece of his last prayer* (John 17). We have numerous prayer efforts already going in our community. How can we link these? How can we support one another in a unified prayer effort?"

Vision Casting Stage

With the Catalyst, the Convening Team senses the strategic relevance of the PC²LN to the city/county. They join their voices with the Catalyst, engaging other leaders and people of prayer.

Representatives of various prayer ministries in the identified geographic area are contacted. Vision is cast – informally. Congregations that have prayer ministry leaders are likewise envisioned. These sessions may be an informal meeting over a cup of coffee or formal vision-casting sessions complete with power-point. A systematic effort should be made to connect with all the divergent streams of Bible-reading believers in the area so that when a formal envisioning meeting occurs, it is a with a diversity of believers who are genuinely representative of the community and have collectively, the credibility to launch the endeavor. And still, that may be the first of many envisioning meetings in different venues, with different sectors of the prayer leadership constituency. The informal sharing escalates to formal vision-casting sessions – some occur in small groups, others among large groups, some in this or that stream. At times, you will find this necessary, before getting the divergent groups under the same roof. It will be very important to have endorsers early in the process, who echo the need for the PC²LN – among different denominational streams, ethnic streams, prayer ministry efforts, etc.

The Constituting Council

The vision-casting sessions lead to the constituting meeting. At this point, all relevant prayer leaders and ministries should have been envisioned.

A date is set for the Constituting Council. This organizational meeting should be about vision. It may take place over the course of a full day. It should creatively tell the story of what is already happening in the community in terms of prayer efforts and perhaps across the nation. In this case, it is a discovery fair, an educational experience designed to show the unseen, but valiant prayer efforts by individuals, organizations and congregations already happening in quiet disconnected ways. The day might be sprinkled with video segments, visuals, and stories. All these various pieces constitute the patch-work, which knitted together, has the potential to blanket the city in prayer.

This meeting will launch the actual process forward, including the commissioning of a leadership team, primary goals, some simple structural model that has the flexibility for expansion. Using support materials, available on-line, the envisioning and constituting meetings move the process of community prayer and unity forward.

It must be remembered that the members of the PC²LN are in their positions due to an appointment by national prayer organizations, local congregations and church agencies, or para-church entities. In some rare communities, there may be no formal national prayer effort – no National Day of Prayer representative, no Moms-in-Prayer group, no SYTP effort, etc. In such a case, the PC²LN will become very strategic in starting those efforts. Where such representatives do exist, every effort should be employed to get them to the table.

The group may need several sessions beyond this initial council gathering in order to approve a working organizational document. Samples are provided, both simple and complex. Some groups may choose to work informally, at least for a season, without a formal organizational constitution or set of by-laws. In some cases, a small team may be appointed to bring back originating articles.

The Leadership Team

At the Constituting Council, a Servant Leadership Team is chosen. Among them, a 'Moderator' for the leadership team, the cabinet and council gatherings is chosen. This leader will guide the general process, provide leadership at most meetings. It is important to find someone with a broad perspective, a person of prayer who also has huge leadership gifts. With the 'Moderator', a Vice-Moderator/Executive Assistant is found along with a Recording Secretary-Treasurer and three-to-five at-large members. Together, they constitute the Servant Leader Team for the PC²LN. The PC²LN may also create an advisory team of three-to-five individuals.

Ambassadors

Once the first team in any geographic region is chosen, they have the wonderful privilege of replicating their effort by assisting the formation of PC²LNs in adjacent communities. The more these efforts are conjoined, networked, the more synergy is possible.

Ambassadors should be selected who can envision catalysts and conveners in adjacent communities. These people serve informally. They use the strength of relational connections to further the PC²LN.

In any concentrated metropolitan area, a collage of PC²LNs working collaboratively would allow for specific township/city/county attention, and then by connection, multi-county, broad coalition efforts. The possibilities of such unity are almost unimaginable. No such prayer construct now exist in most cities.

STORY

When John and Cindi walked into the gym, they could hardly believe it. It looked like a small convention center. There was a rather festive greeting table, a handout with a diagram of displays and booths along with a schedule of events for the day. A welcoming hostess team greeted them, only one of whom they recognized. Only the day before, they had dropped off a few items for the ministry to which they were connected, but the gym looked nothing liked it presented today. Banners. Arrows. Even colored lights. Music was playing. And a crowd had already gathered.

They hurried to find the display table for the Child Advocacy Group, for whom they volunteered, but it was difficult to resist not stopping along the way – Young Christian Men, an organization they had never heard about; Salvation Army, that was familiar. There was an information table for the Crisis Pregnancy Center, the Urban Housing Agency, the Homeless Shelter, Abused and Battered Women, Family Counseling, the Reconciliation Initiative, the After-School

Watch Program, Meals on Wheels, Hospice, Un-reached People Outreach to Franklin County - there were unreached people here? There were displays for Care Coalitions, Bible distribution, Prayer Groups, Bible Study networks, men's and women's faith initiatives. There was even a Cops4Christ chapter. She was blown away by the diversity. There were more than fifty exhibits set up in the gym in rows. Over to one side was a snack bar. Clowns and young people dressed as Biblical characters wandered through the exhibit hall entertaining kids.

Every fifteen minutes, an emcee with a mobile microphone took a few minutes to describe what he saw at one of the booths and have the representative tell their story about what they were doing to impact the community. Every hour on the hour, the small stage was used for a more formal presentation about care agencies in the city. Three youth agencies were interviewed together; and then two women's outreaches; and then a special presentation of collaborative evangelism. All those participating knew it was a Christian event designed to make churches and their people more aware of community care options and to bring the leaders together to interact informally.

Almost a thousand people walked through the exhibits that day. Fifty sponsoring churches had distributed flyers and tickets to the event and urged their people to attend. Prizes and drawings enhanced the day. Each agency made a small contribution to defray the expenses, and together, they identified over two-hundred potential volunteers. One week following the event, these agency leaders met again for a working dinner. This time, they considered the impact of their recent coming together for their first every Community Care Fair, and how they might put feet on collaboration. They formed five Care Coalition Groups with general purposes – Children, Family Stability, Men's Issues, Senior Care, and the Homeless. Each cluster of potential care coalitions caucused, and planned to meet again and develop ideas on how to collaborate.

Brady Wilson, the organizer of the event told a reporter, "I think we leaped forward light years in behalf of the community today." Brady discovered that a similar event had been attempted a few years before, but faith groups had been specifically exempted from the event. This time, faith groups led the event, but they did not exclude secular organizations who chose to participate. "We can always work together for common cause. They do not have to share our beliefs in Christ for us to help a family who has just lost their home in a fire, and we do not have to stop believing because we care. This is a win-win for the community."

In the afternoon, even the mayor wandered through the exhibit hall and received a warm round of applause. The media covered the event with a friendly twist. Almost immediately, a small group of local corporations inquired about a funding mechanism gifts community wide assistance. Derek Rogers explained to Brady, "We give to specific community organizations, but many of us are believers, and to be able to give to a kind of community chest that funded a collaborative approach, multiple Christian organizations, that would be huge". We're not there yet," Brady confessed. "Well, maybe we can help you get there," Derek responded.

PC²LN Collaborating Pastors and Ministry Leaders Guidelines

Purpose: To create a collaborative effort, across the scope of the city/town/area/county, for unified prayer, revival and renewal for America. To support the prayer effort through ministry and congregational involvement in prayer and awakening, with a focus on prayer in the community, local church and multi-congregational events with participation in community prayer efforts.

The PC²LN initiative is a grass roots effort. National prayer organizations provide resources, but each community creates its own prayer and action strategy.

Church/Ministry Participation Goals:

1. Participate, as possible, in all the community prayer initiatives.

2. Conduct community leaders and pastoral prayer gatherings - day-long "prayer summits". Do focused prayer gatherings – business leaders, the medical community, teachers and educators, banks and finance sector leaders

with workers, family/social services, police and fire, the Judicial sector with attorneys, etc. Focus on personal, then community transformation.

3. Call men to pray – across the entire region. Then women, youth, even children. Hold prayer convocations.

4. Sponsor 'days of awakening!' – concentrated seasons of seeking and prayer-action focused on the community.

5. Participate in the nation-wide simultaneous prayer effort, Seek God for the City, in the season of Lent. Appoint an organizer. Look for prayer-walking guides on-line. These excellent reprintable guides have been prepared by Steve Hawthorne, noted for his expertise in this area, and President of Waymakers. Look for similar concentrated prayer efforts. Pray for the 10/40 window. Join the 30 days of prayer for the Muslim world. Retreats work best for these gatherings. Nothing less than a day is genuinely effective.

6. Join Ezra's and Nehemiah's in the area for prayer, pastors and marketplace (work-based prayer leaders) – through prayer gatherings, extensive prayer-walking efforts, prayer unity rallies, small-group (prayer cell) connections and the like.

7. Consider an annual Solemn/Sacred Assembly for your city.

8. Develop a strategy for a prayer meeting in every neighborhood in your community, between every couple at specific points during the year.

9. Encourage work-place gatherings of small prayer cells that aim at inviting the presence of God, in an intentional way, into every conceivable workplace environment in the city – the church scattered being the church!

10. Make your community a "prayed for" community, where an intentional process of prayer (the Great Commitment) is set in place – and out of that a focus on God's caring love (the Great Commandment), and then sharing the good news (the Great Commission).

Process:

1. Each county is part of a national grass-roots network that works in collaboration with the vision of members of the National Prayer Committee.

2. Each Moderator is to function in the context of a team – to resource pastors and Christian leaders, laity and para-church organizations, calling the Christian community to repentance and renewal as an example to the county and its cities, to fresh vision and vitality focused on Great Awakening.

3. Work to identify supporting and collaborating congregations in the county that will call their constituents to prayer and renewal.

4. Work with different denominations, pastors and para-church leaders, to ensure broad interdenominational support of the renewal efforts.

5. Develop a plan for comprehensive prayer walking – that blankets the community. [Imagine thousands of simultaneous prayer walks across the nation on 9-11!]

6. Develop a plan for marketplace-based prayer cell groups embedded throughout the community, praying quietly and passionately, at or near their workplaces during the week of awakening. Target time: Noon, daily.

7. Nurture the idea of on-going prayer and unity efforts in the community.

PC²LN Constituting Meeting and the Leadership Team

Purpose of the PC²LN: To create a collaborative effort, across the scope of the county/city/township (some definitive incorporated/unincorporated geographic area), for persistent prayer that aims at revival and renewal both in the local area and the nation. To support the local expressions of national prayer efforts laced with creative community prayer initiatives along with congregational involvement with a focus on pervasive prayer in the community, in local churches, and in every sector of the defined area. To provide leadership for community-wide prayer and renewal initiatives. To recruit and encourage. To resource prayer leaders, pastors and para-church leaders. To mobilize prayer in the defined community with a goal of 24-7-365 prayer.

While the PC²LN is a local mirror, to some degree, of the National Prayer Committee, it is primarily a grass roots effort. Various national prayer organizations provide resources, but each community creates its own prayer and action strategy.

The Constituting Meeting

The PC²LN consist of local representatives of national prayer organizations, denominational and local prayer organizations, para-church prayer leaders and intercessors, with the prayer leaders of local congregations. Duly appointed and recognized prayer leaders living in the community are invited to participate in the network. Prior to the constituting meeting, every effort should be made to engage and ensure the participation of all these leaders.

The Leadership Team

It is recommended that the PC²LN choose from among themselves a leadership team of 3-5 members in small communities, and as large as 8-12 in metropolitan zones.

This team should be identified early in the constituting process of the PC²LN. All prayer leaders of national organizations and local congregations, by their role and function, are members of the community-wide PC²LN, but a strategic team is necessary to meet more often and provide definitive leadership for the whole.

The PC²LN acting together 'lays hands' on those to be entrusted with the vision and the expansion of the prayer effort. These leaders are empowered by the trust of the larger council. In the beginning, the majority of those who are members of the PC²LN will be present by the appointment of others, as representatives of national prayer organizations and local congregations. By nature, the authority of the leadership team is necessarily relational. The leadership style is servant-based.

The Simplified Message to Community Prayer Leaders and Pastors

"We have created a PC²LN in our city – a place for prayer leaders to connect and support one another in an effort to see prayer events translated into a comprehensive prayer process. Our PC^{2}LN is the local expression of a national grass-roots prayer network whose desire is to see a blanket of prayer covering our entire country, community-by-community, a collage of like-minded networks throughout the country. Prayer and unity are partners. All of our smaller cities and towns have unique needs, but we also desire to see one united movement of prayer across our community/ county/region and the entire country. Prayer has been the catalyst for every nation-impacting Great Awakening in our history! God promises a blessing when his people prayer together (Psalm 133). The centerpiece of the last prayer of Jesus was our unity (John 17)."

Leadership Team Role

The PC^{2}LN Leadership Team guides the process of translating prayer events into a prayer process that seeks to mobilize and network prayer 24/7/365. It should become a servant to the prayer process – the Holy Spirit actually leading it, calling intercessors and believers to more consistent and fervent prayer.

The Leadership Team becomes the primary cheerleader and support team for every established prayer event in the city, and attempts to proliferate them, to multiply them, making the community a genuinely prayer-for area.

The Leadership Team of the PC^{2}LN may be formal or informal. Created materials should be reviewed and then adapted to fit the needs of the local community.

The Officers

The Officers should consist of a Moderator for both the PC^{2}LN gatherings and the Leadership Team. This individual is the point person for the prayer movement in the community. A vice-moderator or executive assistant should also be chosen, carefully considering the importance of unity and the role of this individual as a partner to the moderator. The number of officers may depend on the size of the city and the constituting council. The PC²LN may also choose a secretary-treasurer or elect to allow the Officer Core to choose a person for this role. Advisors may be the choice of the PC²LN or the Officer Core. (See the sample organizational chart).

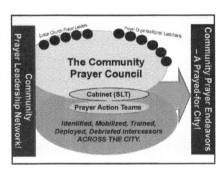

Specific Responsibilities and Qualifications of Leaders

1. Persons of prayer and moral character, team players.
2. Selected by the local PC²LN, commended by the appointment of a national prayer organization of which s/he serves as a local representative or by a commendation from a local pastor as a prayer leader in an area congregation, etc.
3. Agrees with the Lausanne theological declaration – evangelical in theology and missional in nature. (Appendix)
4. Capable of collaborating with all the various prayer efforts in the area in a non-partisan manner, and across denominational, ethnic and para-church lines to create a comprehensive collaborative effort.
5. "Agenda-free" in terms of motive – except for the noble goal of a "Great Awakening!" in the nation.

Moderator Responsibilities

The responsibilities of the Moderator include calling meetings of the Leadership Team and the PC²LN, providing agendas, and recording meetings. The PC²LN should meet at least 3-4 times annually. The Leadership Team should meet monthly (10 times annually). The Moderator is the leader for both groups and the custodian of the vision, though he may share or delegate that role.

He serves as a resource person and cheerleader to the various task-teams that lead different prayer efforts in the city.

As new prayer-initiatives are envisioned, new leaders will be identified and empowered. A sense of quantifiable vision and mission should emerge – with measurable goals. Such goals should be a stewardship priority for the Moderator.

Along with the PC²LN and the Leadership Team, the Moderator may recommend the creation of a number of ad-hoc committees.

Executive Assistant (Vice Moderator)

The Executive Assistant should be an active member of the PC²LN who exhibits dedication and strong leadership qualities. In the absence of the Moderator, the Executive Assistant would temporarily fulfill the Moderator's duties. Assistance to the moderator and task-force leaders, to ad hoc committees, as well as on-going prayer efforts would be a part of this role.

Leadership Team Members

Depending on the size of the area served and the membership of the PC²LN, 3-7 at-large members should be selected to serve along with the Moderator, Executive Assistant, Recording Secretary-Treasurer as Servant Leaders (SLT/Officer Core). All should meet the criteria above.

Advisors

Advisors are drawn from three sources. The two sectors of the Christian community – Ezra's (pastoral leaders) and Nehemiah's (community leaders), along with well-known and proven intercessors. Responsibilities of the advisors include attendance at Officer Meetings and significant participation in the community prayer effort. Involvement in the leadership processes. General prudent advice and godly counsel. Advocacy of the Prayer Council's vision to the larger pastoral and Christian business community. Assisting, as possible, in funding the community prayer effort. Note: Some PC²LN's may determine to use Advisors in a more passive role. Others may use them as active members of the Officer Core.

Leadership Team Duties:

1. To identify current prayer leaders, build a team, envision and cultivate a pervasive prayer movement in the local community.

2. To nurture the idea of on-going prayer and unity efforts in the community.

3. To identify supporting organizations and collaborating congregations that will call their constituents to prayer.

4. To promote the various prayer efforts for the community sponsored by national organizations, and do so together, through local ministries, and congregations.

5. To work with various denominations, pastors and para-church leaders, to ensure broad interdenominational support of prayer efforts.

6. To identify prayer resources for pastors and community organizations with prayer resources, especially those that call the Christian community to repentance and consecration as an example to the geographic area, to fresh vision and vitality focused on Great Awakening.

7. To be aware of the web-based resource materials, print out samples for distribution to pastors and other leaders. Encourage the use of the materials wisely and broadly.

8. To serve as a local expression of a national grass-roots network working in collaboration with the vision of the National Prayer Committee. And yet, the nexus of renewal always bubbles out of the heart of the individual – the Ezra (pastoral leader) or Nehemiah (civic/vocational/ professional/lay leader), or a Joel (prophetic/intercessory leader). With a sensitivity to national prayer efforts and events, understanding the value of unity and simultaneous prayer, allow the Holy Spirit to lead your local team in developing a vision and strategy for your area.

9. To provide reports of your community efforts and support in various prayer events.

10. To maintain a connection with national organizations through their representatives and the PC²LN network to hear about developments in other areas – and to share your plans with others. Let's keep the lines of communication open.

Leadership Cabinet

The real power of the prayer effort is endowed in those who lead specific prayer ministries. In order to synergize and expand the local prayer effort, the moderator, acting with the Leadership Team, may choose to name a 'Cabinet' consisting of leaders of strategic prayer initiatives who are not members of the Officer Core. The Cabinet should consist of different task-team leaders. They would meet with the Officer Core as needed, some seasonally, to connect the various components of the larger prayer effort.

PC²LN Moderator Guidelines

Moderator's General Role: To provide leadership for the PC²LN initiative in the local community. To recruit and encourage, and to mobilize prayer. To raise awareness of the deep spiritual need of the Church and our country. To seek God's forgiveness and an outpouring of His Spirit in a sweeping revival in the Church. To seek God's intervention in our nation to reverse our worsening moral decline and convert the lost. To unite believers in our communities in intense and intentional prayer toward those ends. To lay a foundation for continued local efforts toward united prayer and evangelism.

Qualifications:

1. A person who is commended by a life of prayer and Christian character, a born again disciple of Jesus Christ.
2. A representative of a national prayer organization or a duly appointed prayer leader of a local congregation or para-church ministry.
3. Commended by a pastor or Christian leader, chosen by

peers in a constituting meeting.

4. Agrees with the Lausanne theological declaration – evangelical in theology and missional in nature.

5. Capable of collaborating with all the different prayer efforts in the area in a non-partisan manner, and across denominational, ethnic and para-church lines to create a broad collaborative effort.

6. "Agenda-free" in terms of motive – except for the noble goal of a "Great Awakening!" in the nation.

Specific Duties:

1. To convene a PC²LN composed of community prayer leaders.

2. To embrace and carry the vision of the PC²LN – to articulate it, grow it, engage it, and see its fulfillment. To envision a prayed-for city. And systematically plan to see that vision fulfilled.

3. To provide prayerful servant leadership to the entire PC²LN, including the Leadership Team, Cabinet, ad hoc and standing committees, the strategic vision and planning team. To expand the prayer process creatively, by multiplying competent and mature community prayer leaders and networking them. To identify supporting and collaborating prayer leaders in community congregations that will trumpet the call to prayer and consecration.

4. To promote unified prayer efforts aimed at a Great Awakening. Nurture the idea of on-going prayer and unity efforts in the community.

5. To be a friend to pastors and community leaders – a prayer partner with community intercessors and people of prayer. To locate and create resources for prayer to be used by pastors and Christian leaders, laity and para-church organizations in calling the Christian community to repentance and consecration as an example to the community,

300

to fresh vision and vitality focused on Great Awakening.

6. To be Spirit-led, guided by Scripture and informed by underlying research regarding the history, present trends and plans in the community, its purpose and promise, its problems and possibilities – to discern with leaders the spiritual destiny on the city.

7. To support existing prayer efforts by para-church, denominational and congregational groups, national prayer movements and local efforts.

8. To engage spiritual mappers and interface intercessors who are systematically informed with helpful data to direct their praying as watchers on the wall of the city, and then debriefed.

9. To envision the professional and vocational tribes of the city as an important focus for week-day prayer. To work to create a culture of prayer in the city.

10. To refuse to cocoon –to keep the local prayer effort connected to the region, the state, and the nation.

11. To keep the national facilitator in information loops, emails, etc. To import and export prayer ideas. Confirm contact data on the web data-base. Provide a listing of team members and their contact data. File a report on the success of your efforts with the appropriate national ministry. Provide the Prayer Council National Office with stories of renewal, unity and breakthrough.

12. To develop a budget for the local prayer effort.

The PC²LN Moderator and Core Team

T he Moderator and Core Team must subscribe, above all else, to the mission of the PC²LN.

The mission of the PC²LN is to synergize and facilitate prayer efforts in collaboration with national/state/regional prayer organizations in the nation, typically, the local representatives of member organizations of the National Prayer Committee and others they invite to the table, working with pastors, ministry leaders and congregational prayer leaders, along with intercessors and believers in every community to improve the spiritual and moral vitality of the congregations and the community through a unified, strategic prayer network that unwraps a seamless prayer process aimed at edifying the saints and evangelizing the cities.

General Qualifications for Servant Leaders (Officers)

1. A stellar reputation as a Christian believer and a person of prayer.

2. A representative of a national prayer organization with credentials and commendations, or a denominational prayer leader resident in the community, or a pastoral/ prayer leader representing a local congregation or ministry.

3. A dedication to and active involvement in the community-wide prayer ministry as determined by the members of the cabinet.

4. Faithfulness in attendance at meetings and community prayer efforts.

5. Exemplification in life, of the principles and goals of the PC^{2}LN and its parallel nation-wide double, the National Prayer Committee.

6. Experience in 'prayer' ministry and service on the PC^{2}LN, if not the Cabinet, are preferred for the Servant Leader Team (Officer Core).

Specific Qualifications and Responsibilities of the Servant Leader Team Members (Officers) Moderator

1. Calling and leading the SLT meetings at least once per month (Approximately 10 times a year).

2. Creating an agendas for the meetings – adequate planning and preparation.

3. Providing vision and leadership for the movement.

4. Relating to the Prayer Team leaders of existing prayer ministries.

5. Creatively envisioning addition Prayer Team leaders who lead new community-focused prayer efforts.

6. Encouraging goals for the expansion of the prayer effort by every team. Setting and keeping track of annual and semi-annual ministry goals.

7. Responsible, in cooperation with the council, to provide oversight for the creation of ad-hoc committees.

Vice-Moderator/Executive Assistant

1. Regular attendance at all meetings including temporary fulfillment of Moderator's duties in his or her absence.
2. Assistance to the moderator and task-force leaders, to ad hoc committees, as well as on-going prayer efforts.

Recording Secretary-Treasurer

1. Creation of records of Servant Leader Team meetings, Council and Cabinet meetings, and others as directed.
2. Distribution of minutes, task-assignments, etc.
3. Assistance to the moderator and task-force leaders, to ad hoc committees, as well as on-going prayer efforts as requested.
4. Accounting of funds, receipts and distributions as directed by the Moderator, consistent with Cabinet/Council policy.
5. Regular financial reports.

Members At Large

Depending on the size of the area served and the membership of the PC²LN, 3-7 at-large members should be selected to serve as Servant Leaders (Officers).

Members may also be representatives of Prayer Organizations or themselves Prayer Team leaders or members.

They should meet the criteria of Officer Standards described in Section V.

Advisors

Advisors are drawn from three sources – Ezra's (pastoral leaders) and Nehemiah's (community-based spiritual lay leaders), along with known and proven intercessor(s).

Responsibilities of the advisors will include:

*   Attendance at Officer Meetings and significant participation in the community prayer effort.
*   Involvement in the leadership processes.
*   General prudent advice and godly counsel.
*   Advocacy to the larger pastoral and Christian business community.
*   Assisting, as possible, in funding the community prayer effort.

Note: Some PC²LN's may determine to use Advisors in a more passive role. Others may use them as active members of the Officer Core.

Meetings

The Officers Should meet monthly, if at all possible (ten times annually).

Some Officer Meetings may be conducted in conjunction with meetings with the Cabinet.

The PC²LN Expanded Leadership Team

General Purpose: To work with the PC²LN Leadership Team (Officer Core) to provide comprehensive leadership for the community-wide renewal and awakening effort. To serve as assigned, in collaboration with other team members, with the goal of an effective pervasive prayer covering in and over the entire area.

The Identity

The Expanded Leadership Team is comprised of point leaders for various prayer efforts who are not members of the Officer Core. Some may serve national ministries. Others may have been identified and empowered locally, by the PC²LN, as new prayer efforts are initiated.

The Cabinet may expand and contract. These leaders of different prayer projects and efforts are invited to join the Leadership Team, depending on the seasonal prayer activities being planned and promoted. The expansion of this team is dynamic, often seasonal and situational.

The Cabinet

The real power of the prayer effort is endowed in those who lead specific prayer ministries. In order to synergize and expand the local prayer effort, the moderator, acting with the Leadership Team, may choose to name a 'Cabinet' consisting of leaders of strategic prayer initiatives who are not members of the Officer Core. The Cabinet should consist of different task-team leaders. They would meet with the Officer Core as needed, some seasonally, to connect the various components of the larger prayer effort.

Component Elements of the Cabinet
Publicity

1. Work to open avenues for promoting community awareness of the area-wide, multi-denominational prayer effort.
2. Connect with local congregations, Christian-entities, Charitable efforts that express Christ's love, various denominational offices, para-church ministries, particularly those with a prayer component, to assist in awareness of the community-wide prayer movement and local prayer events.
3. Be aware of web-based support materials for promoting various prayer events – a great place to look is the National Prayer Committee site or www.prayercouncils.org.
4. Release press announcements through PSA channels, television and radio, to insure general community awareness of prayer events and efforts.
5. Connect with the local ministerial associations, some county-wide, some city-wide to ensure their awareness and solicit their support.
6. Find the local representatives of state and national prayer organizations – NDOP leaders, SYATP, Aglow, Concerned

Women, Moms in Touch, Prayer Summits (International Renewal Ministries), Mission America initiatives, Global Day of Prayer leaders, Intercessors for America, Cry Out America leaders, and various denominational, and state prayer and unity organizations. Assist as possible.

Congregational Involvement Advocate

1. Seek the involvement of all the Bible-believing congregations in your community, but set a baseline for the involvement of at least 20-25% of the congregations in the defined area. Work toward some level of diversity – geographically (every neighborhood/sector of the definitive area represented, denominationally and ethnically. Consider a pastor's envisioning event to solicit congregational involvement from across the area. Get an audience before the ministerial association. [Why 20-25%? Consider it a bare minimum – but also remember, about three-five percent are visionaries. Another 12-15% are early adapters, meaning they more quickly than others see the benefit of trends and movements. Identify the visionaries and early adapters who will advocate for concerted and unified prayer – and with them, the others will come!]

2. Work at creating a broad coalition of evangelical churches that represent the geographic, denominational and ethnic diversity of your county.

3. Encourage pastors to own the process of calling their constituents to repentance and renewal, through community-wide spiritual renewal.

4. Study the resources available on-line in order to better promote prayer events in local churches, specifically resource materials that can be used by the pastors of the churches – bulletin inserts, preaching-teaching materials.

5. Transform public prayer events into a process aimed at spiritual renewal and awakening.

6. Call pastors together for periodic prayer, envisioning and information. Allow the pastors to creatively shape collaborative renewal efforts across the city/county. Envision new pastors who regularly come into the community (As many as 20% of all churches change pastors annually).

7. Get a broad buy-in for public prayer efforts.

Public Prayer Rallies/Resource Assistant

1. Many community prayer rallies and events are local expressions of national prayer organizations which provide program resources and support materials. These national prayer event websites will usually contain program information offered as a resource for the local program team. Any program going forth under a national prayer ministry should reflect the essence of the recommended program and the spirit of the particular event. The goal of the PC^{2}LN is to make these even more successful and to lace the various prayer events together, translating them into a process.

2. Each prayer effort should be an opportunity for an earnest heart-felt collective plea for divine forgiveness, first with the Christian community in view, then the geographic area and the nation – a plea for a Great Awakening.

3. Prayer events should have historical elements – our identity as a people, our Christian heritage. And contemporary elements – our current moral and spiritual crisis. And Biblical elements – the hope for a nation that reckons with God. And the concern for one that does not do so!

4. The public prayer programs should be well-planned, and yet flexible – allowing for "God-moments!" in which he might break-in and break our hearts for the nation. Develop a time-line for elements of the event, but be open to spontaneous Spirit-moments. Such times are the sparks that can ignite a Great Awakening!

5. The participant-leaders should be reflective of the diversity desired in the Christian community, without being driven by political correctness. Authentic leaders, pastors and laymen, political and community leaders, should participate – but all who do so should share a heart for vital spiritual and moral renewal in the county.

6. Work to make prayer events – 'prayer' events, not preaching rallies. Avoid sermons, including long prayers. Sponsor community prayer services.

7. Coach the "pray-ers" at your events to pray, really pray, and not to make statements or declarations, to be sensitive to the multi-denominational nature of the event. Have them pray "brief 1-2 minute prayers from the heart! Focus on our sins – the sins of the church. The community needs to hear us repenting "for us" and not "for them." Avoid sermonizing prayers.

8. Have a small team of intercessors praying for the event even as it progresses – quietly and without fanfare.

Youth Prayer Coordination

1. Solicit the involvement of youth pastors and local para-church leaders, SYATP, Youth for Christ, Christian Schools – and release them to plan youth prayer events and form youth prayer groups.

2. Consider a "Midnight Fire!" rallies. Kids like to stay out late. Encourage soul-searching prayer aimed at personal repentance and the life-transformation of young people.

3. Consider prayer events at or near schools.

4. Link local church youth groups for prayer efforts.

5. Don't forget the nearest campus or university.

Para-church Organizational Involvement

1. Discover the para-church organizations at work in your

community. These organizations are not as easily located as churches, but they often work across denominational lines and can be critical partners in the prayer mobilization process. Many of them have prayer teams – or need them.

2. In addition, denominational leaders or associational offices may also be partners in the process allowing you to mobilize a number of congregations more readily.

3. Para-church organizations often move more easily in and out of the work-place environment. And they can be great assistants in the grass-roots prayer mobilization process.

4. Some representatives of para-church organizations will not have an office or phone listing. You will need to look for them through relational channels. Key partners for our process include the local representatives of such organizations as: County/City National Day of Prayer Coordinator; Global Day of Prayer Coordinator; SYATP; Moms-in-Touch; Intercessors for America; Prayer Summit leaders; Mission America members and unique state prayer movements.

5. A gathering for para-church leaders and pastors is a great idea. Announce your event. Gain their support and collaboration.

Christian Business Leaders

1. Bill Bright called them the 'Seven Mountains' of culture. Each city has them – sectors of city/county life. Think of these as professional/vocational tribes, each with leaders, with ranks, with tenure, with criteria for advancement, licensure and educational training, etc. - Government (County Commissioners, Mayors, City Councils, etc.), Judicial and Police/Sheriff with Fire/Safety personnel, Business, Banking/Finance, Retail/Services Sector, Manufacturing, Agriculture/Farming, Medical, Education,

Arts and Entertainment, Media, Social/Family Services. Ask: Who are the Christians in each of these sectors (vocational tribes)? Who are the people of prayer? Every sector/tribe needs embedded intercessors! And missionary intercessors.

2. Get representatives of each sector/tribe together! Have them dream: What would our city look like if it were redeemed, if we prayed, if a Great Awakening came here?

3. Empower the leaders in each sector to dream about renewal efforts throughout the city/county. For example, what work-place based prayer events could take place to encourage believers to be humble, and yet bright witnesses of Christ? What could happen if teachers and lawyers, business leaders and construction workers were pausing, if only for 5-10 minutes of unified prayer, on their jobsite. Inviting God "to come" to the marketplaces of the community! Specific example: What would the medical community look like, if nurses and doctors, medical technicians and staff, regularly prayed together for their professional/vocational tribe, its people and its purpose? As the same question about education, social/family services, the media, etc.

4. Be creative! Allow sector (professional tribal/vocational) leadership to develop in each venue. Emphasize the "goodness of God" that leads to repentance. Pray for a city/county-wide spiritual awakening. Develop on-going prayer covenants embedded in the different sectors of the culture that connect Christians across denominational stream during the weekdays, for the purpose of entertaining God in the marketplace.

5. And yes, encourage business leaders to support the financial needs of the community initiative.

Mobilizing Intercessors / People of Prayer

1. Encourage each pastor to submit the names of interces-

sors to create an area-wide intercessory network to pray, in unity, for a Great Awakening!

2. Discourage, when possible, the destabilizing movement of dissatisfied people from church-to-church or the proselytizing of members, particularly among the people of prayer. Make it safe for pastors to participate. And yet, emphasize the one-church of the city!

3. Remember, Great Awakenings began with unified prayer that reached across various divides. And around the world, the great renewal efforts taking place are driven by unified prayer.

4. Link intercessors by email. Do intercessor rallies – hundreds of intercessors praying together two-to-three times a year. Do monthly smaller focused on-site deployment of intercessors with a specific focus on this place or that, this promise or that pain. Don't allow the intercessors to be bogged down by a myriad of typical prayer requests. Don't use the intercessor team to replace the work of members and intercessors in local congregations.

5. Develop prayer plans – prayer chains, 24-7 on-going prayer efforts.

6. Plan prayer walks and missions in the area. Then, gather intercessors and debrief, sharing the results of their prayer excursion. In some cases, you may be able to systematically deploy intercessors to prayer walk/drive each part of the city.

7. Do research on the area. Send teams to every significant site in the county – places of pain and promise, places of darkness and light, places of bondage and liberty, seats of power – political and spiritual.

8. Organize intercessors into small, efficient networks (small - 3-5; large 8-10). Pass assignments through intercessory captains. The communication will keep intercessors engaged. It provides a point of release for watchers on the wall – someone is taking their intercession seriously. It

directs the prayer process.

9. Make a list of the 100 most influential people in your county – people in positions of power, and people who are influential by means of the wealth or status, by the company they own and the people they employ. Create a brief profile on each and have the intercessors pray for them. In the course of three-to-four months, the complete list can be covered. These people then receive the attention, the gift of prayer, three times annually. Develop prayer ambassador teams – men and women of peace. Send them out during the week. Teams of 3-5 people, made up of pastors and gracious believers from a variety of churches, go bearing gifts – a flower, a Bible, a Christian book, information on the multi-denomination prayer effort, etc. Greet these leaders in behalf of the Christian community. Offer a prayer, asking for God's blessing and favor. Ten teams making two visits per day during one week of outreach can touch the 100 most influential people in your county. Ten teams making two visits per week can cover the list in a year. Tip: Pray for believers and unbelievers, skeptics and believers. Bless. Smile. And look for divine surprises – the believer secretary next to the person of power, the assistant, the doorkeeper. Bless them, as well. Develop Prayer Ambassador support materials.

Finance/Budget

1. Develop a budget for the community prayer effort.

2. Each community must raise their own funds for the local PC²LN initiative.

3. Make sure your funds are duly accounted for and all the bills are paid.

4. Consider having a church or an existing 501 (c) 3 organization whose purposes are consistent with those of your initiative manage the finances. If necessary, the organization can file a DBO (Doing Business As) for the prayer

initiative and open a separate bank account. Be good and trustworthy stewards.

5. Contributions that qualify for a tax deduction must be to a legitimate non-profit organization with a tax exempt status.

6. At least annually, provide an accounting for all funds to the entire council. The leadership team should get monthly financial reports.

7. Send notes of thanks to all contributors to the event.

8. Do not incur debt in the name of any national prayer organization.

Ethnic/Gender Diversity

1. Do simple computer research on the demographics of your county. You will quickly discover the ethnic/racial diversity, the religious and denominational range.

2. Work to assure a leadership team that is reflective of the area. In some counties, you may want to consider bilingual prayer gatherings. In other cases, the ethnic diversity may be so pronounced, that a team reflecting the different nations in your community would number a hundred or more – it is the spirit of diversity that we want to achieve. The church here should resemble the church around the throne in heaven.

3. Look for ethnic leaders/pastors that have influence within some ethnic stream in the geographic area. Have them carry the banner for prayer in that stream.

4. Recruit, in every ethnic stream, collaborating pastors.

5. Look for business leaders in the community from different ethnic streams.

6. Ethnic church and pastoral involvement will only be accomplished by finding leader-advocates within each stream.

7. The church, diverse and unique, standing together public-ly. Repenting, asking God to come to the city/area, these are a powerful witness to the community.

Suggestions:
Communication

1. Over-communicate! Use email. Develop multiple lists – pastors, prayer leaders, intercessors, for your area! Use conference calling. It's free.
2. Use the resources of the website.

Prayer

3. You can't pray too much! Pray, then pray, then pray again!
4. Identify and organize intercessors. Mobilize them.

Local Vision

5. Be creative! Each PC²LN is part of a national grass-roots network that works in collaboration with the vision of the member organizations of the National Prayer Committee. And yet, the nexus of renewal always bubbles out of the heart of the individual – the Ezra (priestly leader) or Ne-hemiah (civic leader), or a Joel (prophetic leader). With the guidelines in view, allow the Holy Spirit to assist in developing local vision for your multi-city, county-wide, multi-denominational renewal effort.

Pass Out Resources

6. Resource pastors and Christian leaders, laity and pa-ra-church organizations in calling the community to re-pentance and renewal as an example to the city, to fresh vision and vitality focused on Great Awakening.

Build a Supporting Network of Congregations

7. Identify supporting and collaborating congregations that will call their constituents to prayer and renewal, and participation in various prayer efforts – the minimal goal: At least 20% of the community congregations collaborating in the prayer process. At such a minimal goal, in more than 35,000 communities and townships in the nation and 330,000 congregations, some 65,000 churches would be collaborating, and that could represent the largest revival and renewal collaborative effort in modern American history.

Show Up

8. Promote various prayer events – and show up for them.

Send in a Report

9. Make sure the national offices of the various prayer events get a report of what happened in your community – for the NDP, SYATP, Call2Fall, etc. And post a report on the Prayer Council website, as well.

10. Have someone video-tape prayer events. Pan the crowd, repeatedly during the taping. Show audience breadth and response. Interview participants. Have them talk about their heart for revival in the community and the country.

11. Get copies of newspaper articles, ads, newspaper releases, TV news coverage and media time, interviews, and share them with the national sponsors.

Use the Web-Based Support Materials

12. Be aware of the web-based resource materials. Print out samples for distribution to pastors and other leaders. Encourage the use of the materials wisely and broadly.

Keep Renewal Going

13. Build a team and keep the renewal process going. Nurture the idea of on-going prayer and unity efforts in the community. The goal is not a successful rally or even a significant crowd turnout. The goal is a Great Awakening, a revival that sweeps the nation!

Expand

14. In addition to national prayer representatives and local church prayer coordinators, other prayer teams may be formed to steward on-going community prayer efforts, such as: Intercessory Mobilization; Neighborhood Lighthouses of Prayer; 24-7 Prayer Walls, Chains; Community Prayer Hot-lines; Church Prayer Leader's Fellowship; Collegiate Prayer Task Force; Association of Prayer Room Leaders; Community Leader's Prayer Partner Project; Mayor's Prayer Breakfast Task-Force; Interracial Prayer Fellowship Network; Prayer Summit/Prayer Retreat Coordination; Marketplace Prayer Networks (8 Sectors); Embedded Unreached Peoples/Missional Prayer (Unreached Peoples in the community); Youth Prayer Network; Family Prayer Advocacy Team; Men's Prayer Group Network; Community Healing Rooms; Adopt a School Program.

15. Some prayer efforts might be seasonal: Community Events (needing a special prayer covering); Seasonal Events (Holidays, Special Efforts, Anniversaries, i.e. "200th Anniversary of the City!"; Special Outreach (Which may evolve into a permanent Prayer Team, i.e., prayer support for a crusade, witnessing effort, etc.); Special Needs (Community crises warranting a special prayer effort, i.e., missing child, rampant drug rates, murder or crime spree, discovery of some community anomaly that deserves prayer, i.e., skyrocketing unemployment, plant closure, racial tension, rioting, etc.); Solemn Assembly – Every community should consider an occasional Solemn Assembly to gather to honor God, to right community wrongs before heaven's throne.

First Year Efforts

The Big Picture

1. Define major public prayer events to be mutually supported by the PC²LN. *Examples: The National Day of Prayer, the Global Day of Prayer; the Call2Fall; Cry Out America; 30 Days of Prayer for the Muslim World; Seek God for the City; See You At the Pole; Prayer for the Peace of Jerusalem; Day of Prayer for the Persecuted Church, etc.*

2. Get representatives of these nationally resourced prayer events/efforts to the table for collaborative envisioning.

3. If no representative exists and that prayer effort is considered essential to the overall prayer strategy, consider who might lead the effort and suggest them to the national group.

4. Calendarize these events. Translate them into a seamless prayer process for the city/county.

STAGE TWO: Engaging the Movements

1. Convene the leaders of prayer movements (non-event

networks, relational movements, etc.). *Examples: Moms-in-Prayer; Christian Educators Prayer Network; Adopt a School; Neighborhood Prayer; Aglow; Intercessors for America.*

2. Spend time allowing each to explain to the others their efforts in the community, the extent of their network, their resources, their vision.

3. Pray together.

4. Consider how each prayer ministry compliments the others, and develop a strategy for mutual support.

5. Practice the principle – Don't copy, collaborate; don't duplicate, cooperate; don't separate, synergize!

6. Consider the different contribution of these prayer movements in the city contrasted with prayer events. Find the common connection between them.

STAGE THREE: Engaging the Congregations

1. Convene the pastors and/or prayer leaders of every Christ-exalting, Bible reading congregation in the community.

2. Give them a report of your efforts.

3. Share the resources available.

4. Envision a 'prayed-for' community – a 'Great Awakening!'

5. Develop a strategy to support congregations in being houses of prayer for the community and the nations. Find your existing models. Champion them. Connect them to other pastors and congregations.

   • Focus: At-home prayer; church-wide prayer meetings; church prayer-rooms; a network of city-wide, church-based prayer rooms/centers; cooperative prayer evangelism efforts.

STAGE FOUR: Mobilizing
Intercessors City-Wide

1. Identify intercessors across the city – in connection with their congregations, geographically, vocationally, in terms of passion and intercessory calling.

2. To move from random intercession to informed intercession – do some basic research on the city.

    A. What is the strength of the church in the area?

    B. How many congregations are there in the defined area?

    C. What is the ratio of congregations to the population? (Typical: 1 – 1000; Ideal: 1-750; Significantly Under-churched: Less than 1 – 1500; Densely churched: More than 1 – 500.

    D. How many people in the defined area are in church on any given Sunday?

    > Percentage of the population in church on any given Sunday (National average – 17%).

    > It is estimated that some five percent of all believers have a specific call to intercession. With that as a standard, how many intercessors should you be able to identify in your community, given the strength of the Christian community?

    > All believers are called to pray – and to pray for those in authority. Set a reasonable goal (recommendation – 10%) of the Sunday attendance, and begin to mobilize them in prayer.

3. Issue a citywide call to all intercessors to gather to pray for their community.

4. Remember, prayer events test our capacity to mobilize. And the prayer events themselves often reveal training-teaching gaps. And prayer events demonstrate the community prayer strength.

5. Consider 3-4 such prayer gatherings annually.

STAGE FIVE: Gathering Data

1. Map congregations involved in the prayer process. Map congregations not involved.
2. Map the location of keep intercessors.
3. Begin a basic spiritual mapping project.

STAGE SIX: Strategic Prayer Evangelism Deployment

1. Focus groups:
   A. Educators
   B. Government Workers
   C. Social Services
   D. Medical
   E. Arts and Entertainment
   F. Media
   G. Banking and Finance
   H. Service Sectors
   I. Trades
   J. Sales/Services
   K. Manufacturing/Industry
   L. Science/Technology

> Pastors are trained by Bible Colleges and Seminaries to interpret Scripture, and they teach others to do the same, but no one gives them the tools to interpret a city, and that is not something they teach their congregations – it is just not on their radar screen.[62]
> ━ ━ ━ ━ ━ ➤

2. Who is the largest employer in your city? What are the moral implications of the work – is it something God can bless?
3. What drives the economy of your entire city?
4. What the character of your city? River, coastal, railroad, resort, interstate, border, retirement, bedroom, educational, medical, banking, blue-collar, manufacturing, welfare, ethnically distinct, historic, tourist? Is it growing or declining? Healthy or unhealthy? Is sin hidden or open? Are

the controlling influencers godly or ungodly?

5. Where does the light need to shine more brightly?

6. Who are the leading Christians in the above city-sectors?

7. Are there organized prayer efforts for or in any of the above sectors?

8. What about the groups without Christian insiders? Crime, drug areas, gangs, prostitution, abortionaries, human trafficking, addictions ... etc.

9. Goal: 5 prayer groups for every 1000 residents of the community. Bare minimum, at least one prayer group inside or in behalf of each of the city-sectors.

PC²LN Ambassadors

General Role Description

The Ambassador is the Johnny Appleseed of an established and constituted PC²LN in a metropolitan area.

The Identity

Ambassadors may function formally or even informally. They spread the word of what is happening in the newly created PC²LN. They are empowered as a result of contacts with other prayer leaders in neighboring communities, and because of their passion for seeing the movement spread throughout a definitive geographic area.

Their role is vision-casting. Their authority is relational. In no sense is there a desire to establish a hierarchy, rather a peer network of like-minded PC²LNs. Each PC²LN should be autonomous, and yet, in metropolitan regions, function as networks.

The Simplified Message to Community Pastors and Prayer Leaders

"We have begun a PC²LN in the city – and it is the local expression of a national grass-roots prayer network. Our passion is to see a collage of like-minded networks throughout our county/metropolitan area, all with the same purpose, to see our community become a prayed-for community. Prayer and unity are partners. All of our smaller cities and towns have unique needs, but we also desire to see one united movement of prayer across the entire county/multicounty area.

"In the very least, we can pray together! *God promises a blessing when his people pray together* (Psalm 133). *And Jesus wants us to be one – it was the centerpiece of his last prayer* (John 17). How can we link our various community prayer efforts? How can we support one another in a unified prayer effort for the entire county/metropolis?"

Identifying Catalysts and Conveners

Once an ambassador has discovered a potential catalyst or convener, he shares the discovery with the established PC²LN leadership team.

They collaborate to use their relational collateral to encourage the effort. Their goal is to assist in the planting of multiple PC²LNs until the entire area is covered in prayer.

1. Determine whether or not other interested parties in that community are already at work to establish a PC²LN.
2. If so, connect them!
3. Register the potential catalysts and convening team.
4. Provide contact information.
5. Provide any credentials, connections – do you work with a national prayer organization (Helpful, but not neces-

sary)? Are you a prayer leader for a local congregation?

6. Provide references!

7. Help them with the process.

National Launch Strategy

STAGE ONE (Months 1-24)
Embracing the vision of the PC²LN
Goals:

- Develop the basic concept, and get it on paper.
- Cast vision to national prayer organizations and get a buy-in.
- Make modifications. Let the vision grow and expand. Build trust.
- Create a national advisory committee to steward the process.
- Develop vision-casting materials.

STAGE TWO (Months 3-18)
Creating the Resources to Launch the Process
Goals:

- Find funding for vision-casting, support processes, etc.
- Create web-presence.

- Create basic promotional materials (mock-ups).
- Build synergies for vision-casting, pilot projects.
- Beta-testing (Find Several Diverse Venues for a Test Models).
- Readjust Models based on field-testing.

STAGE THREE (Months 6-36)
Launch Pilot Projects
Goals:

- Identify trainers.
- Identify 50 pilot city/counties for the project.
- Partner pilot project counties with National Organizations who might be invested in some area, leader, etc.
- Start the process of constituting the PC^{2}LNs.
- Monitor their progress.
- Detail their challenges.
- Work on solutions.
- Recalibrate the model.

STAGE FOUR (Months 18 – 48)
Launch a Nation-wide PC²LN Effort
Goals:

- Trainers are now training trainers.
- Manual is completed for PC^{2}LN.
- Support materials (a kit, has been created).
- State Ambassadors are recruited.
- Regional Ambassadors are recruited.
- Configurations of multi-county areas (metropolitan) are considered.

STAGE FIVE (Months 48-60)

Recalibrate the PC²LN
National Leadership Team
Goals:

- Leadership moves from strategic envisioning and launch modes, to sustaining growth.
- A National Prayer Council meeting is considered.
- Ways and means to support the infrastructure are in place.
- The connection to the National Prayer Committee, along with constituting national prayer organizations is complete and healthy.

Simple PC²LN
Constitution

I. NAME

The name of this organization shall be the _____
Prayer-Connect Community Leadership Network – the
PC²LN.

II. STATEMENT OF FAITH

The Statement of Faith is that adopted by the Lausanne Covenant from 150 countries at the 1974 International Congress for World Evangelization in Lausanne, Switzerland, a congress called by Rev. Billy Graham. The overwhelming acceptance as a document has provided a new base for collaboration and is being used by hundreds of ministries throughout the world.

III. STANDING

This PC²LN is a grass-roots expression of the fellowship of national prayer leaders who comprise the National Prayer Committee along with pastors and intercessors, prayer leaders and representatives of local/regional ministries, and congregations.

IV. PURPOSE

The purpose of the PC^{2}LN shall be to convene community prayer leaders to create a seamless prayer process in order to make the city/county a prayed-for and blessed place. The Community Prayer Council Table is a common meeting ground for representatives of national/regional/state prayer ministries, as well as local church prayer coordinators to collaborate and conspire for holy purposes in behalf of the city.

V. MEMBERSHIP

Membership in the PC^{2}LN is based on representative status in association with recognized prayer organizations or community congregations and ministries.

VI. LEGAL ORGANIZATION

Each PC^{2}LN is autonomous with respect to IRS status and economic function. Each is responsible for its own actions. The National Prayer Committee, nor any other national prayer organization with representative members, nor its members assume any liability for local actions. If the organization chooses to function as a legal entity with tax-exempt status, it must pursue its own status as a 501 (c) 3 organization and all the responsibilities thereof.

VII. GOVERNMENT

The membership and structure of each PC^{2}LN is dynamic. Its membership, officer selection process, is determined by the constituting council. Subsequent adaptation and development are also matters of the local leadership team. In function, final authority shall reside with the members of the Network. They shall approve and/or affirm Biblically qualified leadership, to carry out Network purposes.

VIII. OFFICERS

A slate of officers shall be chosen by the Network to provide servant leadership. The PC²LN shall determine the process of Officer/Leadership selection, as well as the tenure and responsibilities.

IX. PROVISION FOR BY-LAWS AND POLICY MANUAL

If the PC²LN is organized as a legal entity, it grows more complex, and it may need to develop BY-LAWS which embody qualifications for leaders and officers. The BY-LAWS shall also include officers' duties, provisions for the appointment of additional leaders, organizational expansion, conditions for membership, etc.

The By-laws are a separate document, usually more detailed, and easier to change. They should be a dynamic document.

The By-laws provide a vehicle to implement and carry out the purposes of the PC²LN. They explain how the organization functions in terms of boards, committees, officers, membership admission, frequency of meetings and quorums. A description of boards and committees, including their duties and terms of service, should also be included. An organizational chart is helpful.

X. AMENDMENTS

Amendments to this constitution may be made at the annual business reporting meeting, providing a thirty (30) day notice has been provided to members. Or at a special called meeting, given a ten day notice (10 days), and with changes approved by a two-thirds majority.

PC²LN
Complex Constitution
(Model)

Note: This model is only a suggestion. Each PC²LN oper- ates as a 'grass-roots' connection-point, in association with the National Prayer Committee and its member organizations. The power of this movement is 'bottom-up.' We anticipate general agreement in form and purpose, with Spirit-inspired innovation and origination. What we long to see is not a 'top-down' model, but one that is geometric and dynamic, Councils connecting with other councils, created a network, particularly in metropolitan ar- eas, state regions, and the like. Less turf, more collaboration and cooperation.

I. Name

The name of this organization shall be _____ Prayer-Connect Community Leadership Network – the PC²LN.

II. Purpose

To utilize the resources of national prayer ministry organizations with local innovation and creativity, in order to create a seamless prayer process owned and directed by prayer leaders in the community.

III. Mission

The mission of the PC²LN is to synergize and facilitate prayer efforts in collaboration with national/state/regional prayer organizations in the nation, typically, the local representatives of members of the National Prayer Committee and others they invite to the table, working with pastors, ministry leaders and congregational prayer leaders, along with intercessors and believers in every community to improve the spiritual and moral vitality of the congregations and the community through a unified, strategic prayer network that unwraps a seamless prayer process aimed at edifying the saints and evangelizing the cities.

IV. Community Prayer Council
A. Membership

Membership will be composed of representatives of National Prayer Organizations working in the community to advance the cause of prayer (Example: National Day of Prayer Coordinator; SYTP; COA; GDP; Moms-in-Prayer; Campus Prayer Ministries; Intercessors for America; etc.; along with Local Church Prayer Coordinators, denominational prayer leaders, etc.).

Though the spirit of the council is a gracious open door, membership is the privilege of recognized prayer leaders.

B. Meetings

1. The Council will meet as a whole every four months to pray together, learn together, and to plan and envision a prayed-for community, networking and encouraging par-

ticipation in community days of prayer and other prayer efforts, molding them together in a seamless fashion.

2. The agenda for the Council meetings will be set by the Moderator in collaboration with Servant Leader Team and the Cabinet.

C. Organization

1. **SERVANT LEADERSHIP TEAM (SLT)** – The Constituting Council will select from its members an officer core (Moderator, Vice-Moderator/Assistant, Recording Secretary, Members-at-large) to provide servant leadership for the community prayer effort.

2. **PRAYER TEAM/MINISTRY LEADERS** – A select group of prayer ministry leaders may be selected to sit with the officers from time to time in the interest of broader leadership. They serve as a Cabinet, adhered to the SLT. They provide specific direction and focus to the recognized community prayer efforts that take place during the year, so their executive role is strategic.

3. **STRATEGIC PLANNING TEAM** – A Strategic Planning Team is recommended. They would work to provide detailed projections for a 3-5 year period and then decadal projections, answering the question, "What would a prayed-for community look like? What will it take to get there? What are the long-range steps? Short-term?"

4. **CABINET** – The Cabinet consists of select representative leaders of key prayer ministries, congregational and para-church, and/or prayer team leaders along with members of the Strategic Planning Team (Numbers 1-3 above) in conjunction with the SLT. Advisors may also sit with the Cabinet.

5. **COUNCIL** – the Council is open to every duly recognized prayer leader in the definitive geographic area – those who lead or serve with local expressions of national

ministries, congregational prayer ministries leaders, leaders of community prayer efforts recognized by or created by the Cabinet and SLT, as well as select intercessory leaders.

6. **STANDING COMMITTEES** – Standing Committees that work in areas adjunct to the prayer effort may also be named.

D. Advocacy and Promotion

A major component is information sharing on prayer efforts and resources, as well as the promotion of prayer training, the proliferation of prayer resources, the mobilization of prayer efforts, and a camaraderie that owns every prayer effort in the city and champions it for all. In this sense, the PC²LN (Prayer-Connect Leadership Network) is a friend to all Bible-based, Christ-honoring community prayer, its best advocate and promoter.

E. Finances

Each community is responsible for its own funding. They may choose to acquire 501 (c) 3 status, or operate under the umbrella of an existing organization. They may choose to solicit contributions from members. In either case, it is recommended that sound fiscal accounting policies be put in place with regard to monies handled. Regular financial reports are critical, along with a detailed annual financial report. The cabinet should receive a written financial report at each meeting. The finances of Prayer Force Teams should also be monitored – to insure integrity and community honor.

V. Officers (Servant Leader Team) of the Prayer Network

The Prayer Network will select Officers (Servant Leader

Team) of 7-12 representative leaders to provide guidance to the community prayer process.

  A. Overview of the Servant Leader Team (Officer Core)

      1. Moderator

      2. Executive Assistant or Vice-Moderator

      3. Recording Secretary/Treasurer

      4. Members (3-7)

      5. Advisors (3-5)

      See Appendix A for organizational chart.

  B. General Qualifications for Servant Leaders (Officers)

      1. Must have a stellar reputation as a Christian believer and a person of prayer.

      2. Must be a local representative of a national prayer organization with credentials and commendations, or a denominational prayer leader resident in the community, or a pastoral/prayer leader representing a local congregation or ministry.

      3. Must exhibit dedication and active involvement in the community-wide prayer ministry as determined by the members of the cabinet.

      4. Must have shown faithfulness in attendance at meetings and community prayer efforts.

      5. Must exemplify in life, the principles and goals of the PC^2LN. and its parallel nation-wide shadow, the National Prayer Committee.

      6. Two years of experience in 'prayer' ministry, and a year of service on the PC^2LN, if not the Cabinet, are preferred for the Servant Leader Team (Officer Core).

  C. Specific Qualifications and Responsibilities of the Servant Leader Team Members (Officers)

      1. Moderator

         a) In selecting a Moderator, preference will be given to the incumbent, executive assistant or a task-force leader.

    b) Responsibilities of the moderator will include:

       (1) Calling, providing agendas for, and recording meetings which shall occur at least once per month.

       (2) Providing vision and leadership to the task-force leaders in their duties, including a quarterly review of division goals.

       (3) Setting and keeping track of annual and semi-annual ministry goals.

       (4) Is responsible, in cooperation with the council, to provide oversight for the creation of ad-hoc committees.

2. Vice-Moderator/Executive Assistant

    a) An active member of the council who exhibits dedication and strong leadership qualities.

    b) Responsibilities of the executive assistant will include:

       (1) Regular attendance at council meetings including temporary fulfillment of president's duties in his or her absence.

       (2) Assistance to the moderator and task-force leaders, to ad hoc committees, as well as on-going prayer efforts.

3. Recording Secretary-Treasurer

    a) An active member of the council who exhibits dedication and a capacity for attention to details, records and financial responsibility.

    b) Responsibilities of the Recording Secretary-Treasurer:

       (1) Creation of records of Servant Leader Team meetings, Council and Cabinet meetings, and others as directed. Distribution of minutes, task-assignments, etc.

      (2) Assistance to the moderator and task-force leaders, to ad hoc committees, as well as on-going prayer efforts as requested.

      (3) Accounting of funds, receipts and distributions as directed by the Moderator, consistent with Cabinet/Council policy.

      (4) Regular financial reports.

4. Members At Large

   a) Depending on the size of the area served and the membership of the PC^{2}LN, 3-7 at-large members should be selected to serve as Servant Leaders (Officers).

   b) Members may also be representatives of Prayer Organizations or themselves Prayer Team leaders or members.

   c) They should meet the criteria of Officer Standards described in Section V.

5. Advisors

   a) Advisors are drawn from three sources – Ezra's (pastoral leaders) and Nehemiah's (community-based spiritual lay leaders), along with known and proven intercessor(s).

   b) Responsibilities of the advisors will include:

      (1) Attendance at Officer Meetings and significant participation in the community prayer effort.

      (2) Involvement in the leadership processes.

      (3) General prudent advice and godly counsel.

      (4) Advocacy to the larger pastoral and Christian business community.

      (5) Assisting, as possible, in funding the community prayer effort.

Note: Some PC^{2}LN's may determine to use Advisors in a more passive role. Others may use them as active members of the Officer Core.

6.   Meetings

    a)   The Officers Should meet monthly, if at all possible (ten times annually).

    b)   Some Officer Meetings may be conducted in conjunction with meetings with the Cabinet.

VI. Prayer Teams

A. Prayer Team Leaders

   1. Existing National Prayer Leaders are already leaders of a prayer-force in the community. Their leadership should be acknowledged by the PC^{2}LN. They function, by virtue of their appointment by the National Organization with whom and for whom they work, as a Community Prayer Action Team leader, along with their team.

   2. Additional Prayer Team leaders, for efforts unique to the community, are initially nominated by the Moderator and the Servant Leader Team.

   3. General responsibilities include:

    a)   Regular attendance at PC^{2}LN meetings, with a replacement from within the prayer team if absence is necessary.

    b)   The formation of goals for their prayer team in connection with the goals for the entire community.

    c)   Provision of leadership for their specific Prayer Teams including the execution of goals, the growth and development of leaders in the focus area, cooperation with the ministries, churches and sectors of the city served.

B. Leadership

   1. Prayer Team leaders who serve in connection with a National Organization sit on the council at the will of

the National Group they represent.

2. Prayer Team leaders who serve the prayer effort of a local congregation may in some cases by asked to serve on the Cabinet, particularly, if the prayer ministry reach of that congregation is critical to the whole community effort.

3. Prayer Team leaders who lead local prayer efforts, and are chosen to lead those efforts by the SLT may serve a given term, or through the completion of the 'task' or prayer event, or as an on-going advocate of some component of the community prayer process (Prayer-walking, Pastoral Prayer Coverings, Crime-team Prayer Units, etc.).

4. It is recommended that a core-group of at least three leaders be appointed to each prayer leadership team with one designated as the Cabinet liaison.

C. Membership

Each Prayer Team (Core-Group) selects additional team members. Prayer Leadership Teams expand and contract, depending on their activities and the demand for man-power. Membership of the team is dynamic, often seasonal, and situational.

D. Tenure

Locally selected Core-Leaders of the Prayer Teams are reaffirmed each year by a review of the prayer cabinet. It is recommended that at least 20% of all Prayer Team members be fresh recruits annually.

E. Application

1. On-going Prayer Efforts

Prayer Teams may be formed to steward on-going prayer efforts, such as:

a) Intercessory Mobilization.

b) Neighborhood Lighthouses of Prayer.

c) 24-7 Prayer Walls, Chains.

d) Community Prayer Hot-lines.

e) Church Prayer Leader's Fellowship.

f) Collegiate Prayer Task Force.

g) Association of Prayer Room Leaders.

h) Community Leader's Prayer Partner Project.

i) Mayor's Prayer Breakfast Task-Force

j) Interracial Prayer Fellowship Network

k) Prayer Summit/Prayer Retreat Coordination

l) Marketplace Prayer Networks (8 Sectors).

m) Embedded Unreached Peoples/Missional Prayer (Unreached Peoples in the community)

n) Youth Prayer Network

o) Family Prayer Advocacy Team

p) Men's Prayer Group Network

q) Community Healing Rooms

r) Adopt a School Programs

2. Special/Seasonal Prayer Teams

a) Community Events (needing a special prayer effort).

b) Seasonal Events (Holidays, Special Efforts, Anniversaries, i.e. "200th Anniversary of the City!"

c) Special Outreach (Which may evolve into a permanent Prayer Team, i.e., prayer support for a crusade, witnessing effort, etc.)

d) Special Needs (Community crises warranting a special prayer effort, i.e., missing child, rampant drug rates, murder or crime spree, discovery of some community anomaly that deserves prayer, i.e., skyrocketing unemployment, plant closure, racial tension, rioting, etc.)

e) Solemn Assembly – Every community should consider an occasional Solemn Assembly to gather to honor God, to right community wrongs before heaven's throne.

F. Finances

    1. Each Prayer Team is responsible for its own funding, and yet accountable to the Officers and Cabinet, and ultimately the entire PC²LN to retain integrity and honor before the community with regard to money management, payment of obligations, etc.

    2. No Prayer Team should sign a contract, obligating the community prayer effort, without the approval of the Cabinet and its advisors, unless that obligation is both authorized by and guaranteed by the Prayer Ministry they represent. Even so in the Spirit of humility, disclosure is recommended.

VII. Transitions

A. Generational Leadership

The Biblical characteristic of leadership is enduring and typically generational. Neither quick nor robotic tenures are healthy in an organization or its leadership. And yet, fresh leadership is a requisite for growth. The healthy body replenishes and replaces. The rule of thumb recommended is 20% fresh leaders annually.

B. Leadership Transition

Develop a scheme to refresh leadership at the Cabinet and Prayer Team levels without displacing those who have a generational calling as well as the community-wide credibility to convene pastors, business leaders and prayer leaders along with intercessors.

C. The Transition Cycle

A leadership transition is recommended every 2-3 years, with an annual review. Annual terms are not long enough to launch and grow a process as challenging as a community call to transformational prayer.

Each year, however, some persons will need permission to step-aside, and others will have moved or failed to adequately perform their duties.

Solicit commitments, and make appointments for 2-3 year terms, with annual recommitment.

Tenure limitations are not recommended. Sabbaticals are. Every key leader should, after some season, invoke a sabbatical for rest and reflection. Or move to an emeritus role to allow for fresh leadership, at least for a season. Consider leadership cycles. Stay fresh.

Select and/or reaffirm the Officer Core first during each transition and leadership reaffirmation process.

In the 30-60 days following the reaffirmation of the Officer Core, reaffirm Prayer Team Core Leaders, the Strategic Planning Team, Standing Committees, etc. Encourage out-going and on-coming team members to meet together at least once to assure smooth transition.

VIII. Removal and Vacancy

A. Removal of PC²LN Members
   1. By Loss of Position or Representative Status
      a) While the nature of the PC²LN is relational, it is also representative. Therefore, if a member disengages or is replaced by the national ministry that he was representing on the council, he is to yield that seat to his duly appointed successor. The same would be true for a local church prayer leader serving as a representative, etc.
      b) Exception: If the Cabinet approves, the individual may remain as a part of the Community Prayer Council as a 'member at large' and serve and/or lead various Prayer Teams, but not as the 'representative' of some national, regional, or denomination/parachurch ministry.
   2. By Relocation

The nature of the community is grass-roots, local, and demands members who live in the community and contribute to the prayer effort. One who moves away should forfeit their role and simultaneously be encouraged to start one in the community to which they move.

3. For Ethical Reasons

    a) The integrity of the PC²LN, the Cabinet, the Officers and the Prayer Teams are to be above reproach. Should a member experience life-challenges that might in any way affect the ability of the Council to be a pure representative of Christ in the community, they are urged to withdraw – permanently or temporarily.

    b) Reasons for withdrawal or removal include – indictments, church discipline, clear moral failure, marital stress that demands the attention of the member at home for a season to regain personal stability, criminal charges, arraignments, undue negative public and media attention, personal moral challenges that require time for recovery and personal growth, etc.

4. By Action

    a) In the sad event that a member of the Cabinet, the PC²LN, or a Prayer Team refuses to vacate the position, the Moderator may appoint a Reconciliation Panel of at least three individuals (Members of the PC²LN, Advisors or Community Pastors) to meet with the individual to attempt to mediate the matter and solicit a conciliatory withdrawal.

    b) On the recommendation of the Reconciliation Panel, the Cabinet may act, on the recommendation of the SLT and the Advisors, to remove the person.

B. Vacancy of Position

1. Moderator: The Cabinet may select from within its own ranks or from the PC²LN a successor to serve out the term of the Moderator.

2. Vice-Moderator/Executive Assistant: The Cabinet may select from within its own ranks or from the PC²LN a successor to serve out the term of the Moderator.

3. Prayer Team Leaders: The Officers may appoint another member of the Core Leadership Group or from the Prayer Teams to serve in cases where the prayer effort is local. In cases where a prayer leader was representing a National Prayer Ministry, that ministry will appoint a successor. However, not all national ministries are immediately aware that the representative has moved or is non-functioning. A pro-active SLT can offer a great service to national prayer ministries by assuring them of the local support of that particular prayer cause, and urging the appointment of a replacement.

4. Advisor: The Moderator will nominate to the Officer Core a replacement for the Advisor.

IX. Committees and Consultants

Ad-hoc committees may be formed at the discretion of the Prayer Cabinet.

A. Committees: (Examples Only)

1. Recruitment Committee – Focused on enlarging the number of churches participating in the prayer process, encouraging local church prayer leaders, marketplace prayer leaders to join the PC²LN.

2. Budget Committee – Composed of a treasurer (Member of the Cabinet), and either the Moderator, Executive Assistant, and at least one Advisor. The budget is submitted to the Cabinet for review and suggested

changes. The budget committee provides a written budget report (income, expenses, bills due and payable, anticipated obligations and income, balance sheet) for each Cabinet meeting, and at least annually to the PC²LN. The new Cabinet is entitled to a fresh budget report.

3. Community Ambassador Committee – This committee, if deemed necessary, connects with the Mayor, major industries, community leaders, the Chamber, etc. to advance the cause of prayer in the whole community.

4. Prayer Resource Committee – This team works to discover and offer resources and training to the local churches. It partners with local church prayer leaders to assist them in their efforts. It postures inter-denominationally, crossing boundaries, helping congregations from different streams, respecting traditions, not advocating for a 'slice' of theology, but the orthodox core.

5. Spiritual Mapping Committee – This team is researching the city, discovering both its past and its potential, its pain and promise. It provides insights to the PC²LN, to pastors and local church prayer leaders, to the intercessors. The date should be available to all, as much as wisdom will allow.

6. Strategic Planning Committee – A special group should slowly and deliberately be assembled to project the implications and impact of a 'prayed-for' city. This team would develop a multi-year, perhaps, a 10-20 year prayer plan for the city, aimed at godly transformation.

B. Consultants

As the prayer effort grows, the Officer Core along with the Cabinet may identify 'consultants' who are willing to serve the community prayer process. Some may be members of the local community. Others may be outside, but bring some resource or expertise to the churches and prayer ministry efforts.

C. Community Connections

Partnerships with the community are essential! For example, finding a liaison to Law Enforcement could be extremely helpful. Other community connections are vital as well. The agencies and individuals serve to create connection points between the Community Prayer Leaders Council, its associated organizational members and congregations.

D. Discovery Exposition

1. A Discovery Exposition is an event that brings together people of prayer and faith with other community leaders to exhibit resources and envision a changed community.

2. Various secular agencies, together with churches and prayer organizations, Christian ministries, explain programs and resources, interact for the good of the community.

3. The Discovery Exposition consists of an array of table displays, literature, dialogue, organized presentations, panels – all focused on interactive cooperation to make the city/community a better place.

4. The Discovery Exposition last from 2-3 days. It should take place every 2-3 years. It may involve joint planning and give birth to collaborative efforts.

5. The Discovery Exposition should be held in conjunction with the long-range plans of the Strategic Planning Team.

X. Ratification and Amendments

A. This constitution shall be approved by the initial Community Prayer Leaders Network.

B. Amendments shall be proposed to the cabinet and then to the PC²LN for approval.

---

61   Phill Butler, *Well Connected* (Authentic Media, 2005), 23.
62   Bakke, 56.

SECTION FIVE
Appendix

Perspective on Pastors

Pastors are simultaneously, the greatest obstacle to a national spiritual awakening and most remediable. This is not to suggest that pastors are either knowingly or willfully obstacles for city-unity and revival. Admittedly, the paradigm we are suggesting here is new and untried. Traditionally, pastors have been trained to focus almost exclusively on their congregations. Such pastor congregational independence is now hurting, not helping. Simultaneously, Christianity and pastors have been abandoned by the culture as a respected and accepted profession. They are now under incredible spiritual warfare and emotional stress. According to the Schaeffer Institute,[63] pastors in America are in a deep crisis. Dr. Richard Krejcir points out the startling dilemma of the pastoral predicament in an article entitled, "What is Going on with the Pastors in America?"[64] Currently, 70% of pastors are so burned out or stressed that they regularly consider leaving the ministry.[65] During the first five years of ministry, there is huge drop-out rate, "This is not what I signed up for! Not what I expected. Far different than I anticipated. I am not cut out for this." Eighty percent of seminary and Bible school graduates who enter the ministry will leave the ministry within the first five years. As many as 35-40% who enter by some other means - answer a call without professional training, become part-time pastors, pastoral staff-members – also exit pastoral ministry in that early season of ministry. In all, 60-80% will exit after a decade or less of service, and only a fraction will stay in it as a lifetime career.

One statistic suggested that only one percent make pastoral ministry a lifetime career – they start in pastoral ministry and re-tire as a pastor.[66] Seventy-eight percent have been forced to resign from a church at some point in their career. Sixty-three percent have been fired twice or more. Job security then becomes a major issue, and pastors become professionally conditioned not to rock the parish boat. Fifty-two percent cited organization and control issues as the cause for leaving a congregation. The second most cited reason was the pace or degree of change in the congregation, thus a discernment and leadership problem. And finally, there is the lack of relational collateral with the congregation.

In one survey of more than a thousand pastors, every one of them had a buddy who had exited the ministry due to either moral failure, conflict in the church or burnout. Sadly, some of those were no longer serving the Lord.[67] Ninety-percent of the pastors reported frequent, chronic fatigue. Eighty-nine percent had con-sidered leaving the ministry at some point. Fifty-seven percent confessed that they would leave if an acceptable secular job were open to them. This is more than half. They are tired of fighting, don't want to go AWOL, but hope and pray for a graceful exit from the career for which they were willing to sacrifice.

Shockingly, 77% did not feel that they were in a good or healthy marriage. Thirty percent have had an on-going affair or a one-time sexual episode with a parishioner.[68] Thirty-eight percent were divorced or in the process of divorce. *Focus on the Family*[69] has reported that in the United States, we lose 'a pastor a day' be-cause he decides to choose an immoral path instead of righteous-ness. He substitutes a false intimacy for the only satisfying intimacy – spiritual intimacy with God through prayer. About 35% of pastors attempt to deal with their own sexual sin, privately. The more educated and affluent pastors compartmentalize. They have developed the capacity to perform ministry functions and separate personal foibles, to wall off character deficit issues and even sin. They rationalize, "It's the office that is anointed. No one will be hurt if no one knows." Such thinking is outside the bounds of Scripture. It fails to reckon with the spiritual nature of sin, the intangible character of the ministry itself, fraught with spiritual content.

Three-fourths of pastors surveyed felt that the seminary they had attended had poorly trained them for the work of pastoral ministry – the gap between theory and practice was far too wide. Seventy-two percent only studied the Bible for sermon preparation – these were evangelical pastors. They had lost their love for the Word. Only 38% read the Bible devotionally or casually. For the majority, it was not their favorite book. Only 26% have daily personal devotions and feel adequately fed spiritually. Only 23% were happy and content with themselves, their home, and their present station in ministry.

Seventy percent battle chronic depression. Seventy percent do not have close personal friends, and have no one in whom they confide. They are alone. According to the study by psychologist Richard Blackmon, the average insurance cost to churches for dealing with mental breakdowns with clergy is four percent higher than any secular industry. The stress rises from managing personal and church finances, caring for the facility, recruiting and working with difficult volunteers, counseling and visitation. Blackmon suggests that the pastor's chronic exposure to the care component of his work is especially taxing. His solution, sadly, is a professional distance, healthy indifference, not prayer!

Another poll, taken by sociologist Jeffrey Haddan ("Prayer Net" Newsletter, Nov. 13, 1998), involved over 7,400 Protestant ministers. He found that only 13% to 51% of ministers, depending on their denomination, accepted Jesus' physical resurrection as a fact. His poll states between 19% and no more than 60% of ministers believe in the virgin birth of Jesus. The poll goes on to say that between 67% and 95% of ministers believe that the Scriptures are true in faith, history, and practice – difficult to understand if they reject the historicity of the virgin birth and the resurrection. These statistics are extremely despairing, of course, depending on one's denomination. What are these ministers trying to accomplish in God's Holy Church?

One telling sample suggested that a lack of sound theology was like self-inflicted damage to the pastor. Working out of a non-Biblical worldview, he is disadvantaged and vulnerable from the start.[70] Without a healthy vertical relationship and theology that makes the vitality of his relationship with God central to ministry, he starts the journey, asking ministry to do for him what only a personal relationship with God, in Christ, out of Scripture, animated by the Spirit can do. He is lost from the start. The center must be on Christ Himself, Christ alone, and not even on the noble cause of the ministry with its various functions, or his ministry effectiveness. If not, disaster is certain from the beginning.

Granted, it is difficult to separate Christ from the church, from preaching, from caring, from evangelizing or from serving. Indeed, it is impossible. And yet, this distinction is not theoretical. One does not enter the ministry in order to preach and teach, serve and care, evangelize and disciple. If the ministry is only about the horizontal, its supernatural nature has been omitted from the start, and it is reduced to a social institution. If one is in ministry to care, that is fundamentally different from one who is in ministry because God cares, and they convey, rather than create care. Ministry is entered because one does these things out of the overflow of the Christ-life and is, therefore, set-aside to do them full-time. And yet, they are ancillary. What is primary is life in Christ. The personal, not the public. The private intimate relationship, the vertical; not the horizontal reflection.[71]

The Lausanne Covenant

Introduction

W e, members of the Church of Jesus Christ, from more than 150 nations, participants in the International-al Congress on World Evangelization at Lausanne, praise God for his great salvation and rejoice in the fellowship he has given us with himself and with each other. We are deeply stirred by what God is doing in our day, moved to penitence by our failures and challenged by the unfinished task of evangelization. We believe the Gospel is God's good news for the whole world, and we are determined by his grace to obey Christ's commission to proclaim it to all mankind and to make disciples of every na-tion. We desire, therefore, to affirm our faith and our resolve, and to make public our covenant.

1. THE PURPOSE OF GOD

We affirm our belief in the one-eternal God, Creator and Lord of the world, Father, Son and Holy Spirit, who governs all things according to the purpose of his will. He has been calling out from the world a people for himself, and sending his people back into the world to be his servants and his witnesses, for the extension of his kingdom, the building up of Christ's body, and the glory of his name. We confess with shame that we have often denied our calling and failed in our mission, by becoming conformed to the world or by withdrawing from it. Yet we rejoice that even when borne by earthen vessels the gospel is still a precious treasure. To the task of making that treasure known in the power of the Holy Spirit we desire to dedicate ourselves anew.

(Isa. 40:28; Matt. 28:19; Eph. 1:11; Acts 15:14; John 17:6, 18; Eph,. 4:12; 1 Cor. 5:10; Rom. 12:2; II Cor. 4:7)

2. THE AUTHORITY AND POWER OF THE BIBLE

We affirm the divine inspiration, truthfulness and authority of both Old and New Testament Scriptures in their entirety as the only written word of God, without error in all that it affirms, and the only infallible rule of faith and practice. We also affirm the power of God's word to accomplish his purpose of salvation. The message of the Bible is addressed to all men and women. For God's revelation in Christ and in Scripture is unchangeable. Through it the Holy Spirit still speaks today. He illumines the minds of God's people in every culture to perceive its truth freshly through their own eyes and thus discloses to the whole Church ever more of the many-colored wisdom of God.

(II Tim. 3:16; II Pet. 1:21; John 10:35; Isa. 55:11; 1 Cor. 1:21; Rom. 1:16, Matt. 5:17,18; Jude 3; Eph. 1:17,18; 3:10,18)

3. THE UNIQUENESS AND UNIVERSALITY OF CHRIST

We affirm that there is only one Savior and only one gospel, although there is a wide diversity of evangelistic approaches. We recognize that everyone has some knowledge of God through his general revelation in nature. But we deny that this can save, for people suppress the truth by their unrighteousness. We also reject as derogatory to Christ and the gospel every kind of syncretism and dialogue which implies that Christ speaks equally through all religions and ideologies. Jesus Christ, being himself the only God-man, who gave himself as the only ransom for sinners, is the only mediator between God and people. There is no other name by which we must be saved. All men and women are perishing because of sin, but God loves everyone, not wishing that any should perish but that all should repent. Yet those who reject Christ repudiate the joy of salvation and condemn themselves to eternal separation from God. To proclaim Jesus as "the Savior of the world" is not to affirm that all people are either automatically or ultimately saved, still less to affirm that all religions offer salvation in Christ. Rather it is to proclaim God's love for a world of sinners and to invite everyone to respond to him as Savior and Lord in the wholehearted personal commitment of repentance and faith. Jesus Christ has been exalted above every other name; we long for the day when every knee shall bow to him and every tongue shall confess him Lord.

(Gal. 1:6-9;Rom. 1:18-32; I Tim. 2:5,6; Acts 4:12; John 3:16-19; II Pet. 3:9; II Thess. 1:7-9;John 4:42; Matt. 11:28; Eph. 1:20,21; Phil. 2:9-11)

4. THE NATURE OF EVANGELISM

To evangelize is to spread the good news that Jesus Christ died for our sins and was raised from the dead according to the Scriptures, and that as the reigning Lord he now offers the forgiveness of sins and the liberating gifts of the Spirit to all who repent and believe. Our Christian presence in the world is indispensable to evangelism, and so is that kind of dialogue whose purpose is to listen sensitively in order to understand. But evangelism itself is the proclamation of the historical, biblical Christ as Savior and Lord, with a view to persuading people to come to him personally and so be reconciled to God. In issuing the gospel invitation we have no liberty to conceal the cost of discipleship. Jesus still calls all who would follow him to deny themselves, take up their cross, and identify themselves with his new community. The results of evangelism include obedience to Christ, incorporation into his Church and responsible service in the world.

(I Cor. 15:3,4; Acts 2: 32-39; John 20:21; I Cor. 1:23; II Cor. 4:5; 5:11,20; Luke 14:25-33; Mark 8:34; Acts 2:40,47; Mark 10:43-45)

5. CHRISTIAN SOCIAL RESPONSIBILITY

We affirm that God is both the Creator and the Judge of all people. We therefore should share his concern for justice and reconciliation throughout human society and for the liberation of men and women from every kind of oppression. Because men and women are made in the image of God, every person, regardless of race, religion, color, culture, class, sex or age, has an intrinsic dignity because of which he or she should be respected and served, not exploited. Here too we express penitence both for our neglect and for having sometimes regarded evangelism and social concern as mutually exclusive. Although reconciliation with other people is not reconciliation with God, nor is social action evangelism, nor is political liberation salvation, nevertheless we affirm that evangelism and socio-political involvement are both part of our Christian duty. For both are necessary expressions of our doctrines of God and man, our love for our neighbor and our obedience to Jesus Christ. The message of salvation implies also a message of judgment upon every form of alienation, oppression and discrimination, and we should not be afraid to denounce evil and injustice wherever they exist. When people receive Christ they are born again into his kingdom and must seek not only to exhibit but also to spread its righteousness in the midst of an unrighteous world. The salvation we claim should be transforming us in the totality of our personal and social responsibilities. Faith without works is dead.

(Acts 17:26, 31; Gen. 18:25; Isa. 1:17; Psa. 45:7; Gen. 1:26, 27; Jas. 3:9; Lev. 19:18; Luke 6:27, 35; Jas. 2:14-26; John 3:3, 5; Matt. 5:20; 6:33; II Cor. 3:18; Jas. 2:20)

6. THE CHURCH AND EVANGELISM

We affirm that Christ sends his redeemed people into the world as the Father sent him, and that this calls for a similar deep and costly penetration of the world. We need to break out of our ecclesiastical ghettos and permeate non-Christian society. In the Church's mission of sacrificial service evangelism is primary. World evangelization requires the whole Church to take the whole gospel to the whole world. The Church is at the very center of God's cosmic purpose and is his appointed means of spreading the gospel. But a church which preaches the cross must itself be marked by the cross. It becomes a stumbling block to evangelism when it betrays the gospel or lacks a living faith in God, a genuine love for people, or scrupulous honesty in all things including promotion and finance. The church is the community of God's people rather than an institution, and must not be identified with any particular culture, social or political system, or human ideology.

(John 17:18; 20:21; Matt. 28:19,20; Acts 1:8; 20:27; Eph. 1:9,10; 3:9-11; Gal. 6:14,17; II Cor. 6:3,4; II Tim. 2:19-21; Phil.

1:27)

7. COOPERATION IN EVANGELISM

We affirm that the Church's visible unity in truth is God's purpose. Evangelism also summons us to unity, because our oneness strengthens our witness, just as our disunity undermines our gospel of reconciliation. We recognize, however, that organizational unity may take many forms and does not necessarily forward evangelism. Yet we who share the same biblical faith should be closely united in fellowship, work and witness. We confess that our testimony has sometimes been marred by a sinful individualism and needless duplication. We pledge ourselves to seek a deeper unity in truth, worship, holiness and mission. We urge the development of regional and functional cooperation for the furtherance of the Church's mission, for strategic planning, for mutual encouragement, and for the sharing of resources and experience.

(John 17:21,23; Eph. 4:3,4; John 13:35; Phil. 1:27; John 17:11-23)

8. CHURCHES IN EVANGELISTIC PARTNERSHIP

We rejoice that a new missionary era has dawned. The dominant role of western missions is fast disappearing. God is raising up from the younger churches a great new resource for world evangelization, and is thus demonstrating that the responsibility to evangelize belongs to the whole body of Christ. All churches should therefore be asking God and themselves what they should be doing both to reach their own area and to send missionaries to other parts of the world. A reevaluation of our missionary responsibility and role should be continuous. Thus a growing partnership of churches will develop and the universal character of Christ's Church will be more clearly exhibited. We also thank God for agencies which labor in Bible translation, theological education, the mass media, Christian literature, evangelism, missions, church renewal and other specialist fields. They too should engage in constant self-examination to evaluate their effectiveness as part of the Church's mission.

(Rom. 1:8; Phil. 1:5; 4:15; Acts 13:1-3, I Thess. 1:6-8)

9. THE URGENCY OF THE EVANGELISTIC TASK

More than 2,700 million people, which is more than two-thirds of all humanity, have yet to be evangelized. We are ashamed that so many have been neglected; it is a standing rebuke to us and to the whole Church. There is now, however, in many parts of the world an unprecedented receptivity to the Lord Jesus Christ. We are convinced that this is the time for churches and para-church agencies to pray earnestly for the salvation of the unreached and to launch new efforts to achieve world evangelization. A reduction of foreign missionaries and money in an evangelized country may sometimes be necessary to facilitate the national church's growth in self-reliance and to release resources for unevangelized areas. Missionaries should flow ever more freely from and to all six continents in a spirit of humble service. The goal should be, by all available means and at the earliest possible time, that every person will have the opportunity to hear, understand, and to receive the good news. We cannot hope to attain this goal without sacrifice. All of us are shocked by the poverty of millions and disturbed by the injustices which cause it. Those of us who live in affluent circumstances accept our duty to develop a simple life-style in order to contribute more generously to both relief and evangelism.

(John 9:4; Matt. 9:35-38; Rom. 9:1-3; I Cor. 9:19-23; Mark 16:15; Isa. 58:6,7; Jas. 1:27; 2:1-9; Matt. 25:31-46; Acts 2:44,45; 4:34,35)

10. EVANGELISM AND CULTURE

The development of strategies for world evangelization calls for imaginative pioneering methods. Under God, the result will be the rise of churches deeply rooted in Christ and closely related to their culture. Culture must always be tested and judged by Scripture. Because men and women are God's creatures, some of their culture is rich in beauty and goodness. Because they are fallen, all of it is tainted with sin and some of it is demonic. The gospel does not presuppose the superiority of any culture to another, but evaluates all cultures according to its own criteria of truth and righteousness, and insists on moral absolutes in every culture. Missions have all too frequently exported with the gospel an alien culture and churches have sometimes been in bondage to culture rather than to Scripture. Christ's evangelists must humbly seek to empty themselves of all but their personal authenticity in order to become the servants of others, and churches must seek to transform and enrich culture, all for the glory of God.

(Mark 7:8,9,13; Gen. 4:21,22; I Cor. 9:19-23; Phil. 2:5-7; II Cor. 4:5)

11. EDUCATION AND LEADERSHIP

We confess that we have sometimes pursued church growth at the expense of church depth, and divorced evangelism from Christian nurture. We also acknowledge that some of our missions have been too slow to equip and encourage national leaders to assume their rightful responsibilities. Yet we are committed to indigenous principles, and long that every church will have national leaders who manifest a Christian style of leadership in terms not of domination but of service. We recognize that there is a great need to improve theological education, especially for church leaders. In every nation and culture there should be an effective training program for pastors and laity in doctrine, discipleship, evangelism, nurture and service. Such training programs should not rely on any stereotyped methodology but should be developed by creative local initiatives according to biblical standards.

(Col. I:27,28; Acts 14:23; Tit. 1:5,9; Mark 10:42-45; Eph. 4:11,12)

12. SPIRITUAL CONFLICT

We believe that we are engaged in constant spiritual warfare with the principalities and powers of evil, who are seeking to overthrow the Church and frustrate its task of world evangelization. We know our need to equip ourselves with God's amour and to fight this battle with the spiritual weapons of truth and prayer. For we detect the activity of our enemy, not only in false ideologies outside the Church, but also inside it in false gospels which twist Scripture and put people in the place of God. We need both watchfulness and discernment to safeguard the biblical gospel. We acknowledge that we ourselves are not immune to worldliness of thoughts and action, that is, to a surrender to secularism. For example, although careful studies of church growth, both numerical and spiritual, are right and valuable, we have sometimes neglected them. At other times, desirous to ensure a response to the gospel, we have compromised our message, manipulated our hearers through pressure techniques, and become unduly preoccupied with statistics or even dishonest in our use of them. All this is worldly. The Church must be in the world; the world must not be in the Church.

(Eph. 6:12; II Cor. 4:3,4; Eph. 6:11,13-18; II Cor. 10:3-5; I John 2:18-26; 4:1-3; Gal. 1:6-9; II Cor. 2:17; 4:2; John 17:15)

13. FREEDOM AND PERSECUTION

It is the God-appointed duty of every government to secure conditions of peace, justice and liberty in which the Church may obey God, serve the Lord Jesus Christ, and preach the gospel without interference. We therefore pray for the leaders of nations and call upon them to guarantee freedom of thought and conscience, and freedom to practice and propagate religion in accordance with the will of God and as set forth in The Universal Declaration of Human Rights. We also express our deep concern for all who have been unjustly imprisoned, and especially for those who are suffering for their testimony to the Lord Jesus. We promise to pray and work for their freedom. At the same time we refuse to be intimidated by their fate. God helping us, we too will seek to stand against injustice and to remain faithful to the gospel, whatever the cost. We do not forget the warnings of Jesus that persecution is inevitable.

(I Tim. 1:1-4, Acts 4:19; 5:29; Col. 3:24; Heb. 13:1-3; Luke 4:18; Gal. 5:11; 6:12; Matt. 5:10-12; John 15:18-21)

14. THE POWER OF THE HOLY SPIRIT

We believe in the power of the Holy Spirit. The Father sent his Spirit to bear witness to his Son; without his witness ours is futile. Conviction of sin, faith in Christ, new birth and Christian growth are all his work. Further, the Holy Spirit is a missionary spirit; thus evangelism should arise spontaneously from a Spirit-filled church. A church that is not a missionary church is contradicting itself and quenching the Spirit. Worldwide evangelization will become a realistic possibility only when the Spirit renews the Church in truth and wisdom, faith, holiness, love and power. We therefore call upon all Christians to pray for such a visitation of the sovereign Spirit of God that all his fruit may appear in all his people and that all his gifts may enrich the body of Christ. Only then will the whole church become a fit instrument in his hands, that the whole earth may hear his voice.

(I Cor. 2:4; John 15:26;27; 16:8-11; I Cor. 12:3; John 3:6-8; II Cor. 3:18; John 7:37-39; I Thess. 5:19; Acts 1:8; Psa. 85:4-7; 67:1-3; Gal. 5:22,23; I Cor. 12:4-31; Rom. 12:3-8)

15. THE RETURN OF CHRIST

We believe that Jesus Christ will return personally and visibly, in power and glory, to consummate his salvation and his judgment. This promise of his coming is a further spur to our evangelism, for we remember his words that the gospel must first be preached to all nations. We believe that the interim period between Christ's ascension and return is to be filled with the mission of the people of God, who have no liberty to stop before the end. We also remember his warning that false Christs and false prophets will arise as precursors of the final Antichrist. We therefore reject as a proud, self-confident dream the notion that people can ever build a utopia on earth. Our Christian confidence is that God will perfect his kingdom, and we look forward with eager anticipation to that day, and to the new heaven and earth in which righteousness will dwell and God will reign forever. Meanwhile, we rededicate ourselves to the service of Christ and of people in joyful submission to his authority over the whole of our lives.

(Mark 14:62; Heb. 9:28; Mark 13:10; Acts 1:8-11; Matt. 28:20; Mark 13:21-23; 1 John 2:18; 4:1-3; Luke 12:32; Rev. 21:1-5; II Pet. 3:13; Matt. 28:18)

CONCLUSION

Therefore, in the light of this our faith and our resolve, we enter into a solemn covenant with God and with each other, to pray, to plan and to work together for the evangelization of the whole world. We call upon others to join us. May God help us

by his grace and for his glory to be faithful to this our covenant!
Amen, Alleluia!

National Prayer Organizations

- Global Prayer Connection
- The 4/14 Window - Uniting the Global Prayer Movement to target the challenge of making disciples of the 4/14 Window and equipping them to transform the world in the power of Christ.
- 4-14 Window Global Initiative - The 4-14 Window refers to the demographic group from age four to fourteen years old, which is the most open and receptive to every form of spiritual and developmental input. God is calling us to a new missional focus: the 4-14 Window golden age of opportunity to transform the world. God is calling us to radically change the way we view children and to respond to the 4-14 Window strategic importance and rightful place in His Kingdom.
- 24-7 Prayer - There are various 24/7 Prayer Watches worldwide
- American Bible Society - American Bible Society uniting the world in prayer through a Worldwide Circle of Prayer
- Australian Children's Prayer Network - The vision of this network is to mobilize and network praying Christian children
- Australian Prayer Network - News and prayer info from Australia
- Awaken the Watchmen 24-7 Prayer
- Bethany World Prayer Center
- Bible Online - The Bible Society is an advocate for the Bible in

contemporary cultures, resourcing and influencing those who shape society and making the Bible heard by all.

- Caleb Project - Providing media tools and training experiences to equip the body of Christ for strategic ministry to unreached peoples.
- Call2all - All2all is a partnership of hundreds of the top missions agencies, denominations, and organizations in the world, including tens of thousands of Christian leaders, all working together and strategizing to complete the Great Commission in our generation. Working together, we accomplish what could not be finished if we all act alone.
- Children in Prayer - Teaching children to hear the voice of God through the discipline and practice of prayer and be trained as worship leaders, intercessors, and evangelists as God so chooses.
- Children's Prayer Journal - A must for the parents and teachers of Children in Prayer
- Children's Prayer Network, South Africa - Our passion is PRAYER. Our focus is CHILDREN.
- Childrensprayernet - To raise up a generation of young leaders who know how to reach heaven through intersession.
- Christian Solidarity Worldwide - CSW is a Christian organization working for religious freedom through advocacy and human rights, in the pursuit of justice.
- Christians Concerned for Burma (CCB)
- CryOut - Calling believers from all corners of the earth to pray and fast for people and cities in Lebanon, Syria, Jordon and Iraq.
- Ethnê to Ethnê . . . This Generation! - Learn more about the 6,900 "least-reached by the Gospel groups" in the world
- Every Home for Christ - Participate actively in taking the Gospel of Jesus Christ to every home in the whole world
- Global AIDS Prayer Network - Pray to God to end AIDS
- Global Day of Prayer - To call Christians from all Nations to unite in repentance and prayer and work together as God's servants for the blessing and healing of the Nations
- Global Harvest Ministries - Powerful prayer, spiritual warfare, and spiritual mapping could literally change the spiritual atmosphere over nations, cities, and people groups.
- Global Mapping International - GMI is to produce and present world-class research that fuels emerging mission movements and leaders

- Global Prayer Digest - The Global Prayer Digest is a unique devotional booklet for each day.
- Gospel Communications - 300 individual online ministries working to use technology and the Internet to reach the world with the message of Jesus Christ
- Hollywood Prayer Network - Christians around the world are invited to catch the vision of the HPN to pray for Entertainment professionals.
- Hope for Europe - Hope for Europe is a relational movement networking followers of Jesus in many fields across the continent, partnering for transformation of life and society.
- Humanitarian International Services Group - Worldwide disaster relief and community development operations of HISG.
- In Jesus' Name Productions - A not-for-profit ministry created to be the world's first Christian movie studio. We bring together leading Hollywood filmmakers to create and release films designed to be both compelling entertainment and high-quality ministry tools for the purpose of maximum spiritual impact throughout the world.
- Intercessors for America
- Interprayer - Partnering in prayer and action towards transformation of the nations
- Jericho Walls International Prayer Network - Connecting people, mobilizing prayer and transforming the world
- Joel News - Aiming to supply encouraging and reliable news about what God is doing worldwide.
- Joshua Project - To spread a passion for the supremacy of God among all unreached peoples
- Kids in Ministry - The purpose of Kids In Ministry International is to impart vision to children and adults of how God sees children as His partners in ministry worldwide
- Kidspray - To mobilize and network praying Christian children
- Muslim Prayer Focus - 30-Days of Prayer for the Muslim World coinciding with Ramadan each year
- National Pastors' Prayer Network - Not just for pastors
- Neighbourhood Watchmen - An initiative to encourage Christians to pray for their local community.
- Open Doors International - Open Doors' vision is to strengthen and equip the Body of Christ living under or facing restriction and persecution because of their faith in Jesus Christ, and to encourage their

involvement in world evangelism

- Operation World - The primary purpose of Operation World is PRAYER!
- Prayer Week - Make the week, a prayer week for churches or fellowships, so that as many churches as possible throughout the world are praying together with a similar purpose.
- Praying Through the Window - Praying through the 10/40 Window
- Teach us to Pray - Learn through fun to pray
- The National Day of Prayer for America - To communicate with every individual the need for personal repentance and prayer, mobilizing the Christian community to intercede for America and its leadership
- The Cause - Helping kids change the world
- The Persecuted Church - They were called to help acquaint His Free Church with His Persecuted Church
- The Sentinel Group - The Sentinel Group is a community of cutting-edge researchers, filmmakers and ministers dedicated to the task of preparing needy communities for spiritual revival and societal transformation.
- Thirty-Second-Kneel-Down Prayer Revolution - Transform the history of campuses by calling a generation to pray each morning before school
- U.S. Prayer Center - Discipling the nations for Christ
- Viva Network: Children's prayer for children at risk - Find out how you can equip and encourage children to pray for children at risk
- Voice of the Martyrs - A vision for aiding Christians around the world who are being persecuted for their faith in Christ, fulfilling the Great Commission, and educating the world about the ongoing persecution of Christians.
- Way Makers - A mobilization ministry focused on seeing Christ glorified by obedient, worshiping movements in every people group.
- World Prayer - Praying for the world by the world
- World Prayer Assembly - To bring together prayer leaders, intercessors, church and marketplace leaders, and children and youth to accelerate the development of an ongoing, interactive global prayer movement towards the fulfillment of Habakkuk 2:14, that "the earth will be filled with the knowledge of the glory of the Lord".
- World Prayer Centre - As the Church begins to strategize and think globally, so we must pray globally.

- WorldWide Prayer - Luke 18:7 "and shall not God avenge His own elect which cry day and night unto Him"; WorldWide prayer offers many prayer resources, prayer focus points, and updates.
- Xtreme Prayer - How do you raise up a new generation of radical worshipers who will change the destiny of their world through a lifestyle of prayer . . . ?

Annual Calendar of Prayer Days
Establish a rhythm of prayer, using these prayer events: daily, monthly, quarterly, annually.

First Friday Prayer Focus
First Friday of Each Month
www.ifapray.org

JANUARY

Great Days of Prayer
First Sunday in the Quarter
www.praycog.org

Fasting for His Favor
Join over a million Christians who begin the year with a concentrated fast.
January 10-31
www.praycog.org

FEBRUARY

Collegiate Day of Prayer
Fourth Thursday
www.collegiatedayofprayer.org

Seek God for the City
Devotional produced by Waymakers

40 days before Palm Sunday
www.waymakers.org

MARCH

Seek God for the City continues

40 Days for Life
www.40daysforlife.com

APRIL

Great Days of Prayer
First Sunday in the Quarter

Seek God for the City concludes

MAY

National Day of Prayer
First Thursday
www.nationaldayofprayer.org

Pentecost Sunday
Varies according to Easter

Global Day of Prayer
Pentecost Sunday
www.gdopusa.com

JULY

Great Days of Prayer
First Sunday in the Quarter

Call 2 Fall
Sponsored by the Family Research Council
First Sunday
www.call2fall.com

AUGUST

30 Days of Prayer for the Muslim World
Varies according to Ramadan

www.30-days.net

SEPTEMBER

Saturation Prayer Campaign
September 1-30
www.projectpray.org

Operation: 9-1-1
Pray at 9AM/9PM for one minute, with one purpose – a national spiritual awakening.

Patriot Day
Sponsored by Cry out America
September 11
www.awakeningamerica.us

See You at the Pole
Fourth Wednesday
syatp.org

OCTOBER

Great Days of Prayer
First Sunday in the Quarter

Day of Prayer for the Peace of Jerusalem
First Sunday
www.daytopray.com

Global Day to Pray for Unreached People Groups
Sponsored by Billion Soul Network
Last Sunday
www.billion.tv

NOVEMBER

International Day of Prayer for the Persecuted Church
Second Sunday
www.idop.org

The Process

Here is another look at the process, a slightly different model. The early questions: Where are we now? What do we know – how well do we know the state of the church and the city – and what do we need to know? Where do we want to go? What is important to us? What will the task look like when it is finished, how will we measure success? Who needs to be in the room to make this happen? How do we develop a long-range plan? What do we do first?

Defining Mission

It is always out of deep dependence on God that mission must arise. Always. If you allow your creative team members to put forth mission ideas, there will likely be no small number on the table. *Good* ideas. Even *great* ideas, but not necessarily God ideas. Prayer, corporate prayer, gives birth to mission. This means creating opportunities for pastors to gather in prayer in increasing numbers. For laymen to gather across denominational lines to connect for extended times of prayer, which will be historic. Christians, gathered consistently to pray for their city. And then, to connect to one another in their vocational sectors – teachers praying together,

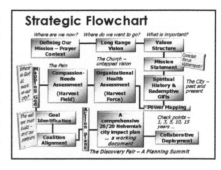

doctors and nurses, business leaders, members of the financial sector, judges and attorneys, on and on. The more you pray together, the greater unity will grow. The healthier the relationships will become. The higher trust levels will develop. That is due, in part, to the view we have of one another in the context of prayer. It is prayer that gives us the clearest look into one another's hearts – not our idea sharing in dialogue. It is when we hear someone sincerely talking to God that we see their heart most perceptibly – broken, humble, hungry, dependent, strong, committed, yielded, ready, open. Moments when we see one another's hearts bind us together!

Vision and Values

Out of prayer comes a sense of mission, and it is in prayer that unity for the mission is forged. Direction is determined in the crosshairs of mission and vision. Mission feels and says, it is passionate and articulate; vision sees. Values help us sort through the mission-vision elements, giving priority to what is most important. With values defined, and a vision of

what can be along with a clear, you are now ready to forge a clear, crisp mission statement. This is, a concise declaration of your purpose for existence and your intentions going forward. It should be succinct enough to memorize quickly and every strategic leader should determine to be able to articulate it to others.

The value of LOVE AND UNITY - The gospel you offer is a gospel of reconciliation. You may have some sharp conflicts in your journey. At times, these will center on differences of doctrine and style. At other times, they may rise out of deeply held feelings about the mission itself, its priorities and leadership issues. Keeping everyone in the room may not be possible. Nevertheless, a spirit of conciliation

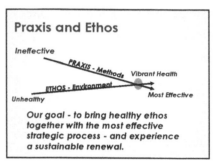

Praxis and Ethos

Ineffective

PRAXIS - Methods   Vibrant Health

ETHOS - Environment

Unhealthy   Most Effective

Our goal - to bring healthy ethos together with the most effective strategic process - and experience a sustainable renewal.

should always prevail and a door for renewed relationship should be open. Two terms, noted earlier, are critical – *praxis* and *ethos.* *Praxis* has to do with practices, tools and the process itself, with outcomes. It is pragmatic. It gets one caught up in doing. Intoxicated by action. It wants to abandon the ineffective, move toward the more effective, reaching to the most effective. *Ethos* is the intangible. It is difficult to measure. It is often unnoticed until it is unbearable, because it is the environment in which the action, the praxis is unwrapped. It is not a natural focus point, but something to which we pay indirect attention. It is the *spirit,* the attitudes, the underlying emotional messaging, the acceptance and approval, the love, in which the individuals and teams operate. It is how they treat and respect one another. *Praxis* is about *quantifiable* results; ethos, about the *qualitative* relational process – and that affects the outcome in ways that are sometimes not immediately discernable. If we get a gospel team on the doorsteps of every home in the city/

county, but we do so in a manner that is inconsistent with the gospel of peace itself, we have failed. "My how those Christians love one another" should be heard in the community.

Research

Now, you move forward with your initial research. You know where God wants to take you (mission) and what it will look like when you get there (vision), and you have so clearly defined your values, that you know the behaviors that are important along the journey. You recognize that what you must embrace is not merely *praxis,* new improved methodology, tools to transform the church and the city, but *ethos,* the intangibles that change a culture, the essence at the heart of all you do! To fulfill the mission in a manner that does not honor Christlikeness, humility and grace, is to fail in the mission!

The Past and Present - In order to move forward with your mission, you need to survey the city. What are its needs? What is the present condition? Who is in the city? To what degree is it Christian? The initial study is largely demographic – population levels/growth trends, households/married/single/seniors, age median, income – all the things we have noted earlier in this document. You want to review the harvest field (city/county) and the harvest force. Once you have a reliable overview of the current status on the harvest field and force, you need to look back. What is the history of the city/county? Revivals? What is its history with regard to the gospel? Significant moves of God? What is its nature? A river town, a railroad town, an interstate town, a valley town, a tourist spot, a lakeside community, a mountain village, an industrial center, a banking center, a transportation hub, a high-tech epicenter, a recreational center, a gambling/casino town, an entertainment mecca, a college town, a capitol, a headquarters city, a medical center, an ethnic collage, an international community? The nature of the city/county will have about it a spiritual shadow. It affects the dynamic of the city in more than an obvious way. What is its reputation? What is the root of its founding? Who were its earliest influencers? Who are its most famous people? What does it take pride in?

You not only want to map the potentially negative, but also the positive. What are the redemptive gifts of the city? What does the city offer other cities, the nation? Goods, products, services, medical care, etc.? Why do people come to your city/county? Why do people beyond your boundaries know about you, depend on some company or someone in your city – for good purposes? What is your city/county offering the state? The nation? For example, is it the home of a state hospital for the elderly, of a VA treatment center? Is it home to an orphanage? Does it manufacture parts used in a certain industry across the nation? Is it a leading producer of a certain resource distributed widely? Perhaps, it houses a unique family restoration complex. Or it is the home of a retreat center used in a five-state region. Maybe your horses and horse farms are internationally known. Perhaps, you have a loan, processing center that handles a huge number of loans for the entire state. Or, you manufacture housing for a five state area. Every area is known, in a positive manner, for its contributions to others.

The Harvest Force and Field
(Congregations/Christians and the City/County)

Your next two steps are to determine the organizational health of the church (harvest force). Are you up to the mission? Are your churches growing? Are pastors in unity? Are there evident signs of spiritual vitality? How healthy are the congregations of the city? Then, you want to be aware of the compassion needs of the city/

county (harvest field)? If you were to make a tangible impact in the area of felt needs, where is the community need the most severe? Housing (affordable, safe housing; abandoned housing restored), employment, family infrastructure, men/fathering, teen sexuality, abortion/adoption, violence/crime, food (meals on wheels, pantries), poverty, safe children's areas/playgrounds, racism, predatory businesses, transportation (for the poor, elderly), hospice volunteers, teen mentoring – and more. In the city is extraordinary pain; and in the church are huge levels of untapped potential and promise. Both must be discovered. Each corresponds to the other.

Mapping God

Remember, God leads the process – not you and your ideas. Not you and your data. Be *informed;* then let your strategy *be formed* by the Spirit. Pray. Ask this question – Is God already at work in our community in caring for the hurting? Where is he working, and how can we join him in his work? There may be evidence of God's work in teens, among men, a stirring among intercessors, benevolent activity by a group that is not overtly Christian, but their work is an act of common grace. How can we join God in what He is doing in our city/county? This may require some probing. Some stirring of the fire? How has God moved in the past in our area? How is He perceived in the marketplace? Pray for ancient wells to be opened, ancient altars to flame up again with holy fire from heaven. Reach back to promises and prophecies spoken but not completely fulfilled. If the way is not clear – pray! Don't race ahead. Seeing God at work will inspire more energy than see the need. The needs you uncover will overwhelm you, but seeing God at work will also energize and inspire you. Remember the words of Jesus, we 'look on the harvest field, seeing it white unto harvest,' and then we lift our eyes to the 'Lord of the harvest, and pray, that he might thrust out laborers.' Responding to the needs will be fatal to your mission. It will degenerate into a humanitarian effort. Noble, but lacking transformational power. Responding to God, going with his cue, being 'thrust' by the Spirit into the harvest, that is a wholly different dynamic. See the harvest, then pray. Weep over whitened fields and hurting people, then cry out to God.

Goal Identification/Coalition Alignment

Now you are ready to do goal identification. This is a matter of strategy. What must be done first, in order to accomplish subsequent tasks? And yet, this is more than the mere sequencing and timing of your effort, it is an assessment of how the various efforts fit together, how teams must relate, how collaboration and unity must emerge. It is far too easy to move from an overly simply mission and shallow vision to 'one thing' you can do together, a tactic, which is often far too narrow! You need a strategic, a big picture plan. Not everyone needs to struggle with either this concept or its design. However, your leadership team needs to buy into the big picture and its plan. The next step is to build the coalitions that can own the various component parts. These will be, in some cases, already in existence. The church may be the late comer – and reluctantly admitted to the table, for example, on solving the community's housing and poverty needs, its concern for afterschool childcare for latchkey kids. With coalitions and partnerships in place, you move to tactical deployment, each church, each agency, each team owning the rebuilding of its portion of the wall. This requires an action plan.

A Comprehensive Plan

Eventually, you want a 2020/2025 Nehemiah Plan. What are

our goals, what does God want us to do in our county/city by 2020/2025. Could we impact crime? Get the gospel to every door? Reach ethnic groups who have never heard the message? Reduce the abortion and divorce rate? Launch a citywide men's prayer and discipleship endeavor? Partner with schools to create safe zones for after-school care? What do we want our city/county to look like, be like in ten to fifteen years? Will we be like the generation before Nehemiah, content to live in the rubble?

Collaborative Deployment

With a comprehensive working document, which will take as much as 6-12 months to produce, you are ready for a multi-day discovery fair, in which you tell the story of your city/county – its past, its present, and its future, given the grace of God at work in your work. Out of such a conference, you are now ready for long-term collaborative action.

You will want checkpoints along the way – one year, three years, five years, etc. Each time you will revisit your mission, re-calibrate your strategy, realign your tactical teams. You will continue to do objective measurements of your effectiveness.

Your research is no small part of the process. In ancient warfare, there were three non-negotiable essentials for the development of strategy. Know the target opposition, its strength and capabilities, and its position. Know your own force and resources. And know the terrain. Beyond that, generals prayed for good or bad weather, high or low water at fords and crossings. Rain or snow, or no rain and no snow, in valleys and mountain passes. The weather, the unseen, the unpredictable, the hand of God, was the wild card. David and Goliath moments happen. And God may give you one! But to make the exceptional common and avoid the hard work of research is telling of the lack of resolve and interest in the community by the church.

Elements of the City Transformation Process

Out of research, your collaborative process should be carried forward by the linkage and partnership of interdependent teams. There should be a lively **pastoral prayer movement.** The city-wide prayer council should be in action, proliferating prayer, encouraging congregations to become 'houses of prayer for the unreached'. **Intercessors** should be linked across the city. **Prayer**

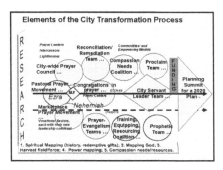

leaders of various prayer days and efforts, and para-church organizations should now know one another and be collaborating. Your **Marketplace** initiative should be alive in a number of sectors. This means you have identified key Christians, from the communities different congregations, who want to see the city impacted for the glory of God, people come to Christ, the moral character of the city improved, the crime rate dimensioned, and more. These people, lay-leaders of the Nehemiah stream, must become peers to pastoral leaders, serving in the church extended, the church in the city, the vocationally engaged form of church (diaspora). In every vocational sector, these leaders need to emerge – men and women of character, of prayer, with compassion and a passion to see people saved.

Critical to your success is the empowerment of multiple 'strands' of prayer and ministry, all interwoven. Pastors and congregations need to be envisioned and engaged, as do new marketplace leaders. A relational construct of laypeople across the city need to be linked and strategically engaged to reach the neighborhoods where they live and the marketplaces where they shop and work. They are our mission force in a mission field increasingly distant from the church. **Prayer evangelism** teams need to be trained in contemporary evangelism approaches. A plan needs to be developed to engage every household in the city/county with the gospel in specific time period. As prayer spreads across the city, efforts need to be set forth to assist in helping **churches** become **houses of prayer,** and not merely places of praise and preaching. Congregations that establish prayer rooms and prayer centers need to linked.

As the process moves forward, it will become clear that there are relational chasms. Some will exist between pastors and congregations, some between Christians in the city, some between the church and the city, and others in the city itself. The gospel we offer is one of reconciliation – it is at the heart of our message. Paul reminds us that our feet are to be shod with the preparation of the gospel of peace. To press the metaphor, we walk in peace. We are to leave a trail of peace, footprints of peace. We are agents of peace. Sadly, the church is rarely the agent of reconciliation in the middle of a community crisis. Who are the people who can be empowered to be peacemakers. Every city needs **a reconciliation team.**

The **Proclamation Team** looks for avenues to proclaim the gospel. This is the more public approach to evangelism, but should be combined with prayer evangelism. This team might sponsor a businessmen's evangelism event, a community youth revival, a children's summer witness-in-the-parks campaign, a special family-life revival for the city. There are so many creative approaches.

One of the most powerful components of your impact process will be the **compassion coalition.** You will want to determine what activities are already occurring to touch the pain and need of the city, and what areas are not being addressed. Then, getting those folks in the same room and finding ways to collaborate will be critical. A number of groups will exist and be effective that will not be explicitly Christian, but Christians will typically be on such teams. Find ways to synergize, collaborate and give birth creatively to meet needs not now being addressed. When needs are met, cups of water given 'in the name of Jesus' – you press the mission forward and open hearts to gospel.

One of your greatest needs will be a **resource and training team** – actually teams. But these teams must be given to the city. A team specifically effective in helping families reestablish a family altar is needed in every congregation in the city. A team capable of assisting in resourcing youth pastors in the prayer-care-share strategy is needed by every youth pastor. Find opportunities to collaborate, to train across the entire city.

The **prophetic team** is one that might create discomfort for some, and it may seem to be at cross-purposes with the reconciliation-peace process. But love can never muzzle truth. Nor should truth eclipse love. There is a prophetic message to which the church is bound. Critical situations may emerge in the process that need a clear, reasoned, Biblical response. Often, the voice of the church is silent or agitated. The prophetic team considers, "What is the message of God to the church, and to the city?" It engages society with truth! It speaks gently, but without compromise. It speaks truth, in the spirit of love.

The City-Servant Leader Team is a composite of all the various team leaders or representatives. They are all moving toward the 2020/2025 goals.

National Prayer Committee
Mission, Values, Call and Covenant

Mission

Centered on the Lord Jesus Christ, America's National Prayer Committee exists to provide collective servant leadership to the national prayer movement.

Values

TO FOSTER A RESTORATION OF CHRIST'S CENTRALITY AND FULLNESS throughout the Body of Christ, and specifically within the national prayer movement.

TO PROMOTE THE BIBLICAL HOPE of revival in the Church, leading to the intervention of God in mercy, justice, righteousness, reconciliation, and completion of the Great Commission of Christ.

TO PROVIDE A FORUM FOR PRAYER LEADERS, both national and regional, from all ethnicities and denominations, to synthesize an interactive vision for revival, leading to awakening, evangelism, and discipleship.

TO DEVELOP A UNITED VOICE AMONG PRAYER LEADERS that speaks lovingly to central issues in prayer and revival, preparing the way for a supernatural work of God in our churches and our nation.

TO "WATCH AND PRAY" OVER THE PRAYER MOVEMENT fostering and protecting it as we intercede for it and for one another.

TO FACILITATE COLLABORATIONS IN MINISTRY among national prayer leaders as we serve the prayer movement together.

TO COMMUNICATE WIDELY developments in the prayer movement, as well as God's answers to our prayers, in support of an acceleration of the moving of God in our land.

TO SERVE, LEARN FROM, AND ENCOURAGE those who are advancing the prayer movement on every front and level, both nationally and worldwide.

TO OFFER COUNSEL AND ENCOURAGEMENT to those who are advancing the prayer movement on every front and every level.

TO ENCOURAGE THE DEVELOPMENT OF RESOURCES, spiritual, educational, and material that are needed to strengthen and equip the national prayer movement.

TO FACILITATE A BROADER NETWORKING between prayer leaders and other Christian leaders committed to a national spiritual awakening to Christ.

Our Call

We recognize our absolute dependence on God and our desperate need for divine intervention.

We believe God is urging us to call all Christians of America to unite in humility and repentance across ethnic and church boundaries to pray persistently for a moral and spiritual awakening in the Body of Christ.

We believe this will greatly advance His Kingdom in our nation and worldwide.

Our Covenant

- We covenant to obey this call by taking the following actions: We will promote this call as broadly as possible.
- Individually, we will commune with God and pray with faith daily.
- We will encourage and participate regularly in corporate, believing prayer.
- We will fast as God prompts us.
- Feeling incomplete without embracing God's family from all races, we will seek reconciliation and participation with all brothers and sisters.
- We will pray until God sovereignly acts.

Calling the Church to a Rhythm of Prayer for Revival

In response to our desperate need for revival in the Church and a spiritual awakening in our country, America's National Prayer Committee, the Awakening America Alliance, and OneCry are issuing a call to believers to join a national Rhythm of Prayer.

The National Prayer Accord was first issued during the First Great Awakening in the United States during the 1730s and '40s. This Prayer Accord is now reissued in this dark hour as a simple pattern of prayer we can embrace in unity to ask Jesus Christ to once again pour out His Spirit on the Church.

THE NATIONAL PRAYER ACCORD

In recognition of:

- Our absolute dependence on God
- The moral and spiritual challenges facing our nation
- Our national need for repentance and divine intervention
- Our great hope for a general awakening to the Lordship of Christ, the unity of His Body, and the sovereignty of

His Kingdom

We strongly urge all churches and all Christians of America to unite in seeking the face of God through prayer and fasting, persistently asking our Father to send revival to the Church and spiritual awakening to our nation so that Christ's Great Commission might be fulfilled worldwide in our generation.

We resolve to promote as an ongoing Prayer Rhythm:

- Weekly—one-half-hour to one-hour private or small group prayer
- Monthly—one- to two-hour individual church prayer gatherings
- Quarterly—one- to two-hour local, multiple church prayer gatherings
- Annually—The National Day of Prayer (first Thursday of May), Cry Out America prayer gatherings (September 11).

Prayer Connect and other ministries are in the process of setting up website that will include multiple resources, news, and a sign-up to register your commitment to follow the rhythm. Keep checking back to see what is added.

Statistical Benchmarks
and Averages

CHRISTIAN MEDIA (RADIO, TV and the WEB)

- About 46% of Christian adults tune in to Christian radio; 91% tune into general radio.
- Nearly two-thirds of those who listen (of the 46% above, thus around 30%, do so at least several times per week).
- One third, 15%, tune in to Christian radio each day (about 20 million), significant, but less than seven percent of the US population.
- Listeners are predominantly women 45-54 years of age, frequent churchgoers, Pentecostal/Charismatic, residents of the South, politically conservative, and self-described activists.
- One in four (23%) of those who listen, don't tune in for Christian programs, they say they are not interested in 'Christian content' (listen mostly for the music)/
- One in five (20%) prefer other content such as news and sports. Eleven percent prefer to get their Christian content elsewhere. Read more at http://www.christianpost.com/news/survey-only-3-in-5-christian-radio-listeners-tune-in-for-music-33305/#2VLDsygpksSaXoR7.99 Read: at http://www.christianpost.com/news/survey-only-3-in-5-christian-radio-listeners-tune-in-for-music-33305/#2VLDsygpksSaXoR7.99

- Sixteen percent of adults spend time on faith-oriented websites monthly. Evangelicals: 41%; compared to 18% - other born again Christians; and 10% of non-born again Americans. The younger a person is, the more likely they are to visit a faith-oriented site. Western states and African-Americans are the groups most likely to check out these resources.

- The same people groups that resisted faith-based radio and television - mainline Protestants, Catholics, Asian-Americans, and the unchurched - were also the least likely visitors to these locations on the worldwide web. See: http://www.barna.org/barna-update/article/5-barna-update/183-more-people-use-christian-media-than-attend-church

- The percentage of adults who watch Christian television programming has remained unchanged since 1992 (An estimated 45% tune into a Christian program in a typical month).

- About seven percent watch Christian television daily.

- Forty-one percent 'never' watch such programming. Christian television draws its strength from people in their 60s and older, females, residents of the South, African-Americans, people with limited education and income and 'born again' Christians.

- Two-thirds of the 'born again' population views Christian programming monthly, more than double the proportion of non-born again adults (30%). Those most likely to watch include mainline Protestants, Catholics, unchurched people, Asian-Americans and college graduates.

- More unchurched people watch Christian television than listen to Christian radio, although the margin of difference is small.

- Slightly more than one-fourth of the unchurched - about 20 million adults - tune in to these shows each month. See: http://www.barna.org/barna-update/article/5-barna-update/183-more-people-use-christian-media-than-attend-church.

CHURCHES and CHRISTIANS

- No one knows the number of churches in the US, speculation places the number between 300,000 to 350,000. For our purposes, we have used the number 330,000. [Source: Rebecca Barnes and Lindy Lowry, 7 Startling Facts: An Up Close Look at Church Attendance in America, http://www.churchleaders.com/pastors/pastor-articles/139575-7-startling-facts-an-up-

close-look-at-church-attendance-in-america.html? Accessed December 16, 2013.]
- That translates to 105 churches per county.
- Using current statistical data, there is a ratio of one church in the US to 937 people. For our purposes, we are using the benchmark of one church per thousand population.
- Seventy-five percent of the US Population self-report as Christian (The Pew Forum, has that number at 73%].
- Almost 50% of Christians attend 10% of the largest churches. Most churches are small, single-cell congregations.
- Nationally, the church attendance mean is 75, meaning half of all churches are smaller or larger than 75.
- About 90% of all churches are less than 350 congregants.
- Nationally, only 10%, some 33,500 churches, 10.6 per county are larger than 350.
- The number who identify as Christians has fallen precipitously from 89% in 1990, to the present 73-75%.
- Fifteen percent of the population do not claim a faith – and they are the most vocal group.
- Sixty-two percent of the US population claim to be members of a church. [Finke, Roger; Rodney Stark (2005). The Churching of America, 1776-2005. Rutgers University Press. 22–23. ISBN 0-8135-3553-0. online at Google Books.]
- The number of non-Anglo congregations in the Southern Baptist Convention has jumped by more than 66% since 1998, according to the North American Mission Board's Center for Missional Research. 10,049 out of 50,768 congregations in the convention identified themselves by an ethnicity other than Anglo in 2011. Also, Hispanic and Asian SBC congregations have risen by 63% and 55%, respectively. (Baptist Press 1/23/13)
- LifeWay Research recently asked more than 4,000 Protestants in the U.S. and Canada, "In the past 6 months, how many times have you made a decision to obey or follow God with awareness that choosing His way might be costly to you in some way?" 37% reported zero times, 36% said 1–2 times, 14% did it 3–5 times while 13% did so 6 or more times. (Facts & Trends, Fall 2012)

CHURCH ATTENDANCE

- On any given Sunday, about 17.7% of the US population attend the nation's churches.

- For many years, the Gallup Poll reported that 40% or more of Americans were in church every Sunday – a figure based on self-reporting by individuals polled. There was no cumulative hard data to substantiate that number until recently. The figure of 17.7% is extrapolated from hard data, based on real attendance counts [Study by Olsen].

- Gallup pollsters, reflecting on the 40% or more of the population who say they attend church each Sunday, note: "No matter how we ask the question to people, we get roughly 40% of Americans who present themselves as regular church attendees".

- In 2005, The Journal for the Scientific Study of Religion published a study by sociologists C. Kirk Hadaway and Penny Long Marler — known for their scholarly research on the Church. Their report revealed that the actual number of people worshipping each week is similar to study conducted by Olson who postulated that 17.7% of Americans were in the pews on any given Sunday. "We knew that over the past 30 to 40 years, denominations had increasingly reported a decline in their numbers," Marler says. Even with still-growing denominations, most mainline denominations were reporting a net loss, and at the same time, the Gallup polls had remained stable. The data was inconsistent. What was at play was "the halo effect" — the divide between what people tell pollsters and what their actions. Americans, it turns out, tend to over-report socially desirable behavior like voting and attending church and under-report socially undesirable behavior like drinking. [Rebecca Barnes and Lindy Lowry, 7 Startling Facts: An Up Close Look at Church Attendance in America, http://www.churchleaders.com/pastors/pastor-articles/139575-7-startling-facts-an-up-close-look-at-church-attendance-in-america.html? Accessed December 16, 2013.]

- There is a growing trend toward worshipping in non-traditional ways, such as small groups. There are informal churches that meet in gyms, storefronts, social halls or even homes.

- Non-denominational independent churches, if considered together, now constitute the third largest segment of congregations in the US, behind only Catholic and Southern Baptist movements.

- In another study, Marler and Hadaway discovered that while the majority of people they interviewed do not belong to a local church, they still identify with their church roots. "Never mind the fact that they attend church less than 12 times a year," Marler observes. "We estimate that 78 million Protestants are in that place." [Source: Rebecca Barnes and Lindy Lowry, 7 Startling Facts: An Up Close Look at Church Attendance in America, http://www.churchleaders.com/pastors/pastor-articles/139575-7-startling-facts-an-up-close-look-at-church-attendance-in-america.html? Accessed December 16, 2013.]

- Fifty percent of all church attenders crowd into the largest 10% of our congregations.

- The broad definition of regular church attendance is someone who shows up at least three out of every eight Sundays, and only 23–25% of Americans fit this category.

- The number of 'regular-irregulars' [every three out of eight weeks] is 23-25%. Gallup's number is 40%. The number of cultural Christians (people who call themselves Christians) is 75%. Ed Stetzer, missiologist and director of the Center for Missional Research at the North American Mission Board of the Southern Baptist Convention recently finished a study on alternative faith communities. The study found that 24.5% of Americans now say their primary form of spiritual nourishment is meeting with a small group of 20 or less people every week. "About 6 million people meet weekly with a small group and never or rarely go to church," Stetzer says. "There is a significant movement happening." Thus, for every nine people in church each Sunday, there is another somewhere in a non-traditional Christian worship, growth or prayer group.

- One church strength assessment postulates, one person in the pew (core strength) equals an additional casual attender. In addition, for each core (the 17.%) and casual attender (Olsen, 25%; Gallup 40%), there is yet another person who in some way identifies with the church (Pew, 75%, cultural Christians).

- Using the above as a model, though it may be generous, optimistic, for every regular attender you then have an irregular attender; and for every regular and irregular attender, you have a 'prospect.' That is ratio calibration of 1:1:2. Using Olsen's number, for every approximate two in the pew (the 17.7% in church each Sunday), we have another one (23-25%) who is irregular. The model falls between Olsen (23-25%) and Gallup (40%). Another church growth model uses the categories – those in close orbit (every Sunday), moderate orbit (irregular), and distant orbit (Easter and Christmas, or less, they are in some direct or indirect way connected to your church).

- The individual in distant orbit is typically an Easter/Christmas/ funeral/ wedding attender. Their grandmother attended the church. A brother was married there. A family member was buried in the church cemetery. They went to Vacation Bible School at a church of the same denomination, but in another city. The close orbit constituency attends almost every Sunday; the moderate orbit constituency – attends irregularly; and with the distant orbit constituency, these three groups constitute the 60-70% of American's who indicate they are involved in the life of some church.

- Countywide, based on Olsen's count, about 17,700 of the 100,000 population (county average) are in the pew each Sunday and that means a whopping 82,300 are NOT. Even if you speculate, that twice that number is in the regular-irregular category, core and casual attenders/close and moderate orbit, you still arrive at only 35.4% of the population, leaving a vast harvest field.

- To average 100, a congregation now needs about 200 attenders (the core and casually committed together).

- In the typical county, Therefore, we would conjecture, that 35,400 people in the county go to church, regularly to irregularly – and yet these are not the never-attenders or the seasonal attenders, the Easter and Christmas crowd. That number – core, casual, cultural/close, moderate/distant – is 70,800, a slightly more conservative number than the 75% who identify as Christian.

CHURCH/CHRISTIAN HEALTH

- It is estimated that some 80-85% of the 330,000 churches are in maintenance mode and not considered, in terms of community impact, life-giving churches.

- Almost 60% (59) of churches draw less than a hundred for Sunday worship. Another 35% draw less than 500. That means that 94% of the churches are smaller than 500 attenders.

- About 6 million people meet weekly with a small group and never or rarely go to church [Stetzer].

- Just 16% of U.S. Christians say they are totally committed to engaging in personal spiritual development.

- Sixteen percent of U.S. adults say they have been hurt by experiences in church.

- Only two percent of church members invite an unchurched person to church.

- Churches that are smallest (attendance 1–49) and the largest churches (2,000-plus) tend to be growing. The small single-cell churches grew 16.4% in a recent study; the largest grew 21.5%, both above the national population growth of 12.2%. However, mid-sized churches (100–299), declined one percent.

- According to some studies, the average Protestant church in America is 124. Some sources project a national average per congregation of 184.

- Half (52.5) of all congregations have fewer than 75 attendees each Sunday.

- Small does not mean unhealthy or ineffective. One study found that 98% of church satisfaction was found in measuring the number of intimate Christian friends within the congregation- relational health. More than the size or the quality of the church programs, even the level of preaching or the inspiration factor, the bottom line is found in the quality of the relational connections. Another factor is ministry opportunity. People who find avenues for service which are consistent with their gifts and passions, they are more fulfilled and motivated to grow in their relationship with the Lord.

- Based on national averages, about 15-20% of the churches are vibrant. According to George Barna, only 10 to 15% of churches are effective in the area of evangelism, thus healthy enough to influence any city or county. Others are stagnant or processing some crisis.

- Nineteen percent of American Protestant churchgoers read the Bible daily, 25% a few times a week, 14% once a week, 27% once a month and 18% rarely or never.

- Sixty-eight percent of U.S. adults celebrate Easter as a religious holiday. While 31% of Americans aged 18–27 celebrate Easter as a non-religious holiday.

- 7 in 10 seniors (65 & older) are white Christians compared to 1 in 10 Millennials (18–29).

- There are more than 5,000 multi-site churches in North America. That's more than 5,000 different churches, each of which has 2 or more different geographic campuses, according to data from a Leadership Network survey. (Advance 9/11/12)

- Churchgoers and Building Relationships - 74% U.S. Protestant churchgoers say they have significant relationships with people at church, but less than half are intentionally helping other believers grow in their faith, claims a LifeWay Research study. 53% intentionally try to get to know new people they meet at church. Yet just 42% intentionally spend time with other believers in order to help them grow in their faith while 28% do not. The research reveals the characteristic that best predicts better building of relationships at church is attendance of small classes or groups of adults. 33% of churchgoers attend classes or groups for adults four or more times in a typical month. 14% attend two or three times a month. 41% do not attend such groups at all, while 12% do so once a month. 40% do not attend church groups. (Baptist Press 4/25/13)

- According to a New LifeWay Research Survey, 66% of American churchgoers believe Christians should seek out honest feedback about their spiritual life from other Christians. 57% say they openly discuss their difficulties with Christian friends. Only one in four does not, according to the survey. Only 34% surveyed indicate they pray for fellow Christians they know every day. 10% do this "once a month" or "rarely/ never." (Baptist Press 5/23/13)

- On average, 20% of pastors will change pastors in a given year.

- Each city/county has committed Christians, casual Christians and cultural Christians. Some 25-30%, the cultural Christians, are disengaged and typically disinterested.

- Soft growth is measured congregation-by-congregation in the movement of families from one church to another, usually in the casually committed, moderate orbit group, but that does little to change the overall impact of faith in the larger culture. What is needed is hard-growth measurements – the number of the uncommitted and the disinterested who become engaged in the faith; the transition of cultural Christians to committed status; and the intensification of the casually committed and distracted to more fervent faith practice. That is a task that can only be accomplished in a collaborate effort.

- America's churches are not keeping pace with population growth of 12.2%. Between 2000 and 2004, the net gain in churches, those opened less those that closed, in evangelical circles, was 5,452.

- Mainline and Catholic churches experienced a net loss of 2,200.

- Combined, all new churches, the net gain of churches in America was 3,252.

- Olson says, approximately 3,000 churches closed every year in the last decade, a number far less than others have speculated, still, this is .9%, just south of one out of every 100 churches.

- Out of new church plants, only 3,800 survived. The net gain in terms of new churches, contrasted with church closures, in this century is 800 each year.

- Consider this – from 2000 to 2004, to keep pace with population growth, a net gain of 13,024 churches was needed.

- Using the population growth as the benchmark, Christianity incurred a deficit of almost 10,000 churches in the period of 2000-2004.

- The U.S. Census predicts a population of 520 million in 2050. At the current growth trajectories, the church will increasingly lose ground. The harvest is growing.

- Some denominational churches no longer include a denominational reference in their name. In fact, among the 20 largest Protestant churches in America, just six have a name that references a denomination. In a new study, Grey Matter Research looked at how a denominational reference (or the lack thereof) in a church name impacts perceptions, particularly among the unchurched. (Grey matter Research 2/21/13)

- Fewer than half of churchgoing Americans realize their house of worship offers official membership, according to a new Grey Matter Research study. 33% believe their church does not offer any sort of official membership, 19% weren't sure, and 48% believe their church does offer official membership. Among the original 48% who believe their church offers membership, 78% are members, with 21% saying they attend but are not members. That translates to 37% in total who claim to be official members of their church and 10% who say they are non-members. The 10 largest Christian denominations in the U.S. all offer some sort of official membership, but only 44% of people belonging to those faiths knew that. About 39% believe their church doesn't offer membership, and 19% are not sure. Those with evangelical beliefs were most likely to believe their church offers membership (72%). (Non-Profit Times 8/29/12)

- Greg Hawkins and Cally Parkinson, in their extraordinary study, identified church attenders on a spiritual continuum in four categories. First, those who were exploring Christ; second, those who had made a faith decision and were growing in Christ; third, those who felt close to Christ; fourth, those who were Christ-centered. The telling mark of the most devoted Christians, almost 80% of them agreeing very strongly, was that they "love God more than anything." What sets them apart is the characterization of their relationship – not as duty or faith, but as love. Sadly, a full third of those 'love God more than anything' do not serve the church frequently.

- According to Hawkins and Parkinson, "Best practice churches don't simply serve their community. They act as its shepherd, becoming deeply involved in community issues and frequently serving in influential positions with local civic organizations. They often partner with nonprofits and other churches to secure whatever resources are necessary to address the most pressing local concerns."

- Those who were in church, but still exploring Christ and on the perimeter of faith fall into active explorers and passive attenders. The five things the exploring Christ segment wants from the church are:
  - Help in developing a personal relationship with Christ (68%);
  - Compelling worship experiences 68%);
  - A feeling of belonging (68%);
  - Help in understanding the Bible (67%);
  - Church leaders who model how to grow spiritually (66%).

- The study by Hawkins and Parkinson points to the extraordinary differences in personal perceptions of their spiritual growth.
  - Fifty-eight percent of the Christ-centered group perceive themselves to be growing at a pace they describe as moderately-to-rapidly in their Christian experience. That almost six-in-ten. These are highly charged individuals, more deeply satisfied.
  - In contrast, only eighteen% of those who are exploring Christ feel that they are growing moderately-to- rapidly, a significant difference.
  - In the group who say they are growing in Christ, 27% classify their growth as moderate to rapid.

- Of those who are close to Christ, 47% classify their growth has moderate-to-rapid.

- The evidence seems compelling, growth in Christ is related to a perception of closeness; moreover, a perception of closeness propels spiritual growth and development. It is relational.

- If an individual attends church for more than five years and is still *exploring* Christ, more than 40% of those in this group feel stalled, stuck in their spiritual quest. A *decision* is necessary to move from exploring to growing in Christ. The longer a person stays in church, without making the decision, the higher the level of dissatisfaction grows.

- Approximately 10% of church attenders are *"exploring* Christ". Some 38% are *growing* in Christ. Another 27% feel *close* to Christ. About one fourth, 25%, consider themselves *Christ-centered.*

- One of the differentiating factors between those who are *exploring* Christ and those who are *growing* in Christ is the level of service. Fifty percent of those who feel that they are growing in Christ commit to a service function in the church at least once per month. Eighty-five percent of them attend church three out of four weekends. Forty-seven percent participate in a small group and at least 50% of them serve in some capacity.

- The factor that separates those who feel *close* to Christ from those who are *exploring* Christ is the daily practice of prayer. Those who believe they are close to Christ pray daily for guidance. Almost half confess their sins daily. The amount of frequency in daily engagement with God in prayer and Bible reading, in spiritual reflection, in solitude in the *close* to Christ groups is more than twice that of the *growing* in Christ segment. It becomes clear, that personal time devoted to prayer and Scripture is the most powerful catalyst for spiritual growth and satisfaction.

- In the areas of Bible reading ("I read the Bible"), reflection on Scripture ("I reflect on the meaning of Scripture in my life"), and solitude ("I set aside time to listen to God") – each of these activities is at least twice greater than in the groups who are merely exploring or growing in Christ. Moving from growth in Christ to rapid growth, to feelings of closeness with God, and deeper satisfaction – is not a *feeling* issue at all, but an *action* issue.

- When a believer feels close to Christ, there is also an increase in their love for others.

- Some 25%, one-in-four church goers, are in the Christ-centered segment. They excel all other groups – they serve the church more, serve those in need, evangelize more frequently, and they tithe more consistently and at higher levels than any of the other three segments. Their sense of love for God and being loved by God is significantly higher than the close to Christ segment. They also feel more equipped to share their faith. And they are more aware of their spiritual gifts.

- When individuals move from *exploring* Christ and *growing* in Christ to feeling *close* to Christ, their satisfaction with the church's role escalates to some 67%.

- The more an individual progresses to a *Christ-centered* life, the more concerned there is for the community, for friends and family around them who may not know Christ. In the beginning of the journey to spiritual development, the focus is on reading the Bible, reflecting on its meaning, personal purity and confession of sins, studying the Bible for truth and direction for their lives, prayer for guidance, setting aside time to listen to God daily.

- As one moves from being merely *close* to Christ, to being *Christ-centered,* they report that God is calling them to be involved in the lives of the poor and suffering, and they begin to invite non-Christians to participate in faith experiences and to know Christ. The more Christ-centered life they live, the more personal initiative for evangelism there is in their own lives. A higher level of personal faith satisfaction with areas that rises out of their own personal experiences and become less reliant upon the church and more reliant upon Christ. Moving from being merely *close* to Christ, to *Christ-centered* means daily reflection on Scripture and time in prayer. A growing trust in the authority of the Bible. A congruence between their own personal sense of self and their identity in Christ. The placing of Christ first in all made in Christ as Savior but is Lord. And finally, the giving of their life away in service to other people from the cause of Christ.

- According to Hawkins and Parkinson, some 26% of church members are stalled or dissatisfied with either the church or their own personal spiritual development. Precisely, some 18% self-classify as dissatisfied; and some 13% self-classify as spiritually stalled or stagnant. There is a five percent overlap. The segment in which stalled Christians show up in greater abundance is in the growing in Christ group. Fifty-two percent of all stalled Christians are in this second segment. Their inability to transition to a relationship in which they feel close to Christ and further, into a Christ-centered life seems to be source of frustration and dissatisfaction.

- Specifically, why do Christians stall? Why have those in the exploring Christ segment of the Hawkins/Parkinson study stalled? Dominating the data is their lack of discipline in daily spiritual practices. Every day busyness crowds out prayer. Other activities take precedence. The lack of spiritual discipline applied daily, time with God, reading the Bible, pausing for reflection, is the dominating factor. It is more decisive than a lack of church community. It is more decisive than ineffective church leadership at the church they attend. It is more of an issue than any personal emotional concerns. It is greater than any doubts about faith.

COMPASSION, GIVING and CARE

- Many Americans would feel the pain of unmet needs for basics such as food and clothing, not to mention a slow-down in disaster recovery efforts, were it not for local churches. *Outlook for Outreach,* a new study by Christianity Today and Brotherhood Mutual Insurance Company, shows 58% of churches in America provide hands-on assistance for causes throughout the nation. Of those, 75% engage in national disaster relief efforts. Nearly all U.S. churches (96%) are serving those in their local community, especially in feeding and clothing the poor. 54% send teams on in-country mission trips and are engaged in housing construction projects. 70% are involved in international outreach efforts and 60% fund building projects overseas, , while 53% travel abroad to physically assist with the construction work. 90% allow other organizations to use their facility for outreach programs, so churches are opening their doors for others to serve, too. They also take care to select suitable volunteers and provide adequate training before doing hands-on ministry. Although finding enough funding and volunteers are the two biggest obstacles to doing outreach locally, nationally and internationally, 41% of churches report volunteerism is up for outreach ministries, and 45% expect their church budget for outreach to increase in the coming year. 62% report the mainresult of serving others is a sense of maturing discipleship among those involved. 35% say more previously unchurched people now attend their church because of their outreach efforts. (ToddRhoades.com 1/1/13)

• Ministry generosity expert, Brian Kluth, has discovered that on average a church's givers are likely to be as follows; 1/3 give $0 per year, 1/3 give under $500 per year, and 1/3 give over $500 per year. In larger churches, with 1000 or more in attendance, 1/2 probably give $0, 1/4 give under $500, and 1/4 give over $500 per year. He has developed a Giving Statistics Worksheet that allows any church to easily determine the stats for its congregation. www.miac.membershipclicks.net. Maximum Generosity, 9/27/12).

• Research by Brian Kluth's *Maximum Generosity* in cooperation with *Christianity Today,* finds in a poll of 4,413 U.S. church tithers, 42% tithe from their gross plus financial blessings, 28% from the gross, 17% from the net and 13% are not sure. (Maximum Generosity 4/13)

• Tithers are Financially Better Off - There are an estimated 10 million Christians in the U.S. who tithe more than $50 billion annually, according to the fifth annual State of the Plate report. Tithers were compared to non-tithers using nine financial health indicators, and researchers found tithers were better off in every category. Among tithers, for example, 80% have no unpaid credit card bills, 74% owe nothing on their cars, 48% own their home and 28% are debt free. 97% of tithers make giving to their local church a priority, and 63% started tithing between childhood and their 20s. 70% give based on their gross rather than their net, and 77% give 11% to 20% or more of their income. Brian Kluth, founder of the study and Maximum Generosity, said, "Without this group of givers, most churches would cease to exist within months." Tithers make up between just five percent and 20% of the givers in a typical congregation, yet they donate 50% to 80% of the money. Among non-tithing Christians who struggle to give, 38% say it's because they can't afford it, 33% say they have too much debt and 18% say their spouse doesn't agree with tithing. The complete report, "20 Truths about Tithers" is available on the State of the Plate website. (Christian Post 5/16/13, ChurchLeaders.com 5/17/13)

COUNTY DATA

- There are 3144 counties or county equivalents in the 50 States.
- The USA population is 313,847,465 million and the average population per county is 99,824. In this book, we have rounded that number up to 100,000.
- Population data reflects the number of males: 151,781,326 (49.2% of pop.); females: 156,964,212 (50.8% of pop.).
- Ethnically: White - 223,553,265 (72.4% of pop.); Black - 38,929,319 (12.6% of pop.); Asian: 14,674,252 (4.8% of pop.); American Indian and Alaska Native - 2,369,431 (0.8% of pop.); Hispanic/Latino [can also be white/black]: 50,477,594 (16.3% of pop.); Native Hawaiian and Other Pacific Islander - 1,225,195 (0.4% of pop.).
- The median age is 37.1 (2012).
- This extrapolates to a population profile in the average county as: White, 72,000; Black, 12,000; Asian, 4,800; Native Indian, 800; Hispanic/Latino, 16,300.
- The average city in America has 8,967 residents [We have used the rounded up number of 9,000] and this is based on the assumption that there are some 35,000 cities, towns and hamlets in the nation, both incorporated and unincorporated. That means, in each county, there are about eleven cities/towns/hamlets. [These are projected averages, intended as helpful benchmarks, as you consider your city/county prayer council.]
- According to the US Census data from 2000, 79.2% of the population lived in urban areas, population clusters of 2500 or more people. Just over 20% (20.7) live in unincorporated areas or towns smaller than 2500.
- There are 153 Urbanized Areas of over 200,000 population, a total of 166,215,889, representing 58.274% of the US population;
- There are 310 Urbanized Areas of 50,000 - 199,999 population, a total of 29,584,626, 10.372% of the population.
- There are 1838 Urban Clusters 5,000 - 49,999 population, a total of 25,438,275, 8.918% of the population;
- There are 1328 Urban Clusters of 2,500 - 4,999 population, a total of 4,717,270, representing 1.654% of the population. - Source: http://www.fhwa.dot.gov/planning/census_issues/archives/metropolitan_planning/cps2k.cfm. Accessed December 16, 2013.
- Nearly 80% of the population of the Western world live in cit-

ies.

- In the US, 212 media market centers reach 96% of the nation's population.

- The ten largest mega-cities contain 23% of the population. Add the next largest twenty, and you have 43% of the US population in thirty mega-cities.

- Out of 100,000 residents, optimistically, 35,400 are regular or irregular, leaving 64,600 countywide who are functionally unchurched. Olsen's number would be slightly higher – 75-77%. We are not considering here home-churches or house churches. That movement is growing significantly. Some estimate that it may comprise as many as 25% of all Christians. However, many of these families remain in some orbit around one or more churches as an occasional attendee; their children may attend a church-based school or participate in a church-based program.

- Approximately 30-40% of the population, 33.4%, are almost completely disconnected from any church. Some from any significant Christian influence. This detached group is the most critical harvest field in the nation. And it is disproportionately young.

- There are 41,801 zip codes in the USA. That is deceiving, in this sense, 29,812 (71.3%) are general zip codes; another 9,363 (22.4%) are PO boxes – that is 93.7% of all zip codes. Military codes number 535 (1.3%). Unique business codes account for 2,091 (5%). 9,897 zip codes cross county lines (23.7%). Eliminating all but general zip codes, with 3144 counties, all things being equal, each county would have some 9.48 zip codes. Based on population ratios, the number of zip codes per county is 12.

- The average population in each zip zone ranges from 7,500 to 10,000 (nation-wide, the number is 7,474 with difference accounting for those who have no physical mail delivery apart from a PO Box.) With a zip-zone designations, the county can be easily analyzed – where are the churches, the schools, crime, the densest population, the bars, drug activity, teen/youth hangouts?

CRIME DATA

- Total nation-wide arrests (2005): 10.369 million. Approximately 3.3 persons per 100.

- That translated to some 3,298 arrests per county; almost 300 (299.8) per city.

- National statistics for annual murders (2005) is 14,860; violent crimes per 100,000 people (2004) was 465.5; and property crimes per 100,000 people (2004): 3,517.1. Homicides per 100,000 people (2004): 5.5.

- That translates, per county, to 465 violent crimes. Property crimes per county, 3,517. Five homicides.

- The number in state, federal, and local prisons was (2005) 2,186,230. Thus about 695 per county.

- In 2009, the number is slightly higher at 743 adults incarcerated per 100,000 population. According to the U.S. Bureau of Justice Statistics (BJS), 2,266,800 adults were incarcerated in U.S. federal and state prisons, and county jails at year-end 2011 – about 0.7% of adults in the U.S. resident population. [Note: the number is up, the ratio is down].

- Additionally, 4,814,200 adults at year-end 2011 were on probation or on parole.

- In total, 6,977,700 adults were under correctional supervision (probation, parole, jail, or prison) in 2011 – about 2.9% of adults in the U.S. resident population.

- In addition, there were 70,792 juveniles in juvenile detention in 2010.

- In 2008, approximately one in every 31 adults (7.3 million) in the United States was behind bars or being monitored (probation and parole).

- In 2008, the breakdown for adults under correctional control was as follows:
  - one out of 18 men,
  - one in 89 women,
  - one in 11 African-Americans (9.2%),
  - one in 27 Latinos (3.7%),
  - and one in 45 Caucasians (2.2%.

- The prison population has quadrupled since 1980, even though hard crime is down. This due, at least partially, to the mandatory sentencing that came about during the "war on drugs."

- In each county, there are an average of 20 bars, taverns, nightspots.

- In each county, there are over 308 places to obtain alcoholic beverages.

- The US bar and nightclub industry's drinking establishments primarily engaged in the retail sale of alcoholic drinks number around 65,000, according to Dunn & Bradstreet, and they generate approximately $20 billion in combined annual sales revenue, with the average establishment accounting for about $200,000 in revenue.
- Taverns are the largest sector with 19,660 drinking places. Combined, they shared more than 32% of the market.
- Bars and lounges represent 19.8% of the drinking places,
- Cocktail lounges are about 11.5% of the drinking places.
- Night clubs constitute about 8.6%.
- Per the U.S. Census Bureau's Statistics of U.S. Businesses, there were about 351,912 people employed within the industry with nearly $4.1 billion in annual payroll in 2005.
- Last year's total Restaurant and Bar Industry Sales accounted for $632 billion with 970,000 locations and are projected to be the same or increase one percent in 2013. Sales of spirits, wine and beer increased 4.9% to reach $93.7 billion in 2011.
- Of the Top 100 survey participants in the US Bar and Nightclub study, 42.8% identified their venues as nightclubs; 70.6% of them described their hotspots as dance clubs. Of those identifying their venue as bars, 31.7% are sports bars and 29.3% are traditional bar/taverns. DJs and live entertainment are featured by 88.3% and 73.6% of total respondents, respectively. Nearly 80% offer a dance floor, 70.1% provide VIP areas and 65% offer bottle service.

CULTURE CLASH

- Eighty-three percent of Americans own a Bible. Eighty percent say it is sacred while 61% wish they read it more.
- Seventy-nine percent of Mosaics (aged 18–28) own a Bible, compared with 95% of Elders (65–plus).
- Eighty percent of Americans identify the Bible as sacred literature vs. just eight percent who think the Koran is sacred.
- Fifty-one percent of U.S. adults are concerned religious freedom in the U.S. will become more restricted in the next 5 years, finds new Barna Group research. The survey found 71% of evangelicals, 46% of practicing Protestants and 30% of practic-

ing Catholics are "very concerned" about this prospect. Among practicing Protestants, 48% say they perceive freedom of religion to have grown worse in recent years, compared with 60% of evangelicals. About 90% of Americans agreed with the statement. (Christian Post 1/19/13)

- The number of Americans who do not identify with any religion is growing at a rapid pace. A new Pew Research Center Forum on Religion & Public Life report finds about a fifth of the U.S. public (and a third of adults under 30) are religiously unaffiliated today. Those are the highest percentages ever in Pew Research Center polling. In just the last 5 years, the unaffiliated have increased from just over 15% to just under 20% of all U.S. adults. Their ranks now include more than 13 million self-described atheists and agnostics (nearly six percent of the U.S. public), as well as nearly 33 million people who say they have no particular religious affiliation (14%). This large and growing group of Americans is less religious than the public at large on many conventional measures, including frequency of attendance at religious services and the degree of importance they attach to religion in their lives. Yet, many of the country's 46 million unaffiliated adults are religious or spiritual in some way. 66% say they believe in God and regular church attendance continues to hold steady at about 40% of U.S. adults. More than half say they often feel a deep connection with nature and the earth, more than a third identify as "spiritual" but not "religious," and 20% say they pray every day. (Charisma News 10/9/12)

- There are an estimated 1500 legal casinos in the U.S. today. Just 35 years ago, Nevada was only place they were legal.

- Ten percent of American workers are willing to get a tattoo of their company's logo in exchange for a 15% raise.

- Fifty-nine percent of American women now have tattoos vs. 41% of men.

- Fifty-one percent of U.S. Christians tend to have attitudes and actions characterized by self-righteousness. Despite their shortcomings, according to a recent Barna study, evangelical Christians are the most likely Christian segment to be categorized as having both Christ-like actions and attitudes (23%). (Barna Group 4/30/13)

- Seventy-five percent of Americans 18–49 agree living together before getting married is a good idea vs. 57% of those 50-plus.

23% of 18–49s say it is not a good idea and 40% of those 50-plus agree. 47% of 18–49s and 43% of 50+s think divorce is so common today because marriage isn't taken as seriously as it used to be. 28% of 18–49s and 23% of those over 50 say it is more acceptable today. 95% of 18–49s and 91% of people over 50 would pick their current spouse again. (AARP Bulletin 6/13)

• Roughly 22 U.S. veterans commit suicide every day, almost one an hour.

• Traditional Values Out of Favor - Gallup.com reports a majority of Americans now say the government should not favor any particular set of values in society and this is the first time the question has been asked in polls since 1993, Americans haven't favored the government's promotion of traditional values. 52% of Americans said the government should not promote any set of values, while 44% believe it should promote traditional values. (ChurchLeaders.com 10/12/12)

• Forty-six percent of Americans believe in the creationist view that God created humans in their present form at one time within the last 10,000 years. The prevalence of this view is essentially unchanged from 30 years ago when Gallup first asked the question. 32% believe humans evolved, but with God's guidance; 15% say humans evolved, but that God had no part in the process. (ToddRhoades.com 5/15/13)

• People Turn to God When Disaster Strikes - A new LifeWay Research study reveals 57% of Americans become more interested in God when a natural disaster occurs. 31% said their interest in God doesn't increase after such catastrophes, and 12% were unsure. 33% of the U.S. adults surveyed said such suffering causes them to put more trust in God. 25% said it makes them confused about God and 16% said they don't think about God at all during such times. Suffering that appears unfair causes another 11% to wonder if God cares, seven percent to doubt God's existence, five percent to become angry toward God and three percent to resent Him. 34% of Americans believe prayer can avert natural disasters while 51% disagree and 32% strongly disagree. (Christian Post 5/30/13)

• Help in Tough Times - When going through a tough time in their lives, 53% of Americans expect their families would be "very helpful." 24% say the same of their local church or religious organization, while 22% think their friends would help that much. Nothing else comes close. Local charities, businesses and all levels of government are seen as very helpful by single digit numbers. (Rasmussen Reports 5/8/13)

EDUCATIONAL INSTITUTIONS

* There are 4,140 2-year, 4-year, public and private colleges and universities, some with graduate programs. That is 1.3 per county.

* Attending them are 17,487,475 students; 724,000 from other nations.

* Total number of public school districts in the nation is 13,809 (Digest of Education Statistics: 2010, Table 91). K-12 schools: 132,656 (Digest 2010, Chapter 1, Table 5); Elementary: 88,982; Secondary: 27,575; Combined: 14,837; Other: 1,262 (Digest 2010, Chapter 1, Table 5).

* The total number of public schools is 98,706; Elementary: 67,148; Secondary: 24,348; Combined: 5,632; Other: 1,587 (Digest 2010, Table 97).

* The total number of charter schools: 5,714 (Center for Education Reform, National Charter School & Enrollment Statistics, November 2011).

* The total number of private schools: 28,220; Elementary: 16,370; Secondary: 3,040; Combined: 8,810 (Digest 2010, Table 63). Catholic Schools 7,400; Elementary: 5,960; Secondary: 1,080; Combined: 370 (Digest 2010, Table 63).

* The total K-12 enrollment: 55,235,000 (Digest 2010, Table 2); Elementary: 38,860,000; Secondary: 16,375,000 (Digest 2010, Table 2).

* The total Public School enrollment: 49,266,000; Elementary: 34,286,000; Secondary: 14,980,000 (Digest 2010, Table 39).

* Total Charter School enrollment: 1,941,831 (The Center for Education Reform, National Charter School & Enrollment Statistics, November 2011).

* Total Private School enrollment: 5,165,280; Elementary: 2,462,980; Secondary: 850,750; Combined: 1,851,550 (Digest 2010, Table 63).

* Home School enrollment: 1,508,000 (estimate) or 2.9% (estimate) of America's school population (Digest 2010, Table 40).

* Catholic School enrollment: 2,224,470; Elementary: 1,457,960; Secondary: 620,840; Combined: 145,680 (Digest 2010, Table

63).

- On-line enrollment: approx. 250,000 (iNACOL Key Stats).
- The number of teachers: 3,219,458; Elementary: 1,758,169; Secondary: 1,234,197; Unclassified: 227,092 (Digest 2010, Table 69). Charter School teachers: 72,000 (Digest 2010, Table 105). Private School Teachers: 456,270; Elementary: 207,230; Secondary: 69,240; Combined: 179,800 (Digest 2010, Table 62). Catholic School teachers: 146,630; Elementary: 94,800; Secondary: 42,400; Combined: 9,430 (Digest 2010, Table 62).
- On average, in each county, there are four school districts and forty-two schools. Thirty-one of those are public schools, two charter schools and nine private schools (religious and non-sectarian). In addition, on average, there are two Catholic schools.
- On average, 15,670 kids go to school in the county.
- Some 617 are in the charter schools. [The largest network of charter schools in the nation is Islamic].
- The average number who attend private schools is 1,643.
- About 500 kids are home-schooled (479 per county).
- Catholic school enrollment on average is 708.
- Approximately 1024 teachers serve students in the public system per county.
- If national church attendance averages hold true, that means that only about 174 (17.7%) of these teachers give themselves persistently, weekly, to the spiritual nurture of their own souls. Double that number with casual attenders, 348. With 'cultural' Christians added, the number rises much higher. No stats are available on the level of active Christians involved in the public school system, but it is thought to be considerable.
- Some 23 teachers, per county, serve the charter schools and in 145 private schools. Catholic teachers, per county, number 47.
- The national average high school dropout rate is nine percent, one in eleven.
- The average district public school per pupil expenditure is $12,744 (Digest 2010, Table 190) compared to Charter School per pupil costs of $8,001 (The Center for Education Reform, Annual Survey of America's Charter Schools, 2010, page 15).

FAMILY/HOUSEHOLD DATA

- According to census data, the number of USA families is 77,538,296.
- The average family size, 3.14.
- Some 65.1% of population own their own home.
- Married couples number 56,510,377.
- The never married number 74,243,000.
- The divorced number 23,742,000. The widowed number 14,341,000. Source: Read more: An Overview of the U.S. Population — Infoplease.com http://www.infoplease.com/ipa/A0004925.html#ixzz2cK1C9HNI
- The number of families per county is 24,662.
- The number of married couples - 17,974; the never married, 23,614; the divorced, 7,551; the widowed 4,561. This is an average.
- A recent Center for Marriage and Families study finds children raised in divorced families or married but severely conflicted households are significantly less likely to attend religious services and express interest in God. Adults raised in happy marriages are "more than twice as likely to attend religious services, compared to those raised in even 'good' divorces" and were less likely to say they have negative experiences with God. The future health of churches may depend on appropriate ministry to divorced, conflicted and non-traditional families. (Church Leaders 2/1/13)
- A married couple's decision to stay together is more influential in lowering the number of teenage out-of-wedlock births, unemployed dads and Americans on the welfare dole than any other factor, finds a new Family Research Council study. Family cohesion is the main factor in determining whether a child will graduate from high school, whether families will end up on welfare, and whether young men will be employed. Living in a family with both parents had a greater impact on teenage out-of-wedlock birthrates than education, including sex education. The study found the more children a man 25-54 had, the more likely he was to be employed. Men with larger families also made more money. (LifeSite News 2/13/13)
- A recent article from the Gospel Coalition sets the record straight about erroneous statistics that have been published on the internet and used as illustrations from the pulpit. The statistic in question was that Christians divorce at roughly the same rate as

the world. The research actually showed couples who regularly practice any combination of serious religious behaviors and attitudes (attend church nearly every week, read their Bibles and spiritual materials regularly; pray privately and together; generally take their faith seriously) have significantly lower divorce rates than mere church members, the general public and unbelievers. The research shows couples who are active in their faith are much less likely to divorce. Catholic couples were 31% less likely to divorce, Protestant couples 35% less likely, and Jewish couples 97% less likely. Read more (Pastors: That Divorce Rate Stat You Quoted Was Probably Wrong by Ed Stetzer, Church Report 9/28/12)

- By age 8, 16% of American kids have a social profile.
- Only 45% of Americans 15 to 17 are being raised by their married, biological parents.
- Based on 2007 data, an average of 1,358 babies were born in each US county. Sadly, nearly 40% of them without a dad either present or immediately anticipated in the life of the child.
- Every day, per county, almost 4 children are added to population - 3.7 a day; 26 a week; 113 month.
- Every day, per county, two more fresh graves can be found in cemeteries - 15 a week and 64 a month (768 annually).
- Fifty-nine weddings take place monthly - two a day; 13 a week; 702 annually.
- Sadly, 360 marriages are terminated annually - 30 a month, almost one a day.
- The number of abortions per resident, per county, are about 411 annually, a bit more than one a day, about eight weekly.
- Nationally: The number of births (2007) were 4,269,000 (14.16 per 1,000 pop.) Deaths (2007): 2,416,000 (8.27 per 1,000 pop.). Marriages (2008): 2,208,000 (7.3 per 1,000 pop.). Divorces (2008): 3.6 per 1,000 pop. Infant mortality rate (2007): 6.37 per 1,000 live births. Legal abortions (2002): 1,293,000. Life expectancy (2007): Total U.S., both sexes, 78; total men, 75.15; total women, 80.97; white men, 75.3; white women, 80.5; black men, 69.0; black women, 76.1 Read more: Vital Statistics | Infoplease.com http://www.infoplease.com/ipa/A0004929.html#ixzz2cK1WmeZ3
- Among unmarried couples living together in the U.S., such relationships are more than twice as likely to dissolve as marriag-

es. Likewise, two-thirds of couples living together separated by the time their child turns 10. (NY Times 2/17/12)

- A 3-year study by the Univ. of Virginia's Institute for Advanced Studies in Culture finds four types of family cultures molding the next generation of Americans. Project co-director James Hunter thinks these family cultures may well be more consequential than parenting styles. They are: (1)The Faithful (20% of American parents) adhere to a divine and timeless morality, handed down through Christianity, Judaism or Islam, giving them a strong sense of right and wrong. Raising "children whose lives reflect God's purpose" is a more important parenting goal than their children's eventual happiness or career success. (2) Engaged Progressives' (21%) morality centers around personal freedom and responsibility. They see few moral absolutes beyond the Golden Rule. They value honesty, are religious skeptics and to train their children to be "responsible choosers," they strategically allow their kids freedom at younger ages than other parents. (3)The Detached (21%) tend to "Let kids be kids and let the cards fall where they may." They are primarily Caucasian with blue-collar jobs, no college degree and lower income. They spend less than 2 hours a day interacting with their children. A family dinner together is often in front of the TV. (4) American Dreamers (27%) are optimistic about their children's abilities and opportunities. With relatively low household income and education, they pour themselves into raising their children and providing them every possible material and social advantage. They view their relationships with their kids as "very close" and express a strong desire to be "best friends" with them once grown. (Newswise 11/15/12)

- Marriage and Religion Research Institute reports among U.S. children, 47% do not reach the age of 17 without a family split. Divorce can decrease the ability of a child to function well in five areas of society: family, school, church, marketplace, and government. Children who have an intact married family are less likely to: Think their father is not warm and loving; get in a fight with a family member; lie, steal or damage school property; hurt someone, get drunk or skip school; have sex before age 14 and have an unwed pregnancy; and have a 2.9 grade point average or higher. (Baptist Press 3/2/12)

- Today 41% of births in the U.S. are outside marriage and 53% for children born to women under 30, according to 2009 National Center for Health Statistics. 73% of black children are born outside marriage, compared with 53% of Latinos and 29% of whites. Educational differences are growing as well. 92% of college-educated women are married when they give birth vs. 62% of women with some post-secondary schooling and 43% of women with a high school diploma or less. Among mothers of all ages, 59% are married when they have children. But the surge of births outside marriage among younger women (nearly two-thirds of children in the U.S. are born to mothers under 30) is both a symbol of the transforming family and a hint of coming generational change. (NY Times 2/17/12)

- 973,250 grandparents in the U.S. have been responsible for their grandchildren for 5 years or more.

- A record 40% of all households with children under the age of 18 include mothers who are either the sole or primary source of income for the family, according to a new Pew Research Center analysis of data from the U.S. Census Bureau. The share was just 11% in 1960.These "breadwinner moms" are made up of two very different groups: 5.1 million (37%) are married mothers who have a higher income than their husbands, and 8.6 million (63%) are single mothers. The income gap between the two groups is quite large. The median total family income of married mothers who earn more than their husbands was nearly $80,000 in 2011, well above the national median of $57,100 for all families with children, and nearly four times the $23,000 median for families led by a single mother. The groups differ in other ways as well. Compared with all mothers with children under age 18, married mothers who out-earn their husbands are slightly older, disproportionally white and college educated. Single mothers, by contrast, are younger, more likely to be black or Hispanic, and less likely to have a college degree. The growth of both groups of mothers is tied to women's increasing presence in the workplace. Women make up almost of half (47%) of the U.S. labor force today, and the employment rate of married mothers with children has increased from 37% in 1968 to 65% in 2011. (Facts and Trends 5/29/2013)

MEGA CHURCHES

- Mega churches constitute less than .5% of American congregations, and some 1600 of them exist across the nation.

- The growth trend has been toward the mega-churches that often function as world to itself, sometimes creating a fellowship of churches beyond the community and their denominational family, if indeed, it is a part of such a theological accord; and even if it is, such churches tend to march to their own drum. (See: http://hirr.hartsem.edu/bookshelf/thumma_article2.html. Also: MegaChurchTrends).

- The larger churches are thriving, despite the tough economy. In 2011, they experienced increased offerings and many planned to hire more staff. 83% of large churches expected to meet their budgets in the current fiscal year. A majority reported offerings that were higher than the previous year. Most mega-churches surveyed spend 10% or more of their budget beyond their congregation on causes ranging from local soup kitchens to world missions. (Charisma News 2/20/13)

- LifeWay Research's Thom Rainer recently cited 7 major trends in megachurches. 1) Further consolidation of people attending church in megachurches and other large churches. While megachurches account for fewer than 0.05% of all U.S. churches, more than 10% of church attendance is concentrated in these churches. 2) A significant increase in the number of megachurches. In 1970 there were approximately 50 megachurches in America vs. 1,600 today. 3) An increased interest in the long-term sustainability of a megachurch. 4) More youthful megachurch pastors. The average age of the pastors of the largest 100 churches in the U.S. is 47. 5) More multi-venue, multi-campus churches. Pastors are becoming increasingly attuned to the stewardship of using more facilities more often. 6) A greater interest in groups. Megachurch leaders have a growing interest in groups as the church mechanism for assimilation, evangelism, fellowship, ministry and more in-depth teaching. 7) A greater interest in the source of megachurch growth. Further analysis of the type of megachurch growth will study: Is it transfer from other churches? Is it unchurched Christians returning to church? Does it represent a true evangelization of the communities in which the church is located? (Thom Rainer, Outreach Magazine 10/2/12)

- 1 in 4 multi-site churches has at least one campus in another language.

- Non-Christian Movements

- There are 2106 Muslim Mosques in the US, as of 2012; .66 per

418

county – two mosques for every three counties.

- The U.S. saw a 74% increase in the number of mosques from 2000 to 2010, from 1,209 to 2,106.
- There are 2.6 million Muslims in the US, 827 per county. Muslim claims of US population in the range of 6 – 10 million are exaggerated; however, the number of Muslims in the past decade, since 9-11, has doubled.
- Estimates for the number of USA Buddhist range from 2.4 – 4 million.
- In addition, there would be about the same number of Buddhist, perhaps more.
- From 1,700 people in 1900, the Hindu population in America grew to approximately 387,000 by 1980 and 1.1 million in 1997. As of 2008, the estimated U.S. population of Hindus of Indian origin is approximately 2.29 million (mainly of Indian and Indo-Caribbean descent). Today's analysis on the US Hindu population. Estimates are that there may also be as many as 1 million practicing American Hindus, not of Indian origin, in the U.S. http://www.hafsite.org/resources/hinduism_101/hinduism_demographics

TEENS/YOUNG ADULTS

- Among Americans aged 18–29, 32% are unaffiliated with any religion. Among the "nones," 88% say they are not looking for a religion that would be right for them. They are not seekers. (The American Church Magazine 1/13).
- Almost 66% of British adults say schoolchildren need to learn about Christianity in order to understand English history, culture and way of life, according to an Oxford Univ. study. (Christianity Today Online 12/4/12)
- A recent survey reported in Biola Magazine revealed that 70% of teens surveyed expressed persistent, measurable doubts that what the Bible says about Jesus is true. Youth expert Mike Nappa, in his survey, confirms 67% of teens say they seldom read their Bibles. (Rock Solid Faith Bible Study for Teens, Zondervan 2012)
- Teens View on Christ's Return 49% of Christian teens don't believe Jesus will return within their lifetimes. 13% refuse to even venture an opinion on the subject. Non-denominational

youth are most likely to say they expect Jesus to return in their lifetimes (54%). 64% of Catholic students are convinced Christ will not return in their lifetimes. Among Christian students who are skeptical of the Bible's trust-worthiness, 77% reject the idea that Christ will return before they die. (The Jesus Survey, Mike Nappa, Baker Books 2013)

- Do Christian Teens Read the Bible? 73% of Christian teens indicate they value daily Bible study as a part of the Christian life. Of these, 31% "strongly agree" with this view. Yet, nearly all Christian teens fail to open their Bibles outside church. A meager five percent study it on a daily basis. More than 1 in 4 Christian students in a church youth group actually reject the idea that Christians have an obligation to study the Bible daily. Belief in the trustworthiness of Scripture has enormous impact on whether or not Christian students place value on studying the Bible daily. Among the overall U.S. youth group population, only 31% believe daily Bible study is very important, although among teens who believe the Bible is trustworthy, that number more than doubles to 63%. (The Jesus Survey, Mike Nappa, Baker Books 2003)

- Why Teens Leave the Faith A 2007 LifeWay Research study found that 70% of young adults who attended church in high school subsequently stopped attending church for at least a year during their college years. Only 20% of those who left the church had planned on doing so while in high school. Surveys by Barna and Gallup have found similar dropout rates, leaving youth and teens experts wondering: What can be done? A new longitudinal study of 500 youth group graduates may provide some answers. Conducted by the Fuller Youth Institute at Fuller Theological Seminary, the study followed the graduates through their years in college or vocational school. The results are compiled in a book, "Sticky Faith: Everyday ideas to build lasting faith in your kids" (Zondervan). Their view of the gospel matters, as well as their connection to the church body, but one result that might surprise some church leaders is that teens who feel the freedom to express doubts about their faith tend to keep their faith. (Baptist Press, 2/20/12)

- The U.S. Department of Labor estimates that today's youth will have 10–18 jobs by age 38.

- Nomads is a term assigned by the Barna Group to 18 to 29-year-olds with a Christian background who walk away from church engagement but still consider themselves Christians. A person in this group typically has trouble identifying with a church or a particular "brand" of Christianity, but would consider themselves, broadly, a Christian. 43% of young American adults with a Christian background believe going to church and having Christian friends is optional. 25% say faith and religion just aren't that important to them. 23% say they used to be very involved in their church, but they just don't fit in anymore. This is the group most likely to say they love Jesus but not the church — or that they are "spiritual but not religious." (Barna Group 5/9/13)

- Prodigals is a term assigned by the Barna Group to 18- to 29-year-olds who have lost their faith. They used to claim a personal faith, but no longer claim any Christian belief. Many say they are as fairly certain they won't ever return to the Christian faith. 21% of Millennials with a Christian background say Christian beliefs don't make sense to them. 20% admit to having had a negative experience in church or with Christians. 19% say their spiritual needs cannot be met by Christianity. This group often gets lumped in with the "Nones," even though they might not be totally opposed to faith and spirituality. (Barna Group 5/9/13)

- Exiles is a term assigned by the Barna Group to 18- to 29-year-olds who struggle with the Christian faith. They have a tough time finding a place in a church setting but choose to remain within an institutional church context. They feel "lost" somewhere between their commitments to church and their desire to stay connected with the world. They struggle to connect their faith or church with their everyday lives, and yet they continue in their Christian faith despite these hurdles. 21% remain Christian and continue to attend a church but find church to be a difficult place for them to live out their faith. 38% say they desire to follow Jesus in a way that connects with the world they live in. One-third say God is more at work outside the church than inside the church, and they want to be a part of that. 32% of American 20-somethings with a Christian background says they want to be a Christian without separating themselves from the world around them. (Barna Group 5/9/13)

- Among U.S. teens that never go to church, 20% are white, 20% are Asian-American, 16% are Hispanic and 15% are black. (Resourcing Christianity)

- U.S. teens 13–17 send an average of 1,742 text messages a month.
- The median teen Facebook user has 300 friends, while the typical teen Twitter user has 79 followers.
- Girls are more likely than boys to delete friends from their social network (82% vs. 66%) and block people (67% vs. 48%).
- Teens Religion Varies by Race - Biola professor and youth researcher Brad Christerson says his research shows a wide diversity of religious belief and practice among teens within each racial/ethnic group. Many Asian teens follow a pattern labeled "relativistic instrumentalism." They pick and choose from different religions; anything they think can help them be successful. Many do not believe in any fixed or absolute morality, but are more likely to live their lives without risky behaviors. "Personalistic absolutism" is how researchers describe the religion of many African-American teens. They are the most likely to be convinced of the absolute truth of their beliefs and that morality is fixed. For them, God is to be obeyed and served. Black teens talk a lot about God and see Him as highly involved in every aspect of their personal lives. "Therapeutic individualism." Describes the religion of many white kids. They display the most diversity of religious belief and denominational adherence. Most are very individualistic in their approach to religion. They talk about "God and me" and about God helping them to be fulfilled and happy. Hispanic kids talk about their families a lot when they talk about their religious experience and beliefs. Many talk about church as something that brings their family together, hence they are termed with "religious familialism." This closeness with family is especially pronounced in the first and second generation kids. They report a strong belief in the Christian religion, and this belief seems tied to their family relationships. Religion for many of them serves as a support and catalyst to family unity. (Brad Christerson, Resources for American Christianity)
- Fewer than 10% of young adults in the U.S. regularly attend worship services.
- For American high school dropouts, an astonishing 83% of first births are outside marriage.
- For American with only a high school degree or some college, 58% of first births occur outside marriage.
- Nearly 40% of 20-something cohabiting parents who had a

baby between 2000 and 2005 split up by the time their children were five years old.

- There are 3.3 million teenage alcoholics of the 10–15 million alcoholics.

UNITY

- Crusades are often the flash point for the unity of churches in a community, at least during the last fifty years, however, rarely to the coalitions of supporting churches achieve even 50% of the congregations in any city – we are a fractured community of Christians and churches.
- About three percent of the churches in any community ever align for a single cause.

63 FASICLD (Francis A. Schaeffer Institute of Church Leadership Develop-
    ment). This quest started in 1989 as a Fuller Institute project that was picked
    up by FASICLD in 1998.
64 Dr. Richard J. Krejcir, Statistics on Pastors, "What is Going On With Pastors
    in America?" http://www.intothyword.org/apps/articles/?articleid=36562
65 Psychologist Richard Blackmon reported in the Los Angeles Times the re-
    sults of a survey in 1985 with one thousand pastors from four major denom-
    inations in California, USA. His research continued to 2004 and revealed
    that over 75% of ministers are extremely or highly stressed. In addition, he
    found that 30% to 40% of ministers ultimately drop out of the ministry.
66 In Blackmon's study, he found that 30% to 40% of ministers ultimately drop
    out of the ministry, a much lower rate.
67 1050 pastors were surveyed from two pastor's conferences held in Orange
    County and Pasadena, Ca-416 in 2005, and 634 in 2006. A similar study
    was conducted for the Fuller Institute in the late 80s.
68 Blackmon's study found that 31.75% of the clergy surveyed had sexual
    intercourse with a church member-who was not their spouse!
69 See: http://www.parsonage.org/
70 Barna Report: "Only Half Of Protestant Pastors Have A Biblical World-
    view" (January 12, 2004). See https://www.barna.org/barna-update/5-bar-
    na-update/133-only-half-of-protestant-pastors-have-a-biblical-world-
    view#.UpEzSFQo7IU
71 I am grateful to R. J. Krejcir, Ph.D. Francis A. Schaeffer Institute of Church
    Leadership Development, 2007. Research from 1989 to 2006. http://www.
    truespirituality.org/